Domestic Abolitionism
and
Juvenile Literature
1830–1865

Domestic Abolitionism
and
Juvenile Literature
1830–1865

Deborah C. De Rosa

State University of New York Press

Published by
State University of New York Press, Albany

For information, address State University of New York Press,
90 State Street, Suite 700, Albany, NY 12207

Production by Judith Block
Marketing by Jennifer Giovani

Library of Congress Cataloging-in-Publication Data

De Rosa, Deborah C.
   Domestic abolitionism and juvenile literature, 1830–1865 / Deborah C. De Rosa
      p. cm.
   Includes bibliographical references and index.
   ISBN 0-7914-5825-3 (acid-free paper) — ISBN 0-7914-5826-1 (pbk. : acid-free paper)
      1. American literature—19th century—History and criticism. 2. Slavery in literature. 3.
   Children's literature, American—History and criticism. 4. Antislavery movements in
   literature. I. Title.

PS217.S55 D4 2003
810.9'355—dc21

                                                                          2002042644

10 9 8 7 6 5 4 3 2 1

Experience, which destroys innocence,
also leads one back to it.

—*James Baldwin*

Contents

Figures

Acknowledgments

First and foremost, I want to thank Joy Kasson for her guidance during the course of this project and for her thoughtful comments. I am grateful to Trudier Harris, who even during her long absence, remained a constant inspiration to my scholarship and my teaching. Many thanks to Philip Gura whose insight especially helped shape an amorphous chapter on biography and publication history. I am also grateful to Robert Johnstone and James Leloudis for their support and insights. I extend a warm thanks to Richard P. Morgan, who willingly located otherwise unknown documents and inspired me in ways I did not think possible. Finally, I want to thank that unnamed child in the Davis Library elevator, on the University of North Carolina (UNC) campus, whose insightful comment inspired this project.

Little of the recovery work would have been possible without the financial assistance of the Elizabeth Cady Stanton Foundation, the W. Bruce Lea Family, the UNC Off-Campus Graduate Research Grant, the Cairns Friends of the Library at Madison Wisconsin Fellowship, the Barnard Alumnae Graduate Fellowship, and the Senior Fellowship at UNC. I thank all of you for believing in my project and for allowing me to make it possible to recover works at the following libraries: the Schomburg Collection, Weidner Library, Schlessinger, Houghton, the Boston Public Library, the Boston Athenaeum, the American Antiquarian Society, the Library Company of Philadelphia, the Historical Society of Pennsylvania, the Massachusetts Historical Society, and the Cairns Women's Collection at the University of Madison, Wisconsin. I would especially like to thank Joanne Chaison and the always helpful and excited librarians at the American Antiquarian Society; Jennifer Tolpa at the Massachusetts Historical Society; Adrienne Petrisko at the Library Company of Philadelphia; and Jill Rosenshield, Susan Stravinski, Barbara Richards, Susan Ehlert, Yvonne Schofer, and John Tortorice at the Cairns Collection. I also want to thank the librarians at Duke University's Rare Book Room; Tommy Nixon at UNC's Davis Library; and Becky Breazeal of UNC's Interlibrary Loan. Gratitude also to Richard Morgan who helped with the recovery of information about Maria Goodell Frost and the American Reform Tract and Book Society.

This manuscript underwent much transformation with the help of critics and supporters at a number of professional conferences. The audience at the "Children's Literature and the Lore of Childhood" session of the National Children's Literature Association Conference offered support and encouragement during the earliest stages. Thanks also go to Melanie Levinson, who chaired the "Voices of Reform, Resistance and Abolition: Antebellum Women Writers" session at the Central New York Conference on Language and Literature; and of course to Lynne Vallone's enthusiasm and warm reception at the "Forgotten Authors: Challenges to Literary History" session at the Modern Language Association in Chicago (1995).

I am indebted to an unfathomable degree to all who helped to bring this project to completion through their constant moral support. I would not have been able to do it without you! Thank you Fr. Joseph Cogo, Mrs. Yolanda Coda, Sr. Margaret, Sr. Rita, and Sr. Gemma for reminding me of times past and giving me a home away from home while I was visiting the various archives. C. C. Ussler, Glen Martin, Fr. Phillip Leech, Sr. Margaret Harig, Kathy Martyn, Brenda Rabelis, Ruda Stankus, and Al West supplied their reassurance, wisdom, and wit during the final stages. To Aaron Butler and Suzanne Bolt, I thank you both for talking, walking, driving, dancing, and skating to keep me level-headed and slim when this project threatened to do otherwise. To Kimberly Myers, where would I be without the constant stream of e-mail encouragement? Of course, I owe deep gratitude to Benita Muth, who patiently read, critiqued, and reread this manuscript always with words of encouragement.

All of this would be meaningless, however, if it had not been for my family. Chiara, Allegro, and Amore, thank you for keeping me laughing. Most of all, thank you Mom; your quiet, enduring love and patience made *all* of this worth it. I dedicate this to you with all of my love.

Abbreviations

AAS	American Antiquarian Society
AASS	American Anti-Slavery Society
ARTBS	American Reform Tract and Book Society
ASSU	American Sunday School Union
BAL	*Bibliography of American Literature*
BFASS	Boston Female Anti-Slavery Society
DAB	*Dictionary of American Biography*
HSP	Historical Society of Philadelphia
LNYFASS	Ladies' New York City Female Anti-Slavery Society
MHS	Massachusetts Historical Society
NUC	*National Union Catalogue*
OED	*Oxford English Dictionary*
PFASS	Philadelphia Female Anti-Slavery Society
RFASS	Rochester Female Anti-Slavery Society

Introduction

This study analyzes the convergence of discourses about women, children, and slavery in juvenile literature between 1830 and 1860. Historical research suggests that nineteenth-century men and women lived under implicit and explicit codes about separate spheres, saw the emergence of the cult of childhood, and faced the dilemma of slavery. However, neither literary critics nor historians have discussed how these three seemingly unrelated factors converge. Perhaps because women comprise a significant number of the authors, critics continue to overlook juvenile antebellum literature as a site of cultural conflict and a genre that gave women activists a voice. The recovered archival texts[1] confirm that Harriet Beecher Stowe, Jane Elizabeth Jones, Hannah Townsend, Maria Goodell Frost, Eliza Lee Cabot Follen, Elizabeth Margaret Chandler, Kate Barclay, Julia Colman, Matilda Thompson, Susan Paul, and other women who signed as "M.A.F.," "S.C.C.," "Cousin Ann," "Grandmother," and "Aunt Lizzie" took advantage of the acceptability of domestic fiction, the rising cult of motherhood and childhood, and the increasing market for juvenile literature as means to create a literary space that would permit them to walk the tightrope between female propriety and political controversy. Through their publications, these authors politicize women and children, transcend the ideology of separate spheres, and enter into the public discourse about slavery to which they had limited access. Thus, recognizing the significance of these nineteenth-century American women's texts supplements and complicates our understanding of women's literary production and reveals how women constructed a "political culture" (Bogin and Yellin 14) by becoming *domestic abolitionists,* women authors who developed a discourse that permitted them to negotiate personal views and cultural imperatives.

Scholars have devoted some attention to abolitionist juvenile literature. The earliest analysis of this genre appears in Anne Scott MacLeod's *A Moral Tale:*

Children's Fiction and American Culture, 1820–1860 (1975).[2] Throughout her analysis of an anonymous woman's *Jemmy and His Mother,* Eliza Lee Cabot Follen's *Sequel to the Well-Spent Hour* and "May Morning," as well as Lydia Maria Child's *Evening in New England* and "Jumbo and Zairee," MacLeod argues that except for Child's short story, "direct assaults upon American slavery were rare" (114). She bases this viewpoint on the belief that

> [t]he appearance of anti-slavery sentiment in children's fiction was . . . *relatively* rare in the *general* book trade; certainly, compared to temperance, the antislavery cause received sparse treatment. Not surprisingly, some of the strongest anti-slavery stories for children were published by *special* presses—The American Reform Tract and Book Society, and the Juvenile Emancipation Society, for instance—most of them in the late 1840s and 1850s. That anti-slavery sentiment which did enter the *mainstream* of juvenile literature was not only unusual, but with *rare* exception, was *muted* and *indirect.* (111, emphasis added)

MacLeod's repeated qualifying statements implying the existence of only a few juvenile abolitionists texts dismiss a significant number of important authors and publishers. As the subsequent analysis will suggest, a significant body of literature *does* exist and it was published by well-known commercial presses and "special" presses with mechanisms in place for widespread distribution. Finally, much of the recovered literature is neither muted nor indirect; rather the domestic abolitionists employ the voices of victimized slave children, resistant slave mothers, rebellious white women, and abolitionist children to critique slavery.

Recent scholarship of a broad range of abolitionist juvenile literature further questions MacLeod's assumptions. The juvenile periodical *The Slave's Friend* has attracted increasing attention: Lou W. McCulloch documents its existence in *Children's Books of the Nineteenth Century* (1979), Yolanda D. Federici provides important background information in "American Historical Children's Magazines of the Nineteenth and Early Twentieth Centuries" [nd], and Shirley Samuels's "The Identity of Slavery" (1992) discusses how in the 250,000 copies published by 1837, *The Slave's Friend* intertwines lessons in reading with antislavery capitalism (164–65). In "The White Supremacy Myth in Juvenile Books about Blacks, 1830–1900" (1988), Donnarae C. MacCann argues that the ideology of white supremacy, firmly established by the 1830s, impacted even the supposedly abolitionist juvenile works by Lydia Maria Child, Eliza Follen, Julia Colman, and Matilda Thompson.[3] Susan S. Williams's study, "'Promoting an Extensive Sale': The Production and Reception of *The Lamplighter,*" recovers one example of this literature in her analysis of the parallels between Gerty and the slave child in the children's adaptation, *The Lamplighter Picture Book; or, The Story of Uncle True and Little Gerty, Written for Little Folks* (1856). Finally, "In 'the gloom of evening': Margaret Bayard Smith's View in Black and White of Early Washington Society," documents Fredrika Teute's discovery of "['Old Betty' (1823)] one of the earliest American antislavery children's stories known to exist"

(40). Based on Smith's personal encounter with a slave woman, Aunt Betty, the narrative critiques slavery, especially slave women's oppression, and counteracts Smith's own complicity for many years in owning and hiring slaves (51–52). Teute writes, "In Smith's children's books, a lost genre in themselves, are the hidden matters of race and slavery that profoundly disturbed her" (54). Yet as my study shows, the field of domestic abolitionism is larger than current scholarship would want us to imagine.[4]

Most scholars and historians have possibly given limited attention to investigating abolitionist juvenile literature because they have focused on studying children's literature for the insight it reveals about nineteenth-century childhood in general.[5] Jane M. Bingham and Grayce Scholt (1980) chart the historical background, publishing developments, and attitudes toward and treatment of children in British and American children's literature from 523 to 1945. Similarly, Monica Kiefer's *American Children through Their Books: 1700–1835* (1948), which admittedly excludes all references to black children (3), uses children's books to document the pre–Revolutionary War period's belief in children's low social status and the nineteenth century's belief that children possessed distinct and innocent personalities. James Clement Stone's dissertation, "The Evolution of Civil War Novels for Children" (1990), analyzes how from 1863 to 1900 authors including Horatio Alger, Oliver Optic, and Thomas Nelson Page wrote increasingly realistic and less moralistic juvenile works about the Civil War. He concludes that authors focus more on events than on the boy protagonists because they lacked distance from the events. Furthermore, Stone argues that these works substitute black protagonists with flat, unindividualized black characters who interact mainly with white characters and with each other. Though adding significant insights to the scholarship on children's literature, these critics do not allude to any domestic abolitionists.

Critics who study images of African Americans in children's literature have also ignored abolitionist juvenile literature. Augusta Baker's *Books about Negro Life for Children* (1963) and *The Black Experience in Children's Books* (1984) are bibliographic compilations of twentieth-century texts depicting African Americans in nonstereotypical and unbiased ways. Similarly, the essays in *Racism and Sexism in Children's Books* (1976) limit themselves to analyses of African American stereotypes in twentieth-century children's literature. The essays in Donnarae C. MacCann and Gloria Woodard's *The Black American in Books for Children: Readings in Racism* (1972) address how many twentieth-century books contain inherent and/or explicit racism and distorted images of African Americans that do not speak to young black readers' experience. Dorothy M. Broderick's book-length study, *The Image of the Black in Children's Fiction* (1973), examines images of African Americans in the books published between 1827 and 1967. However, her sample consists of works written predominantly after 1860 and except for brief discussions of Samuel Goodrich's *Tales of Peter Parley about America* (1827) and Susan Warner's *Queechy* (1852), her chapters entitled "Slavery," "The Happy Slave," and "The Unhappy Slave" exclude discussion of works by antebellum authors.

By overlooking juvenile abolitionist literature, historians and critics continue to silence a fascinating group of antebellum women authors for children. These women remain unrecognized in studies that include women writers of children's literature. Glenn E. Estes's edition of essays in *American Writers for Children before 1900* (1985) includes antebellum women authors such as Lydia Sigourney, Maria Cummins, Martha Finley, and Lucretia Hale; however, she excludes domestic abolitionists. In *A Critical History of Children's Literature* (1969), Cornelia Meigs makes passing reference to Eliza Lee Cabot Follen and Harriet Beecher Stowe in her discussion of predominantly postbellum American women authors like Louisa May Alcott, Rebecca Clarke, and Martha Finley. Anne Commire's *Yesterday's Authors of Books for Children* (1977) and Martha E. Ward, Dorothy A. Marquardt, Nancy Dolan, and Dawn Eaton's *Authors of Books for Young People* (1990) bibliographies each include hundreds of authors of juvenile literature, but only one domestic abolitionist: Stowe. Finally, Jane M. Bingham's *Writers for Children: Critical Studies of Major Authors since the Seventeenth Century* (1988) lists major authors for children like Robert Lewis Stevenson and Louisa May Alcott, but does not mention any domestic abolitionists.

Nor do these forgotten women gain recognition in broad studies of nineteenth-century American women's literary productions. David S. Reynolds's exhaustive study, *Beneath the American Renaissance* (1988), which charts how "major" literary figures responded to and utilized subversive and conventional antebellum literature, mentions neither children's literature nor any of these women, except for Stowe. Mary Kelley's *Private Woman, Public Stage* (1984) identifies twelve best-selling nineteenth-century women "literary domestics" whom historians and critics have ignored.[6] Had Kelley recognized the domestic abolitionists, however, she might have extended her argument from the belief that her literary domestics "necessarily wrote about private, domestic, female lives" (ix) to include those women who consciously chose to write about political issues. A few of the women in this study have attracted the attention of literary historians, but not in their capacity as domestic abolitionists. Moira Davison Reynolds's, *Nine American Women of the Nineteenth Century: Leaders into the Twentieth* (1988) mentions none of the women covered in this study except for Stowe. Nina Baym makes passing references to Follen and Stowe in *Woman's Fiction* (1993) and her *American Women Writers and the Work of History* (1995) includes a reference to Elizabeth Margaret Chandler's historical poetry. Chandler has gained critical attention in various biographical essays[7] and in Mary Patricia Jones's dissertation "Elizabeth Margaret Chandler: Poet, Essayist, Abolitionist," which argues for the recovery and recognition of Chandler's works because she "demonstrated an ability as a poet and essayist that earn her a place in American literary history" (6). Similarly, articles about Eliza Lee Cabot Follen focus on her writings for children and her abolitionist activity, but overlook the intersection of the two.[8] Although Stowe, Follen, and Chandler have attracted some scholarly attention, they and their fellow domestic abolitionists have received little or no consideration from literary critics regarding the abolitionist juvenile literature that includes highly critical, if not seditious, statements about the status of American childhood, motherhood, and womanhood under slavery.

Finally, historians who study women's participation in the abolitionist movement do not explore how writing abolitionist literature for children allowed women, who were otherwise to remain disenfranchised and at home, to circumvent the controversy over women's public, abolitionist activism. Wendy Hamand Venet's *Neither Ballots nor Bullets: Women Abolitionists and the Civil War* (1991) prefaces her discussion of women's political activism during the Civil War with a brief history of their achievements as well as the opposition women faced for their public, abolitionist activism, the schism that women's activism caused in the American Anti-Slavery Society, and the abolitionist movement's impact on the issue of women's rights. In *Black Women Abolitionists: A Study in Activism, 1828–1860* (1992), Shirley J. Yee focuses her discussion on the racial and sexual barriers that antebellum African American women from different regions and economic classes encountered in their independent or joint efforts with white and/or black anti-slavery societies to attain equality in America. Even more specifically, Debra Gold Hansen's social history, *Strained Sisterhood* (1993), discusses the endeavors of the Boston Female Anti-Slavery Society (BFASS), whose members were either upper-class or rising middle-class white women and elite African American women. However, Hansen notes that despite their accomplishments, the BFASS encountered internal turmoil and factionalism because members disagreed over the role of women in politics: the upper-class women desired increasing equality while the middle-class activists "defend[ed] domesticity and motherhood" (11). While these historians work to record this lost history of women's political activism, they focus on larger issues rather than on the political strategies available to women abolitionists.

Jean Fagan Yellin and John C. Van Horne's collection, *The Abolitionist Sisterhood: Women's Political Culture in Antebellum America* (1994), however, is the most thorough study to focus on these women's political strategies. The collection reveals that abolitionist women who turned to gender-segregated, auxiliary female anti-slavery societies found outlets for their political sentiments by engaging in activities ranging from prayer, to organizing abolitionist fairs, to signing petitions.[9] The collection's contributors gauge the extent to which women attained a political voice by evaluating the degree of the public nature of women's activism based upon how much criticism, verbal or otherwise,[10] they received when they published controversial abolitionist works or spoke publicly. The BFASS, with Lydia Maria Child as a leading member, was perhaps the most radical and liberal group of women abolitionists who challenged this limited access by participating in public, political discourse about slavery.[11] The BFASS consisted of some of the wealthiest and most prestigious Unitarian,

Quaker, Episcopalian, and Universalist Boston women (Hansen, "Boston" 61–62) who "were influenced more by the egalitarian traditions of the American Revolution and by the principle of natural rights than by doctrines of sin and salvation" (Swerdlow 36). They engaged in openly public activities such as speaking at lectures, writing political documents, running petition campaigns, and organizing antislavery conventions (Hansen, "Boston" 49–51; 63; 64) where they "adapt[ed] male styles of political action to their own ends" (62). Because it threatened ideas of women's sphere and place, the "[BFASS] was ridiculed by the press as 'petticoat politicians'" (49). For example, Lydia Maria Child's *Appeal in Favor of That Class of Americans Called Africans* (1833) received such harsh condemnation that Child had to suspend publication of the *Juvenile Miscellany,* her children's magazine. Similarly, the Grimké sisters were criticized by other women,[12] the press, and religious leaders[13] for speaking in public against slavery. Although the Grimkés sometimes worried about women's traditional roles, they challenged notions about gender by addressing public audiences on a regular basis and by "publish[ing] a series of public letters" that defended the acceptability of women's public activism (Hansen, "Boston" 52).[14] Because public reaction so adamantly opposed even such high-profile women's entrance into the public (male) forum, one can surmise the hindrances that the doctrine of domesticity imposed upon the average woman's ability to voice her abolitionist opinions.

The Philadelphia Female Anti-Slavery Society (PFASS), less radical than its Boston cohort, encountered less criticism because its members participated in abolitionist activities centered predominantly in the private sphere. Lead by Lucretia Mott and a racially balanced membership (Williams "Female . . ." 160–65), the PFASS balanced the secular and the sacred because they "linked the two issues of political inequality and sin" (Swerdlow 37). This may have been true since "[m]any of the Pennsylvania abolitionists were from Hicksite Quaker backgrounds; they had no strong objections to women working publicly for reform" (Williams 174). However, by the late 1840s, PFASS members shifted their emphasis from public petitioning to gathering in private sewing circles to produce merchandise for the antislavery fair (Soderlund 76–77). Soderlund writes:

> And though the [PFASS] shift of emphasis from arranging the annual fair initially appears to be a retreat from the political arena to the private, in fact the society achieved significant political ends [power] through the sale of sewn articles and other goods. Concentrating on the fair required less disregard of accepted gender roles than obtaining signatures on petitions; still, the Philadelphia society used the impressive proceeds of its fair to gain power within the abolitionist movement, especially the state society, which included women and men. (68)

These women tactfully "transformed female domestic skills into political activities and as a result they faced less public criticism from both men and women (79). Nonetheless, the transition resulted in a separation of spheres within the Pennsylvania abolition movement" (Soderlund 84–85).

Those women who received the least amount of criticism for their abolition-ist sentiments relegated themselves to their "proper sphere"—the home. For exam-ple, New York women "attacked slavery as a sinful violation of female chastity and of the sanctity of the Christian family" (Swerdlow 35); nevertheless, these conser-vative, abolitionist women with antifeminist leanings resented women who left the private realm to engage in public politics. The Rochester New York Female Anti-Slavery Society (RFASS) and the Ladies' New York City Anti-Slavery Society (LNYASS) opposed women's public participation. The LNYASS group stated: "We are opposed to the public voting and speaking of women in meetings, to their acting on committees or as officers of the society with men" (31). Rejecting "thoughts or actions that might weaken the 'God-given' hierarchical family struc-ture" (32), the New York women used scripture and evangelicalism to demarcate the boundaries of their activism. Nancy A. Hewitt reveals that RFASS member-ship dwindled during the early 1840s as women either returned home, rejected public activity, or "limit[ed] their public work to the orphan asylum or the newly established Rochester Female Moral Reform Society" ("On their Own . . ." 27).

The fierce debate over the nature of women's political voice and public activism in the culture as a whole and even within female antislavery societies sug-gests the tightrope many domestic abolitionists had to negotiate. For the women struggling to find an abolitionist voice while maintaining the codes of gender and respectability, writing children's literature suggested one solution to circumventing barriers and doing necessary abolitionist work. Writing for children was safe (or at least safer) work for domestic abolitionists like Kate Barclay, Julia Colman, Hannah Townsend, and Matilda Thompson because this audience situated women in the domestic realm, their appropriate sphere, as did much of the per-missible domestic fiction women published. Speaking about Margaret Bayard Smith's abolitionist juvenile story, "Old Betty" (1823), Fredrika Teute argues:

> Writing children's literature, like adopting anonymity, offered a halfway house sheltering female authors from exposure to public scrutiny. What could be more domestic than producing stories inside the household, usually about mothers and their children at home, to be read by mothers to their children within the home? At the same time, such literary endeavors offered women an outlet for their personal aspirations outside the home. (43)

Children's literature appeared nonthreatening, much like the domestic fiction to which the culture gave its nod of approval because it established ordinary people at home in ordinary situations (Baym, *Novels* 203).[15] Except to men like Hawthorne who saw literary women as "the d——d mob of scribbling women" who threatened his financial success, most women authors did not appear to challenge the ideology of separate spheres.[16] Women authors were exhorted to remember that "[t]heir domestic duties came before their [literary] work and lit-erature was the garnish of their life, not its food" (Welter 76). Contemporary ideals dictated that those women driven to the pen

> may write as much as they please providing they define themselves as women
> writing when they do so, whether by tricks of style—diffuseness, gracefulness,
> delicacy, by choices of subject matter—the domestic, the social, the private—or
> by tone—pure, lofty, moral, didactic. (Baym, *Novels* 257)

Therefore, as long as women writers "made clear their primary identification as
True Women" (Coultrap-McQuin 16) and did not write about "a topic identified
as political—and therefore male" (Bardes and Gossett 41), they escaped much
criticism and might even achieve best-seller status with domestic novels like
Maria Jane McIntosh's *Blind Alice* (1841) and Susan Warner's *The Wide, Wide
World* (1850).[17] Like Margaret B. Smith's audience, domestic abolitionists may
have been able to address such taboo topics because their young domestic audience seemingly fell outside the realm of public influence and was extraneous to
the political bureaucracy.

Furthermore, writing abolitionist literature for children may also have
seemed harmless because it cast these domestic abolitionists as "mothers" given
the responsibility for American children's moral and civic education. The religious and legal changes that came as a result of the Industrial Revolution transformed motherhood into "the heart of women's domestic duties" (Cott 46) and
"the moral center of culture" (Shaw, "Pliable" 76). Cott indicates that the nineteenth-century gender ideologies, shaped by changing religious and secular
beliefs, resulted in women gaining increasing control over domestic, familial, and
moral concerns, previously under male sovereignty (200).[18] Furthermore, Mary
Ann Mason documents how the American legal system seems to have empowered women because by the end of the colonial period, "[f]athers no longer
enjoyed paramount common law rights to custody and control of their children.
Instead, the law emphasized the best interests of the child, with a presumption
in favor of mothers as the more nurturing parent" (81). Although circumscribed
to the private sphere, motherhood became one outlet through which to exert
power in the public realm because they could use their supposedly superior moral
status to socialize their children into educated and moral individuals who would
become good citizens (Cott 85). Thus, consciously or unconsciously, domestic
abolitionists assumed the role of the representative American "mother" who
adhered to religious, legal, and social ideologies that defined her new gender role.

The period's emphasis on the mother figure may have also worked in con-
junction with the changing view of the child. Nineteenth-century Europeans
developed new, often romanticized, notions of childhood that transformed
American perceptions and images of children. According to Barbara Kaye
Greenleaf, the late eighteenth century witnessed a decline in adherence to John
Locke's child-rearing notions, stressing a discipline of enforced self-control and
reason. Greenleaf writes:

> [The Romantics] rebelled against the exaltation of reason and promoted the
> validity of *feelings* instead. They wanted emotions to have full play, to be free of

the tyranny of the mind. The Romantics . . . seized upon the child as a symbol of all they believed in: nature, goodness, joy in living, human progress, instinct, and original innocence, not original sin. (62)

Adults perceived nineteenth-century children as innocent rather than depraved and thought they possessed "a more profound awareness of enduring moral truths" (Grylls 35). Americans adopted these European romantic notions, which allowed "the cult of childhood"[19] to replace the traditional Calvinistic belief in a child's innate depravity. MacLeod states: "If the nature of children was not evil inborn, but neutral or potential, then characters could surely be influenced for the good by wise and conscientious adults" (*American Childhood* 94). With this reformation, Americans came to view childhood as a crucial period during which adults worked to insure sound characters for America's future (Finkelstein 130–33).[20] Domestic abolitionists clearly considered that learning about the evils of slavery might secure America's sound future.

Finally, this new outlook on childhood expanded the market demand for children's literature, an opportunity that women—especially domestic abolitionists—seized. Just as Margaret C. Gillespie argues that English women avidly participated in the production of juvenile literature "[a]s it became evident that juvenile books were a marketable commodity" (85), Anne MacLeod suggests that American women constituted a large force behind the trend to educate children through juvenile literature because they "found ready acceptance in the field of writing for children" (*Moral* 31). The nineteenth century witnessed a surge in the publication of less ominous picture books, series books, illustrated magazines, paper novels, and magazines (Bingham and Scholt 145–47) that may have appealed to the nineteenth century's rising middle-class child who had more leisure time and access to larger sums of expendable, parental income.[21] Furthermore, utilitarian approaches compelled children toward increased consciousness through juvenile literature that replaced harsh Puritanical texts with religious tracts, publishing and distributing as many as 50,000 penny tracts as early as 1827 (Cable 67–69). Yet although juvenile literature began to implement Rousseau's belief in "allow[ing] the child to develop naturally according to his interests, in practice youngsters were often burdened with pressure of information" (Bingham and Scholt 142). For example, based on the belief that the child would influence America's future, many juvenile works asked children to confront, in order to guard against, "adult" issues such as temperance. Domestic abolitionists joined in this movement and wrote juvenile abolitionist alphabet books, poetry, short fiction, and novels condemning slavery.

Although twentieth- and twenty-first-century critics like MacLeod have dismissed domestic abolitionists, this study will document the women who took advantage of antebellum America's political, ideological, and publishing climate to voice their antislavery views. "'Some Twelve or Fifteen Others . . . The Committee

Would Recommend for Publication': Domestic Abolitionists and Their Publishers" (chapter 1) identifies the domestic abolitionists and surveys available information on the production of abolitionist juvenile literature by sectarian organizations such as the American Reform Tract and Book Society and by commercial publishers like John P. Jewett, Carlton and Porter, and Lee and Shepard. Publishers who accepted these women's manuscripts extended women's influence to a wider audience, helped them to create a "safe" literary space from which to write about slavery when such public displays of knowledge were forbidden them, and acknowledged their sentimental and quasi-seditious critiques of slavery's impact upon American childhood, families, economics, politics, and democracy.

"'Now, Caesar, say no more today; / Your story makes me cry:' Sentimentalized Victims and Abolitionist Tears" (chapter 2) centers on texts echoing Harriet Beecher Stowe's belief that the "one thing that every individual can do" to fight slavery is to "feel right." Domestic abolitionists before *and* after Stowe affected this change of heart by creating a hybrid genre: juvenile texts that adopt the strategies popular in nineteenth-century juvenile narratives, domestic novels, and slave narratives. Eliza Lee Cabot Follen, Harriet Beecher Stowe, Kate Barclay, Julia Colman, Matilda Thompson, "Grandmother," "Cousin Lizzie," and other women who used pseudonyms foregrounded slave children and adults in sentimental stories that arouse emotions and produce tears, rather than an objective, theorized understanding of abolitionist politics.[22] By situating slavery in the context of the heart, these domestic abolitionists did not overstep women's domain because they depicted women involved in emotional, not intellectual, persuasion as a means to educate children—America's future—to political and moral consciousness. Nonetheless, although these domestic abolitionists appear to limit themselves to eliciting tears of sympathy from their readers, they also subtly, but subversively, critique slavery's destruction of the black slave child's innocence and the family unit, especially the mother-child bond. Under a cover of sentimental rhetoric, these authors politicize sentiment: they seemingly remain within the limits of women's proper sphere but also transcend it through their subtle critiques of slavery. These critiques reveal concern for and anxiety over the changing American familial ideals due to the burgeoning Industrial Revolution.

The works in chapter 3, "Seditious Histories: The Abolitionist Mother-Historian," reveal an interesting shift from the political sentiment articulated by the voices and images of slave children and slave mothers in the juvenile abolitionist pseudo slave narratives to explicit critiques from the mouths of abolitionist mother figures. While many authors, including Matilda Thompson and Kate Barclay, rely on sentimental conventions to convey maternal activism, others, like Jane Elizabeth Jones and Eliza Lee Cabot Follen challenge sentimentality through the figure of the abolitionist mother-historian who overtly critiques religious and political corruption and who corrects distorted representations of American history. Thus, while seemingly maintaining the approved role of educating their children, these politicized mother figures voice quasi-seditious rhetoric suggesting that they not only renounce teaching their children patriotism (Bingham, *Fifteen Centuries* 156), but also overstep women's designated private sphere by speaking about American religious, political, and economic principles.

In "'We boys [and girls] had better see what we can do, for it is too wicked': The Juvenile Abolitionists" (chapter 4), I argue that in the mid-1840s, several female authors counteract anxieties about childhood, family, religion, and government with images of reform-minded, abolitionist *children* who attempt to restore American familial, religious, and political ideals. Having trained the children using sentimental and political strategies, domestic abolitionists advocate children's participation in the abolitionist movement. Women writers like Eliza Lee Cabot Follen, Harriet Beecher Stowe, and Maria Goodell Frost include children in the question "What can I do to end slavery?," which proponents of juvenile abolitionism started asking in the late 1830s. The women authors perhaps replicated in fiction the reality they witnessed in juvenile anti-slavery societies, which encouraged children to effect change through activities ranging from liberal, public activism to familial and/or private reflection. Significantly, before 1850, female authors depict both male and female protagonists, only the boys *speak,* while the girls are spoken *about.* After 1850, however, every recovered author casts a girl as the primary force for restoring American ideals. This reconstructed historical context has enabled me to reconsider Stowe's Little Eva as not only a "saintly child," but also as a young abolitionist grounded in political and gender politics. In the 1850s and 1860s, domestic abolitionists adopted and adapted Stowe's Eva and created young female abolitionists whom they situated on center stage both in deed and in voice.

While this project identifies who wrote abolitionist juvenile literature, tries to explain why they wrote it, and reveals the strategies these domestic abolitionists used within the works, it does not resolve all the questions this recovery process raised. First, as Fredrika Teute notes, many libraries and archives have not catalogued this early children's literature for a variety of reasons (41); therefore, we must speculate whether future archival excavations may uncover an even larger sample. Second, we must wonder whether the patterns and strategies remain the same, as they do in the juvenile and adult versions of Stowe's *Uncle Tom's Cabin,* if these works are compared to adult abolitionist literature. Third, we might ask if any of the authors who chose anonymity or used pseudonyms are African Americans (like Susan Paul) or Southerners (like Miranda Branson Moore). Finally, Fred Davis notes that nostalgia arises from a discontent with the status quo (12). Thus, might Southern women, noticeably absent from this genre, have been able to find their voices and write "history" only in nostalgic, postwar fiction?

Despite the unanswered questions, these recovered texts suggest that domestic abolitionists used juvenile fiction as a means to express their views in the public realm when society condemned such expression. The preponderance of such literature reveals how women tried to socialize the next generation to adopt anti-slavery sentiments and adds a new dimension to the representation of the nine-teenth-century child and his/her literature. In addition, recognizing children's lit-erature as documents that domestic abolitionists used to politicize sentiment, motherhood, and children enables us to create an increasingly complex portrait of nineteenth-century America. Finally, these recovered works supply missing information on women's biography and the history of the book, as well as sup-plement and complicate our understanding of women's historical political culture and literary production in nineteenth-century America. Recovering these impor-tant cultural documents gives voice to these women and their writings, extends the boundaries of historical and literary criticism, and most importantly, raises questions about the existence of other potentially important but silenced litera-ture by women.

1

"Some twelve or fifteen others . . . the committee would recommend for publication"

Domestic Abolitionists and Their Publishers

I n 1833, Lydia Maria Child received such harsh condemnation for *An Appeal in Favor of That Class of American Called Africans* that "[she] not only suffered financial ruin and social ostracism, but was also forced to end her *Juvenile Miscellany*" (Roberts 354; see also Bardes and Gossett 41). In 1850, Sarah Jane Clarke Lippincott (alias, Grace Greenwood) lost her job as editorial associate at *Godey's Lady's Book*[1] upon writing antislavery articles for the *National Era*, an abolitionist newspaper (Gray 364; Born 305). Similarly, Jane Grey Swisshelm, editor and publisher of the antislavery *Pittsburgh Saturday Visitor,* "was attacked not so much because she was an editor but because she dared to comment directly on politics, a topic perceived to be the domain of men only" (Okker 16). Like the women who published their abolitionist views, women who addressed mixed audiences did not escape criticism. For example, the Grimké sisters often encountered critical public receptions and Jane Elizabeth Jones did not escape egg-pelting mobs during her lectures (Moser 6). These women's experiences suggest that except for organizing activities such as antislavery fairs and petition-signing campaigns from within all-female antislavery societies, women lacked literary and public platforms that did not transgress the "gendered expectations of bourgeois publicity" (Isenberg 61).

Domestic abolitionists, however, walked the tightrope between the legitimate "literary public sphere" (Isenberg 44) and inappropriate gender behavior by writing antislavery children's literature through which they mapped a space for themselves as other women had done in fiction and women's magazines. Susan Coultrap-McQuin reveals that

> [b]efore 1830 about one-third of those who published fiction in the United States were women. During the antebellum years, almost forty percent of the novels reviewed in journals and newspapers were by women, which suggests that an equally high percentage were being published. Best-seller lists reveal that by the 1850s women were authors of almost half of the popular literary works. (2)

Similarly, Patricia Okker suggests that women created "a market for periodicals by and for women" (6) that gave women a public voice. Although still inherently separatists, "[w]hatever their intentions, women editors employed a version of separate spheres that challenged the association of men with public life and women with private life. In doing so, they exploded limiting definitions of what they— and other women—could do and be" (Okker 15). Domestic abolitionists found a similar "literary public sphere" in abolitionist juvenile literature, a genre which appeared firmly grounded within the domestic realm, the nursery and schoolroom, but transcended into the marketplace. The frequent number of pseudonyms may reveal women's fear or criticism; however, domestic abolitionists negotiated a place within the public, abolitionist debate through the sectarian organizations, abolitionist societies, and commercial publishers who marketed their abolitionist juvenile fiction and thereby sanctioned their political voices.

American domestic abolitionists most likely found inspiration in their British foremothers who wrote abolitionist children's literature in the early nineteenth century. Government proceedings and public consciousness had already led the British to prohibit participation in the slave trade in 1807 and to abolish it in 1833. According to Anne Trugman Ackerman, children's books by Charlotte Maria Tucker (1821–1893)[2] and Mrs. Henry Lynch reflect these national decisions (301), as do works by Eliza Weaver Bradburn, Amelia (Alderson) Opie, Maria Edgeworth, and Mary Martha Butt Sherwood. However, the important connection for American women rests in the path that British women paved to American presses. For example, Amelia Opie (1769–1853), a very well educated member of Norwich's intellectual community, gained considerable popularity (Balfour 79). In 1793, she married John Opie, a poor but rising artist; but when he failed to sustain his notoriety, "Mrs. Opie's pen was most active" (84). Stemming from her interests in writing and abolitionism,[3] Opie wrote *The Negro Boy's Tale: A Poem,* originally published with London-based Harvey and Darton in 1824 and then published and sold at Samuel Wood's Juvenile Book Store in New York. Even more prolific than Opie, Maria Edgeworth (1767–1849), the daughter of an agricultural reformer (Crawford 137), secured an international readership (Hawthorne 1). Of her many children's books, *Popular Tale,* which includes "The Grateful Negro," debuted in England and America in 1804 and appeared repeatedly in the United States under various publishers until 1859.[4]

American women may have had access to works by the most prolific British woman author, Mary Martha Butt Sherwood (1775–1851), whose narratives enjoyed repeated publication in America. According to M. Nancy Cutt, Sherwood's evangelically based didactic tales stressing missions and exposing slavery (38)[5] sustained popularity until the 1840s because her evangelicalism complemented the traditional Puritan theology that influenced New England's development (112). As a result, several northeastern publishers willingly produced her abolitionist works. For instance, Sherwood's *The Re-Captured Negro*[6] was published by the following: S. T. Armstrong from Boston in 1821; the Protestant Episcopal Sunday and Adult Society of Philadelphia in 1822; and Ansel Phelps, from Greenfield, Massachusetts in 1834.[7] In 1827, Boston-based James Loring boldly advertised *Choice Gems for Children Selected from Mrs. Sherwood's Writings. Never before Published in This Country,* which included "The Poor Little Negroes." His support bolstered his business interest: (1) he gained recognition for publishing many English authors during his twenty-two-year partnership with William Manning (Thesing 347) and (2) he distinguished himself as an independent publisher of children's literature from 1815 to 1837 (Mahoney 294). Finally, Mahlon Day at the New Juvenile Bookstore in New York published and sold Sherwood's *The Babes in the Wood of the New World* (1831). Considering the potential criticism that could arise from publishing her political beliefs in the 1820s, the fact that Sherwood's works often appeared may have spurred American publishers to consider works by American women.

Publishers' willingness to print English women's abolitionist works in the early decades of the nineteenth century most likely opened doors for American domestic abolitionists. By the time the British abolished slavery in 1833, Americans had established the beginnings of an abolitionist movement. Publication rates suggest that British women stopped publishing such works after slavery's abolition and only renewed their commitment to the cause after Harriet Beecher Stowe published *Uncle Tom's Cabin* (Ackerman 290 n45).[8] With British women's silence and American's strengthening abolitionist efforts, American women had publishers' increasing attention.

THE AMERICAN SUNDAY SCHOOL UNION

Well-educated, middle-class British women's presence in the American marketplace conceivably opened publishing house doors for American women who dared to walk the tightrope between acceptable and unacceptable political expression. Isabel Drysdale, one of the earliest American domestic abolitionists,[9] submitted her work to the American Sunday School Union (ASSU), established in Philadelphia in 1791 (*The Charter* 3–4). In addition to *The Lucky Stone* ([nd]) and *The African Woman* (1835), two works about slavery by unknown authors, the ASSU published Drysdale's "The Negro Nurse" from *Scenes in Georgia* (1827) and thereby commended her views to a vast audience of all denominations, age groups, and social classes. For instance, by 1819, the Philadelphia Sunday and Adult School Union had 127 schools that enrolled 10,550 white and 660 black children as well as 377 white and 716 black adults (*Fifty-Second . . .* 48). In 1823, they formed a national society and within one year, the ASSU had 49,619 students and 7,300 volunteer teachers (*Fifty-Second . . .* 48; *Charter* 4). Its commitment to making books and tracts available only at "the *lowest price*" (*Sixth Annual Report* 18) to schools, students, libraries, and depositories gave works published for the *Sunday School Library* a wide circulation. Thus, by joining this extensive enterprise that "[b]etween 1817 and 1830 . . . published six million copies of its various titles, many of which were for children" (Taylor 13), Drysdale's views must have gained widespread circulation.

The ASSU perhaps accepted "The Negro Nurse" because Drysdale demands neither colonization nor immediate abolition; rather she shows Northern and Southern children that slaves could attain "freedom" through religious conversion. Through her protagonist, Drysdale suggests that slavery's worst evil stems not from how it deprives personal freedom but from how it threatens religion. Enslaved for forty years, Chloe has forgotten about the "land of her freedom" (29) and her branded cheek serves as the only visible reminder of slavery's brutality. According to Drysdale, neither the forced journey from Africa to America nor slavery's whip threatens to destroy Chloe; rather the hazard arises from her having forgotten her religion, which places Chloe "in the region of the shadow of death" (30). At death's door, Chloe's physical illness prompts her "liberation" when Frances Ridgely, the white child whom Chloe views as "a superior being" (31), encourages Chloe's religious conversion. Frances visits her dying "mammy," articulates basic religious principles, and reads Scripture selections. Chloe survives her illness and when she eventually accepts Frances's religious lessons, she "receive[s] that freedom which cometh down from above, and walked in the liberty and light of the gospel" (43). This gesture of "liberation" allows the slavocracy to mask Chloe's literal enslavement and defend her contentment since "the months and years glided peacefully over the happy family at Fair Lawn" (42). One must wonder whether the ASSU published Drysdale's narrative because it advances spiritual rather than literal liberation or because the organization hesitated to support the abolitionist movement just getting underway by 1827.

On the other hand, did the ASSU in actuality censor and/or revise a more radical narrative depicting a female liberating a slave? The ASSU's publication policies could explain the nonradical nature of Drysdale's narrative, which never extends beyond the religious and didactic rhetoric compatible with ASSU goals. According to the Pennsylvania Charter, the ASSU supplied their schools and libraries with reading materials that would "confe[r], gratuitously, moral and religious instruction on that part of our population, who, from their poverty, ignorance, or misfortunes, are unable to obtain these valuable acquisitions through the ordinary means, but more especially on the youth" (6). Thus, the ASSU only

"circulate[d] works which . . . do the most *good*" (*Sixth Annual Report* 18), meaning that they had to have "a decidedly religious character" (*Seventh Annual* 15).[10]
Furthermore, to insure that all denominations found its books, tracts, and juvenile magazine *(The Youth's Friend)* acceptable, the ASSU formed a Committee of
Publication consisting of no more than two members each from Baptist,
Methodist, Congregationalist, Episcopal, Presbyterian, Lutheran, and Dutch
Reformed churches. The committee rejected, expurgated, censored, and edited
manuscripts (*Seventh* 14) before it unanimously approved them for publication
(Taylor 13; *Charter* 8; *Sixth Annual* . . . 13). According to the *Sixth Annual Report,*
"In many instances, words, phrases, and even pages of our books have been
altered or expunged, on the suggestion that they might reasonably occasion
offense or misapprehension" (16). To reach their audience, ASSU contributors
clearly had to observe a strict rhetoric that stressed religious rather than political
and social aims. By 1833, the ASSU planned to establish Sunday schools and to
extend its publications in the South; however, they refused to exert any political
power or to reform civil rights violations (*Southern Enterprise* 1833). One must,
therefore, question the degree to which the committee influenced and/or modified Drysdale's narrative as the title suggests they did to her later work: *Evening
Recreations: A Series of Dialogues on the History and Geography of the Bible. Written
for the American Sunday School Union. Revised by the Committee of Publication.*

THE AMERICAN ANTI-SLAVERY SOCIETY

Whereas the ASSU often censored antislavery texts, the American Anti-Slavery
Society (AASS) created a rhetoric and a print campaign to circulate their opinions on a national and international scale. On January 6, 1832, William Lloyd
Garrison convened with twelve other men in the basement of Boston's African
Baptist Church to organize the New England Anti-Slavery Society (Cain 13),
the foundation for the national American Anti-Slavery Society (1833–1865). In
its *Declaration of Sentiments* (1833), the AASS employed language synonymous
with the rhetoric of both the church and ideal womanhood. For example, its *Declaration* states: "Ours shall be such only as the opposition of moral purity to moral
corruption—the destruction of error by the potency of truth—the overthrow of
prejudice by the power of love—and the abolition of slavery by the spirit of
repentance" (American 45). Having "adopt[ed] the printing, distribution, and
organizational methods of the Bible and Tract Societies" (Nord 23), the AASS
vowed to spread its message of purity, truth, love, and repentance in order to "circulate, unsparingly and extensively, antislavery tracts and periodicals" (American
48). With the editorial experience Garrison had gained from working on Benjamin Lundy's newspaper, he started publishing the Boston-based *Liberator* on
January 1, 1831.[11] Notwithstanding its perceived radicality, the *Liberator's* readership steadily increased. It had five hundred subscribers after the first volume in

1831, between 1,000 and 1,500 by the third volume, and 2,300 by spring 1834 (Grimké 197). Archibald Grimké states that the 2,300 copies printed in 1834 were distributed as follows:

> Philadelphia, four hundred; in Boston, two hundred, in other parts of the free States, eleven hundred; and that of the remaining three hundred, one-half was sent as exchange with other papers, and eighty of the other half were divided equally between England and Haiti, leaving seventy copies for gratuitous distribution. (199–200)[12]

Furthermore, Nord states:

> In 1835 the society flooded the mails with more than a million pieces of antislavery literature, sent free to people all over the country, including the South. The materials ranged from four new monthly journals and a children's newspaper to tracts, woodcuts, handkerchiefs, and even chocolate wrappers. This great "postal campaign" . . . was in many ways simply another campaign in the tract war that the Tappans and others had been waging for more than 10 years. (23)

Thus, while Drysdale may have had to edit her work to benefit from the ASSU's extensive distribution patterns, domestic abolitionists who subscribed to Garrisonian rhetoric and tactics may have had far-reaching influence, especially since subscription numbers do not account for those who shared the newspapers with nonsubscribers.

Extending a hand to women authors, the AASS appeared to recognize women's precarious tightrope walk. In contrast to the AASS's auxiliary all-female societies, the AASS and Garrison's decision to publish a children's column in the *Liberator* and a poetry collection created domestic and appropriately "female" spaces for women's abolitionist sentiments. Within its decidedly male, public, and political realm, the *Liberator* printed several women's voices in the "Juvenile Department," a weekly column devoted to presenting children with poems and stories about slavery. The April 9, 1831, issue contains Mary Russell Mitford's "The Two Dolls," which originally appeared in the London edition of *Our Village: Sketches of Rural Character and Scenery*.[13] Beginning on January 22, 1831, the *Liberator* published U.I.E.'s "The Family Circle," a series with titles such as "The Family Circle; or, the Story of Helen, George, and Lucy" and "Helen, George, and Lucy: The Eclipse." Although it remains almost impossible to identify U.I.E., the attribution of these two titles in *The Edinburgh Doll and Other Tales for Children* (1853) to "Aunt Mary" partially resolves the question of gender. Other female contributors also used pseudonyms: "Medora" wrote "On Hearing a Child Say 'Father'"; "Margery" claimed the work "Aunt Mary"; Philo Paidos wrote "Letter: The Little Slaves to the Sabbath School Children of New England;" and "Zillah," a young African American woman from Philadelphia, signed her penname to "A True Tale for Children," "For the Children," and "A Dialogue between a Mother and Her Child." The AASS clearly welcomed women's abolitionist juvenile literature in this print campaign; however, the tendency to use pseudonyms reflects the hazardous tightrope women walked. Interestingly, Garrison respected women's predicament and yet he fostered their voices when he republished these and other works in *Juvenile Poems, for the Use of Free American Children of Every Complexion*.[14] Considering that the nineteenth-century society granted mothers responsibility for shaping moral, patriotic, and civic-minded citizens, Garrison probably had few qualms about publishing women's abolitionist fiction for children. Actually, Garrison defended this collection's domestic and patriotic goals, stating:

> The only rational, and certainly the most comprehensive plan of redeeming the world *speedily* from its pollution, is to begin with the infancy of mankind. If, therefore, we desire to see our land delivered from the curse of PREJUDICE and SLAVERY, we must direct our efforts chiefly to the rising generation, whose minds are untainted, whose opinions are unfashioned, and whose sympathies are true to nature in its purity. (*Juvenile* Preface [3])

Sales figures for *Juvenile Poems* have not survived; however, if Garrison used strategies like those for distributing other AASS publications, then these domestic abolitionists' works secured an extensive readership.

Although little biographical information has surfaced about the women Garrison published, we may find an example of their lives in Elizabeth Margaret Chandler (1807–1834), a middle-class woman who opposed slavery and published her views in newspapers, but concealed her identity either due to modesty or fear of repercussions. Chandler was the youngest child and only daughter of Margaret Evans Chandler, who died during Chandler's infancy, and Thomas Chandler, a doctor who died when his daughter was nine years old. After her mother's death, the family moved from Center, Delaware, to Philadelphia, where Elizabeth attended the Friends' School until she turned thirteen and received strict religious training from her grandmother, Elizabeth Evans (Dillon, *Notable* 319; Lundy 8). Her upbringing in this Quaker community, with its tradition of allowing women to speak to mixed audiences, possibly sparked Chandler's abolitionist interests. According to Lundy, Chandler joined the Philadelphia Female Anti-Slavery Society, where

> she did not, in consequence of her retired habits, take a very active part in its *public* proceedings, [but] she felt deep and lively interest in its success. . . . At various times, she expressed her desires for the prosperity of the institution, as well as for the advancement of the cause general, in the most feeling terms. (39)

There, she met other abolitionist women like Hannah Townsend and Lucretia Mott, the latter of whom endured persecution when she endorsed Garrison's demand for immediate emancipation (Hare 104).

Although part of this women's coalition, Chandler exerted her influence *not* by speaking publicly or gathering petition signatures door-to-door, but by addressing women who read the "female" columns in abolitionist newspapers, a public but more acceptable forum. Chandler apparently followed the rules of decorum throughout her literary career. As a child she wrote poetry, some of which her friends and relatives published when Chandler was twelve. By age sixteen, Chandler's articles had appeared in newspapers (Bowerman 613), but Benjamin Lundy reports, "such was her retiring modesty, and native diffidence, that she did not, for a considerable length of time, permit her name to be used publicly, as an author" (10). Despite her modesty, Chandler felt insulted when her first antislavery poem, "The Slave Ship," originally won only third place in the *Casket*,[15] a popular, Philadelphia monthly magazine. Yet this "consolation" prize may have helped her career as an abolitionist spokeswoman. In a letter to her good friend Hannah Townsend, Chandler describes how reprinting "The Slave Ship" led to her association with the Quaker Benjamin Lundy and his newspaper. She writes:

> ["The Slave Ship"] was copied into the "Genius of Universal Emancipation"; when the signature was recognized by a friend of mine, who acquainted the editor (B. Lundy) with the name of the author, and conveyed me a request from him, to write occasionally for the paper. An introduction and acquaintance afterwards followed; and I continued to write, sometimes, for the poetical department, until I was formally installed into the editorship of the "Ladies Repository"—and our own friendship has been the result. (Lundy 11–12)

As her letter implies, Lundy provided Chandler with the forum to link her literary talent, political views, and her awareness of women's "place" to a public, literary sphere. From 1826 to 1834, Chandler wrote for the "Ladies Department" in Lundy's *Genius of Universal Emancipation*,[16] "which in 1827 had a weekly circulation of nearly 1,000 subscribers" (Jones 14). By late 1829, at the age of twenty-two, she became the column's editor. Through her literary talent and her experiences with the Philadelphia Female Anti-Slavery Society and the Ladies' Free Produce Society, Chandler encouraged women to oppose slavery (M. Jones 2; 100–101). Dillon argues:

> Miss Chandler continually encouraged women to make greater use of their intellectual abilities, and in her columns for the *Genius* she appealed to them to take their place alongside men in the fight against slavery. In particular she advocated the free-produce movement, an enterprise especially favored by the Quakers, as a means by which women could make their influence felt most effectively; since women more than men controlled the purchasing of food, clothing, and household supplies, they could refuse to buy goods produced by slave labor. (*Notable* 319)

Adamant that women engage in abolitionist politics like their male counterparts, Chandler wrote "An Appeal to the Ladies of the United States" to awaken female philanthropy and reform efforts (Lundy 16–21; see also Bowerman 613 and

Sklar 323). Even after her move in 1830 from Philadelphia to "Hazelbank" (her family's farm in Lenawee County, Michigan), this private, self-effacing woman continued inspiring women with her pen. She "spread her gospel of abolition among [Michigan] settlers" (Filler 276) and as column editor she sustained her influence over the women (from the midwest to the northeast) who read the *Genius* as well as other newspapers and magazines that republished her works (M. Jones 14–15, Dillon, *Benjamin* 173–74; see also Bowerman 613).

Chandler's connection and friendship with Lundy facilitated her subsequent acquaintance with William Lloyd Garrison. Chandler met Garrison in 1829 while he co-edited Lundy's *Genius*. This close working relationship and their mutual defense of women's rights (Cain 14; Reynolds *Uncle* 77–78)[17] helped Chandler crystallize, as Merton Dillon argues, her support for Garrison's conviction in immediate abolitionism rather than Lundy's support for gradualism and colonization (*Notable* 319). Consequently, when in 1831 Garrison broke ties with Lundy, left the *Genius,* and started the *Liberator,* Chandler gained an entrée into another abolitionist arena. From her Michigan residence, Chandler permitted Garrison to republish her juvenile literature, often forgotten due to the attention given to her essays for women. Except for "The Child's Evening Hymn," which Chandler published in the *Liberator* (May 7, 1831) *before* the *Genius* (June, 1831), and "Oh Press Me Not to Taste Again," which appeared exclusively in the *Liberator* (December 1, 1832), her juvenile poems typically appeared in the *Liberator* approximately a month *after* the *Genius* publication date.[18] Credited to "Margaret," one of Chandler's pseudonyms, "What Is a Slave, Mother?" first appeared in the May, 1831, issue of *Genius* and then in the June 4, 1831, issue of the *Liberator's* "Juvenile Department." "Looking at the Soldiers" (1832), "The Sugarplums" (1832),[19] and "Christmas" (1834) follow this same publication pattern and request for anonymity. Thus, Garrison enlarged Chandler's sphere of influence by publishing her poems in the *Liberator's* juvenile column and later in *Juvenile Poems.*

Even after her death in 1834, Garrison and Lundy continued to place Chandler on the abolitionist podium. Garrison reprinted "What Is a Slave, Mother?," "Oh Press Me Not to Taste Again," "The Sugarplums," and "The Child's Evening Hymn" in his collection, *Juvenile Poems* (1835). Sustaining Chandler's desire for privacy by not attributing the poems to her, Garrison nevertheless presents Chandler's voice and views to another distinctly abolitionist forum and audience, children whose parents supported Garrisonian politics with their purses.[20] Similarly, Lundy printed her collected abolitionist poems and essays in *The Poetical Works of Elizabeth Margaret Chandler* (1836). Lundy calls Chandler

> the first American female author that ever made this [slavery] the principle theme of her active exertions: and it may safely be affirmed, without the least disparagement to others, that no one of her sex, in America, has hitherto contributed as much to the enlightenment of the public mind, relative to this momentous question, as she has done. (12–13)

Assembled with Hannah Townsend's assistance, Lundy, however, finally exposes Chandler's identity as well as the breadth and depth of her abolitionist sentiments.

As it did for Chandler, the AASS extended to Chandler's friend Hannah Townsend (?–1865)[21] the opportunity to move beyond the all-female antislavery society into the "safer" public realm of children's literature when it published the *Anti-Slavery Alphabet* (1846). Townsend does not have Chandler's prolific publication record; yet, these two women's paths intersected. Like Chandler, Townsend's Quaker background may have spurred her participation in Philadelphia's female antislavery society and given her the courage to voice her convictions in this female coterie. John W. Jordan suggests that Townsend

> was an active member with her husband of Abington Quarterly Meeting, she being clerk for several years. About fourteen years after the death of her husband she moved to Philadelphia, and re-united herself with the Friends' Meeting at Fourth and Green Streets, of which she had been at one time clerk. She took an active interest in philanthropic work, was an ardent Abolitionist, and a friend of Lucretia Mott. . . . Sympathetic and kind of heart by nature, and possessed of fine literary taste and talent, she was a welcome visitor in many homes, and her company was much sought after. (1538)

The work with the Female Anti-Slavery Society on Cherry Street in Philadelphia (Lundy 30n) kept Townsend within gender-appropriate politics. It also generated friendships with important women like Mott and Chandler, who later dedicated "Remember Me" to her (M. Jones 84). Townsend continued the intimate friendship through correspondence even after Chandler moved to Michigan (Lundy 10–11; 28). Upon Chandler's death, Townsend helped Lundy collect her friend's works.

Perhaps reading Chandler's feminist and juvenile abolitionist works inspired Townsend to write the *Anti-Slavery Alphabet*. However, Townsend apparently did not emulate her friend's publication habits until she gained access to another gender-legitimate forum: the antislavery fair. According to Jean R. Soderlund, abolitionist women from Philadelphia held their first antislavery fair in 1836 and raised seven hundred dollars in 1839 "by charging a small admission and selling antislavery publications as well as their plain and fancy handiwork" (81). The fair expanded over the years, but the women maintained primary control and "from 1836 to 1853, the women raised about $16,500 from the fair" (82). Lloyd Hare states:

> The annual fairs inaugurated at Philadelphia became in them a Pennsylvania institution. The social attraction of these assemblies induced young persons to mingle in them, and thus were brought within the circle of anti-slavery influence laborers who might not otherwise have been converted. (95–96)

Submitting the *Anti-Slavery Alphabet* to the AASS for the 1846 and 1847 fairs, permitted Townsend to solidify her alliance with an influential Philadelphia institution, to influence young fair-goers, and to secure a large audience for her abolitionist views. Although difficult to determine her financial gains from the publication, Townsend added her voice to a women's organization that made the highest contributions to the state antislavery society and as a result, maintained power and "won a share of authority at the state level" (Soderlund 84). Townsend's experience suggests that the AASS again moved women from all female spaces to public forums while providing them with a "safety net" by claiming that they wrote for the children, an appropriate women's audience.

The AASS also welcomed vocal women, like Jane Elizabeth Jones (1815?–1896), who dared walk the tightrope with and without a safety net. Jones resided in Vernon, New York, and was from an "economically comfortable family" (Moser 7). She taught in Mount Vernon Academy school for boys, but ultimately

> became a pioneer Abolitionist lecturer in New England and eastern Pennsylvania. She first visited Ohio, accompanying another controversial abolitionist lecturer, Abby Kelley. In 1845 the two women arrived in Salem, Ohio, a center of fervent abolitionism, and Hitchcock/Jones quickly became involved; she helped to organize antislavery activists and co-edited *The Anti-Slavery Bugle*, official voice of William Lloyd Garrison's Western Anti-Slavery Society. (3)

In this respect, she resembles Chandler in her influence, but not in her modesty. Chandler (as "Margaret") spread her abolitionist views through female- and child-centered forums. Conversely, Jones risked mob attacks and criticism during her public lectures at abolitionist and women's rights conventions from 1850 until her husband's death in the 1860s (5–6). Although her later feminists writings (*The Wrongs of Women: An Address Delivered Before the Ohio Women's Convention, at Salem, April 19th, 1850* and *Address to the Women's Rights Committee of the Ohio Legislature* [1861)]) have survived, many of her *Anti-Slavery Bugle* articles went unsigned and Moser has not located Jones's abolitionist lectures. Ironically, therefore, Jones's *The Young Abolitionist; or Conversations on Slavery* (1848), remains the only identifiable record of her abolitionist thoughts. Although this children's book represents the "safest" thing Jones ever wrote, its contents underscore her nonconformity, activism, and feminism, evident through its fictional mother-historian who chronicles slavery's history to give her children a more accurate understanding of American history.

As little as we know of Chandler, Townsend, and Jones, we know even less of other women who published through AASS affiliates. Little biographical information has surfaced regarding "Cousin Ann"; however, we can speculate that she held abolitionist principles based on her decision to publish *Cousin Ann's Stories for Children* (1849) through J. M. McKim. According to William Cohen's "James Miller McKim: Pennsylvania Abolitionist," McKim renounced his role as a Presbyterian minister to join the abolitionist movement and ultimately to serve as an AASS agent in Philadelphia (167–68). He lectured for the Pennsylvania Anti-Slavery Society (PASS) and as "corresponding editor," he published descriptions of these traveling lectures in Lundy's *National Enquirer* (181). But he may have stopped doing so when by 1845 he decided to support Garrison fully (219). Moreover, in 1839, Lucretia Mott offered him a job as the organization's publisher. In February 1840, McKim restocked the failing bookstore on 31 North Fifth Street with tracts on temperance and women's rights (229), goods from the Free Produce Society (230), and antislavery tracts, of course. Thus, when Cousin Ann sent *Cousin Ann's Stories for Children* (1849) to him, she affiliated herself with a powerful individual and Garrisonian politics. Furthermore, Cousin Ann probably suspected that her short-story collection would gain wide circulation under McKim. He contributed to the New York based *National Anti-Slavery Standard* (Cohen 235), in which he advertised *Cousin Ann's Stories for Children* until 1858, nine years after the book's original publication. Thus, published by this influential abolitionist with connections to Garrison and other prominent abolitionists, Cousin Ann's antislavery politics reached a large audience.

Finally, in addition to his abolitionist views, Garrison's support of women's rights perhaps facilitated the publication of some women's work when the Pennsylvania Anti-Slavery Society had Merrihew and Thompson publish S.C.C.'s *Louisa in Her New Home* (1854). S.C.C. authored several juvenile texts such as "The Wishing Cap" (which appeared in Eliza Follen's 1847 issue of *The Child's Friend*), *The Wonderful Mirror* (1855), and *A Visit to the Country* ([nd]). The children whom the AASS influenced in the 1830s with its "Juvenile Department," *Juvenile Poems,* and other abolitionist texts had come of age; therefore, by publishing S.C.C.'s novel about a young female protagonist,[22] the AASS offered the post-Stowe generation a female who acted upon her abolitionist beliefs. Moreover, it gave S.C.C. the opportunity to voice her beliefs about women's political actions in a genre that did not appear as threatening

The publication of these recovered texts reveals that for over twenty years the AASS gave domestic abolitionists a "safe" place from which to voice their opinions. Whether through the *Liberator's* "Juvenile Department," its *Juvenile Poems,* or its regional publishing affiliates, the AASS offered women a "safety net" by concealing their names while identifying them as women. For those women like Townsend and Jones who dared to traverse the tightrope without anonymity, it published names. Regardless, the AASS affirmed women's roles as mothers and teachers and yet, in very feminine ways, it allowed them to overstep the boundary that otherwise kept them from the public abolitionist debate.

COMMERCIAL PUBLISHERS

The AASS and its regional offices made an obvious commitment to publishing antislavery works; yet according to John R. Adams, "[a]bolitionist literature was frankly boycotted by many [commercial] publishers" (33), a circumstance that invites examining those who marketed juvenile abolitionist texts. Despite the boycott by some, commercial publishers in urban centers such as Boston, New York, Philadelphia, and Cincinnati disseminated women's abolitionist juvenile litera-ture. Publication and sales figures remain unavailable; yet the geographic decen-tralization attests to some publishers' willingness to support children's abolitionist socialization and to make women's abolitionist voices audible to wide audiences.

Boston commercial publishers accepted many manuscripts from abolitionist white women, but at least one sanctioned an African American woman's aboli-tionist project for children. Susan Paul (1807–1841),[23] a prominent African American abolitionist and feminist from Boston, wrote *Memoir of James Jackson, the Attentive and Dutiful Scholar, Who Died in Boston, October 31, 1833, Aged Six Years and Eleven Months* (1835). Daughter of Thomas Paul, who was an appren-tice for Garrison's *Liberator* (Cain 5), an abolitionist, and founder and pastor of Boston's influential African Baptist Church (Hansen, "Boston" 47–48),[24] Susan Paul followed in her father's activist footsteps. She served as a member of the Massachusetts Anti-Slavery Society, an officer in the Boston Female Anti-Slav-ery Society (one of the few integrated female antislavery societies),[25] a delegate to the 1837 Anti-Slavery Convention in New York, and a vice president of the Sec-ond Annual Anti-Slavery Convention of American Women in Philadelphia. Many famous abolitionist women such as Anne Warren Weston, Lydia Maria Child, Hannah Southwick, and Henrietta Sargent championed Paul.

In addition to Paul's community status and activism, several related factors may have prompted the Boston-based James Loring to publish Paul's *Memoir of James Jackson,* grounded in the experiences at her school for black children. After her father's death, Paul tried with great difficulty to support her mother and other family members by opening a school for black children that "combined general education with religious education" (Yee 65). Loring possibly published *Memoir of James Jackson* to alleviate the Paul's financial difficulties. More likely, however, he published her text because it reflected his interests in Baptist and children's lit-erature. He printed many Baptist works since he and his former partner, William Manning, were the leading printers for New England Baptists (Thesing 347). Paul's narrative also corresponded with Loring's record for publishing many juvenile texts between 1815 and 1837 (Mahoney 294), such as Martha Sher-wood's "The Poor Little Negroes." Their mutual interest in abolitionism may have also influenced Loring's decision to publish Paul's work because he knew her personally since he sold tickets at the *Liberator's* office for concerts given by Paul's students in "Garrison's Juvenile Choir" (Yee 65–66). Thus, Paul's text found a publisher whose business interests as well as religious and political beliefs matched her abolitionist views, thereby allowing her work to circulate in the pub-lic realm.

Like Susan Paul, Eliza Lee Cabot Follen's (1787–1860) status as a promi-nent Bostonian, an "upper-class activist" (Hansen, *Strained* 19) devoted to aboli-tionist sentiments, and a popular children's author may have helped her secure publishers willing to support her abolitionist views. Samuel Cabot's work as a merchant often led to uncertain financial circumstances; yet, neither lack of money nor the distraction of having twelve siblings prevented Eliza from receiving considerable intellectual stimulation through the family's ties to many prominent Bostonians (Schlesinger 157). The family's residence in Cambridge affiliated her with an intellectual community and facilitated friendships with Harriet Martineau, William Ellery Channing, and Catharine Sedgwick. In Sedgwick's home, Eliza met the German refugee and her future husband, Charles Follen. Her friends expressed concern about this engagement to a foreigner, evident in William Ellery Channing's Aug. 23, 1827, letter to Catharine Maria Sedgwick (William Ellery Channing Papers, MHS). However, when Charles Follen's "German fiancée refused to join him, [his] friendship [with Eliza] took a new aspect," and Eliza (then forty-one years old) married him in 1828 (Schlesinger 157; 158). They remained in Boston's intellectual circles because Charles Follen taught German and gymnastics at Harvard and there he "worked actively in the antislavery cause" (Moe 58). But his Harvard career ended when, according to Eliza, their abolitionist efforts provoked Harvard's refusal to continue employing her husband "since many proper Bostonians disapproved of the movement" (Schlesinger 160).

Despite the popular disapproval, Eliza Follen made significant contributions to the antislavery cause. She wrote numerous abolitionist works, including *To the Mothers in the Free States* (1855) and edited the abolitionist annual, *The Liberty Bell*. Follen's contributions to the Anti-Slavery Tract collection include several hymns and songs that approach slavery from diverse perspectives: familial ("Remember the Slave"), religious ("Where Is Thy Brother," "And the Days of Thy Mourning Shall Be Ended," and "Lord Deliver"), and political ("The Land of the Free and the Home of the Brave" and "Auld Lang Syne"). In addition to her written work, Follen was also "an active member of abolitionist society both in Boston and Cambridge, she lectured . . . and helped to organize antislavery bazaars to raise funds for the cause" (Schlesinger 166). As a result of this written and public political activity, Eliza Follen's "life as a radical outcast intensified" (MacCann 142).

Historians have shown new interest in Eliza Follen's abolitionist efforts; yet they overlook how, despite her "outcast" status, she continued to write children's literature. In fact, she probably used her popularity as a children's author to voice her abolitionist views. Phyllis Moe states: "Although her children's poetry is now almost forgotten, F[ollen] was a pioneer who turned from the harsh, morbid verse characteristic of early nineteenth-century American children's poetry to rhymes frankly meant to give more pleasure than instruction" (59). Perhaps best known for "The Three Little Kittens" (*Little Songs* 1833), Follen published children's fiction and poetry as early as 1831 in *Hymns, Songs and Fables for Children*. She also wrote *The Well-Spent Hour* (1827); *The Sequel to the Well-Spent Hour* (1832); *Little Songs* (1833); *Nursery Songs* (1839); and *The Liberty Cap* (1837). When a steamship accident killed her husband in January 1840, she taught school and became a professional writer.[26] From 1843 to 1850, she edited *The Child's Friend* and authored collections such as *True Stories about Dogs and Cats* (1856); *May Morning* and *New Year's Eve* (1858); and a twelve-volume collection entitled *Twilight Stories* (1858). Clearly, publishers promoted her work.

Commercial Boston publishers ostensibly accepted that Follen interspersed these and other juvenile texts with several sentimental and overtly subversive antislavery juvenile works. For example, *The Liberty Cap*, a short-story collection about slavery, went through multiple printings. Consumers purchased this four-by six-and-a-half-inch soft-covered book in 1837 from Boston's Leonard J. Howland and in 1840 and 1846 from Leonard C. Bowles's bookstore. Similarly, in 1832, Boston's Carter and Hendee published *The Sequel to the Well-Spent Hour; or, The Birthday*, which contains a slave's narrative, and a new edition, *The Birthday: A Sequel to the Well-Spent Hour*, appeared in 1848 from Boston's J. Munroe. Another willing endorsement emerges in the publication history of Follen's short story "May Morning." During her tenure as editor of *The Child's Friend*, Follen championed her own voice when she printed this story as "The Melancholy Boy" (1844).[27] However, the Boston-based John M. Whittmore (stationer) and Nichols and Hall (publishers) stereotyped this work at the Boston Stereotype Foundry as a little volume entitled *May Morning and New Year's Eve* and issued it in 1857, 1858, 1866, and 1868. Her frequent appearance in print suggests that publishers considered Follen an important and marketable children's author. Furthermore, by reprinting and reissuing her works from 1830 until after her death, publishers also promoted her abolitionist voice in this "safe," public forum.

The publication history of *Hymns, Songs, and Fables for Children* most effectively epitomizes Follen's acceptability and marketability. This collection includes five antislavery poems: "Remember the Slave," "Children in Slavery," "The Little Slave's Wish," "Billy Rabbit to Mary," and "Soliloquy to Ellen's Squirrel on Receiving His Liberty—Overheard by a Lover of Nature and a Friend of Ellen." Opponents of women's political expression could have silenced these texts; yet, this volume went through several Boston publishers for about twenty years. Varter, Hendee, and Babcock first published it in 1831, followed by Leonard C. Bowles (1833), then William Crosby and H. P. Nichols (1847, 1848, 1851, and 1854).[28] Furthermore, these works also appeared individually under various titles. "Children in Slavery" appeared as "Lines on Hearing of the Terror of the Children of the Slaves at the Thought of Being Sold" in Follen's *The Liberty Cap* (1846). Sometime between 1855 and 1856, Follen republished it as "On Hearing of the Sadness of the Slave Children from the Fear of Being Sold" for the AASS's Tract collection. Follen's "The Little Slave's Wish" (1846) even appeared thirteen years later as "The Slave Boy's Wish" in Julia Colman's "Little Lewis: the Story of a Slave Boy" (1859), which identifies Follen by name (29). Criticized for her public abolitionist efforts, Follen nevertheless maintained her popularity as a children's author by tactfully scattering her abolitionist juvenile literature throughout her works and embedding her attacks on slavery in these gender-appropriate spaces.

Boston clearly offered women several opportunities to publish their abolitionist sentiments in juvenile literature: Susan Paul worked with James Loring and Eliza Follen utilized a host of commercial publishers. In addition, others ultimately found a forum for their political views in one commercial publisher, John P. Jewett. Originally a publisher of textbook, readers, and novels, Jewett "rapidly took on longer novels and expanded into other fields, gaining a reputation as a publisher of religious, temperance, and abolitionist titles" (Shackelford & Everett 226). His fame rests with the fact that when Phillips, Sampson, and Co. considered it too risky to print a woman's thoughts about slavery, Jewett embraced his wife's advice to publish Harriet Beecher Stowe's *Uncle Tom's Cabin* (Hedrick 223). He sold 10,000 within a few days of its first March 1852 issue and 300,000 copies by December 1852 (Shackelford & Everett 226; Lenz 345). His success led him quickly to supplement Stowe's novel with several juvenile renditions,[29] even though Stowe considered the original appropriate for children. Millicent Lentz argues that Stowe "read [the original version] to her own children as she wrote it and shared the first Little Eva episode with her class of school children in September 1851" (345). Furthermore, in the last *National Era* installment, Stowe wrote:

> Dear children, you will soon be men and women, and I hope that you will learn from this story always to remember and pity the poor and oppressed. When you grow up, show your pity by doing all you can for them. Never, if you can help it, let a colored child be shut out from school or treated with neglect or contempt on account of his color. Remember the sweet example of little Eva. . . . Then, when you grow up, I hope the foolish and unchristian prejudice against people merely on account of their complexion will be done away with. (qtd. in Lenz 345)

Jewett, notwithstanding Stowe's opinions, published the child-oriented *A Peep into Uncle Tom's Cabin* (1853), as did the London-based publisher, Sampson, Low, and Sons ("Harriet," *BAL*). Edited by "Aunt Mary," whom Blanck identifies as Mary Low, Sampson Low's daughter,[30] *A Peep* contains an address from Stowe "to the children of England and America" that prefaces an abridged *Uncle Tom's Cabin* (front cover [?]).[31] Jewett also published *Pictures and Stories from Uncle Tom's Cabin* (1853?), the first juvenile work in his "Juvenile Anti-Slavery Toy Books" series (Figure 1). Albeit designed specifically for children, the preface suggests a broader audience:

> The purpose of the Editor of this little Work, has been to adapt it for the juvenile family circle. The verses have accordingly been written by the Authoress for the capacity of the youngest readers, and have been printed in a large bold type. The prose parts of the book, which are well suited for being read aloud in the family circle, are printed in a smaller type. . . . ([2])

Jewett's decision to use two font sizes to accommodate family readings and independent youngsters reveals his conscious marketing to a dual audience. Stressing the text's appropriateness for the "family circle" reinscribed this political narrative into a gender-appropriate sphere; ironically, its publication opened the political arena to midcentury domestic abolitionists.

Jewett's financial success with Stowe's novel and his promise to continue the "Juvenile Anti-Slavery Toy Books" series attracted other women writers. He may have lured them by promising financial gains and an acceptable published forum for their political views. If the financial prospects attracted them, domestic abolitionists perhaps also recognized that Jewett guaranteed a larger market since he could publish their works from both Boston (1847 to 1857) and from Cleveland, Ohio, before the Panic of 1857 closed his business. For example, Jewett's ability "to distribute his books both to the East Coast and to the growing western market" (S. Williams 181) benefited "Aunt Mary's" *The Edinburgh Doll and Other Tales for Children* (parts of which originally appeared in Garrison's *Liberator* in 1831) and the domestic abolitionists who authored *Grandmother's Stories for Little Children* and *The Lamplighter Picture Book*.[32] Similarly, Kate Barclay relied on James M. Alden and J. C. Derby (both from Auburn, New York) and a publisher in Geneva, New York, to publish her earlier works; however, she sent Jewett her antislavery juvenile work, *Minnie May: With Other Rhymes and Stories*. Although now difficult to determine publication statistics, Jewett's success with *Uncle Tom's Cabin*, his advertising campaigns, and his two publishing houses most likely increased publication output and sales of these juvenile texts. Consequently, domestic abolitionists may have profited financially and politically by letting Jewett publish their abolitionist sentiments.

Perhaps hoping for success similar to Jewett's, other commercial houses accepted domestic abolitionists' works from the mid to late 1850s. Two New York publishers joined the enterprise. First, adhering to their reputation for publishing juvenile literature and perhaps encouraged by the popularity of Stowe's narrative, Philip J. Cozans and Vincent Dill (stereotyper) published both *Little Eva, the Flower of the South* (185?) and *Little Eva, the First Book* (1853 & 1855). Second, evident from their "List of Books and Periodicals," New York's Carlton and Porter most likely published several abolitionist juvenile works for the Sunday School Union and Tract Society of the Methodist Episcopal Church since work for such sectarian groups bolstered market sales. They published a children's library that included fifteen-cent titles such as *The African Orphan Boy* (1800 and 1852), *The History of Adjai: the African Slave Boy Who Became a Missionary* (18??), *Martyrs of the South* (1853), and *What Will Become of the Baby? With Three Other Stories about Children in Heathen Lands* (1855). Their youth-oriented works about slavery, which ranged from twenty-five to forty-five cents, respectively, included *History of Little Richard and Life of Africaner* (1856) and *The Earnest Laborer; or, Myrtle Hill Plantation. Being Sketches and Incidents Drawn from the Experience of a School Teacher, A Book for Senior Scholars* (1864). Authorship of the former juvenile texts remains anonymous; however, Carlton and Porter clearly attribute *The Child's Anti-Slavery Book: Containing a Few Words about American Slave Children*

JEWITT & COMPANY, BOSTON, AND CLEVELAND, OHIO.

ANTI-SLAVERY LITERATURE.

Uncle Tom's Cabin. By Mrs. H. B. Stowe.	Paper,	.38
" " " "	2 vols., do.,	1.50
" " " "	Svo. Illustrated,	2.50
" " " "	Svo. Gilt,	3.50
" " " "	Turkey, gilt,	5.00
" " " "	in German,	.50
The Key to Uncle Tom's Cabin.	paper,	.50
" " " " "	cloth,	.75
" " " " "	1 vol., 12mo,	1.00
Cabin and Key, bound together,	cloth,	1.25

We need publish no comments *of the press* in regard to this work. *We have issued* ☞ 310.000 *copies.*

Speeches of Joshua R. Giddings. 1.00

Writings of Judge Jay on Slavery. 1.00

White Slavery in the Barbary States. By Charles Sumner. 50

Life of Isaac T. Hopper. By Mrs. L. M. Child. 1.25

Despotism in America. By Richard Hildreth. 75

The American Colonization Society. By G. B. Stebbins. 38

A Sabbath Scene. By J. G. Whittier. Illustrated. 25

Autographs for Freedom. 75

Nebraska; a Satirical Poem. 13

Know Nothing; a Poem for the Times. 13

Juvenile Anti-Slavery Toy Books.

Pictures and Stories from Uncle Tom (for children.) 13

The Edinburg Doll, &c. 13

Grandmother's Stories. 13

Minnie May, and other Rhymes. 13

The Series to be continued.

FIGURE 1. John P. Jewett's advertised prices for anti-slavery literature, including the Juvenile Anti-Slavery Toy Books series.

and Stories of Slave Life (1859) to Julia Colman and Matilda Thompson.[33] The decision to publish a collection that depicts victimized slave children must have been well received because Tebble finds that the Boston-based James P. Walker and Horace B. Fuller, who published "war books and children's' books with equal success," also published *The Child's Anti-Slavery Book* (433).

Bridging the antebellum and postbellum periods, Lee and Shepard emerged as one of the last Northern, antebellum, commercial houses to publish domestic abolitionists' works.[34] Located down the street from John P. Jewett's Boston bookstore (Kilgour 9), Lee and Shepard, was "a champion of women's rights, a pioneer in educational books" and authors whom others often labeled radical (Tebble 419). Therefore their decision to republish a work that depicts a mother figure voicing antipatriotic, abolitionist sentiments should not surprise. Asa Bullard, the Congregationalist and secretary of the Massachusetts Sabbath School Society since 1834 (Kilgour 37), compiled *Aunt Lizzie's Stories* (1863). The small volume contains the "Fourth of July Address to Children," which originally appeared in Matilda Thompson's "Mark and Hasty" (1859). With their commitment to women's writing and with the "risk" of publishing a new work having passed, Lee and Shepard may have decided to endorse both the author and her abolitionist message.

Commercial publishers from Boston, New York, Philadelphia, and Cincinnati sanctioned women's political voices by distributing their juvenile fiction. Children's book reviewing did not begin until after the Civil War; therefore, it is difficult to determine how these texts were received. But it seems that these authors and their publishers were willing to take the risk.

THE AMERICAN REFORM TRACT AND BOOK SOCIETY

As opposed to the recognized sectarian societies and commercial publishers discussed above, literary critics and historians have known little about the American Reform Tract and Book Society (ARTBS), which Anne MacLeod has dismissed as a "special press" notwithstanding its publication of the greatest number of domestic abolitionists. The ARTBS, an important Cincinnati-based sectarian reform group, combined Christian and antislavery frameworks, as opposed to the American Tract Society, a Christian organization little interested in slavery.[35] The group met at Vine St. Congregational Church in Cincinnati at 10 A.M. on December 17, 1851, and formed the ARTBS ([*Constitution* 2]). Almost one year later, in November 1852, leaders decided to "form a regular incorporation, under the general law of Ohio for incorporating religious and benevolent societies" and at that time the "organization, under State law, was perfected, and the following constitution adopted" (2). According to Walter Sutton, the ARTBS exemplifies one of the "later crusading groups . . . which was organized to combat slavery" (151).

The AASS would have not been born without the support of Garrison and the twelve other leaders who met on a cold Boston day in January 6, 1832; similarly, the AFTBS may have never been realized had it not been for some prominent, abolitionist midwesterners. Reverend John Rankin (1793–1886), the ARTBS's Presbyterian founder and president, wrote letters to his brother opposing slave holding (Coyle 513); housed fugitives in his Ripley house in Ohio, which became the basis of Stowe's story about Eliza Harris;[36] and founded the Kentucky Anti-Slavery Society. He authored several books, including *A Remedy for Universalism: A Present to Families,* and *An Antidote for Unitarianism* (published by Weed at the Bible Tract and Sunday School Book Depository in Cincinnati). Like Rankin, other ARTBS officers had firsthand experience with slavery. For example, Reverend James A. Thome (1813–1873), a prominent Presbyterian minister from Cleveland, advocated abolitionism in rebellion against his slave-owning father. In 1833, Thome studied with Lyman Beecher at Lane Theological Seminary, where he first met Northern abolitionists. "[O]usted from seminary for extreme views," he attended Oberlin from 1835–1836, where he received support for his antislavery views and efforts ("James A. Thome" 966). From November 1836 to June 1837, Thome traveled to the West Indies to research the effects of immediate abolitionism and he published his findings in *Emancipation in the West Indies* (Lesick 184). However, his realization that the church could abolish slavery led him, after 1839, to shift from fulltime to part-time antislavery work (187) with several antislavery organizations, as well as accepting the position as one of the ARTBS's vice presidents.[37] Finally, as the organization's leaders, Rankin and Thome chose prominent men for its various offices. Most noticeably, Levi Coffin (1798–1877) became an AFTBS director.[38] Criticized for conducting a Sunday school for blacks in New Garden, North Carolina, Coffin moved, in 1826, to Newport, Indiana, where with his wife's help, this Quaker assisted fugitives (Coyle 124). John Scott states, "When the Coffins moved to Cincinnati in 1847, they had given help by their own estimate, to two thousand fugitives; and Coffin had won, for his unselfish labors, the title of 'president' of the Underground Railroad" (59).[39]

Just as Garrison supported domestic abolitionists whom the regional AASS presses published, so too, prominent ARTBS leaders and clergymen endorsed these female voices. But domestic abolitionists most likely looked to one man, the AFTBS's secretary and treasurer, Dr. George L. Weed, whose name appears in the society's advertisements and directions for submissions. Originally the publisher at the Cincinnati Bible Tract and Sunday School Book Depository, Weed published religious works,[40] antitobacco treatises,[41] and children's poems.[42] He also collaborated with John P. Jewett to publish Charles Torrey's *Home; or, The Pilgrim's Faith Revived* (1845) and Joseph Banvard's *Stories about Hands and Feet . . .* (1846). Weed's expertise as a publisher at the Bible Tract and Sunday School Book Depository and his interest in publishing religious, reformist, and children's literature placed him in an appropriate role as the ARTBS officer responsible for advertising and securing copyright for ARTBS publications that predominantly advocated abolitionism.

With Weed at the helm, the ARTBS employed print media to oppose organizations that the society called "the defenders of slavery, either by direct teaching, or by refusing to place it on the catalogue of sins" (*Constitution . . . Organization* 8). The ARTBS condemned the official silence by organizations such as the American Sunday School Union, the American Tract Society, the Methodist Book Concern, and the Presbyterian Board of Publications, who had widespread influence but whose intent to please public taste resulted in their habitually eliminating antislavery passages from books or falsifying history. Therefore, on February 1, 1856, the officers explained the society's origins and publishing goals in the circular of Frost's novel, *Gospel Fruits:*

> THE AMERICAN REFORM TRACT AND BOOK SOCIETY . . . is the offspring of necessity, brought into existence to fill a vacuum left unoccupied by most other Publishing Boards and Institutions—its object being to publish such Tracts and Books as are necessary to awaken a decided, though healthful, agitation on the great question of Freedom and Slavery. This is its primary object, though its constitution covers the broad ground of "promulgating the doctrines of the Reformation, to point out the application of the principles of Christianity to every known sin, and to show the sufficiency and adaptation of those principles to remove all the evils of the world and bring on a form of society in accordance with the Gospel of Christ." (Frost [189])

Counter to many commercial and sectarian publishers who censored information about slavery, the ARTBS pledged to "strike no sin from the catalogue of iniquities, because it is popular and powerful. It proposes to deal with slave holding as with other sins, bestowing upon it attention according to its importance" (*Constitution* 11). The ARTBS clearly saw itself as a mechanism that would combat the apathy and perceived dangerous tactics of other groups with its publications.

The ARTBS adamantly viewed the press as a powerful mechanism through which to voice the truth. The organization vowed to give readers, including children, access to truthful material that reflected abolitionist sentiments (*Constitution* 6–7; 10–11) and would do this through their press. Their *Constitution* states:

> The influence of our religious literature, in newspapers, tracts and books, and particularly books for Sabbath schools, is so great that no reform can be carried successfully forward in opposition to their teachings, except through a counteracting power from the press itself. Such is the rapidity with which thoughts are repeated and circulated, and so universal and implicit is the reliance placed by the majority upon these sources of information, that it is almost literally true, that the printing press does the thinking of the age.
>
> The power thus exerted in molding the public thought, is measureless, as well nigh irresistible. . . .

> Any attempt to create or sustain a public sentiment, by whatever instru-
> mentalities, without the aid of the press, must necessarily and utterly fail. How
> much more idle to calculate upon success in any reformation, not only without
> the press, but against its all-pervading power. (7)

The seriousness with which the society defended the press becomes evident in
the yearly reports and advertisements that document how it broadcasted a
reformist message through diverse materials. The ARTBS began by publishing
the *Christian Press,* which shifted from a weekly to a monthly newspaper when
its publication threatened the society's financial viability. By January, 1858, they
announced their success:

> To spread these principles the Society has issued more than twenty Bound
> Books and forty Tracts, has 3,500 pages stereotype plates on hand, and sends out
> 6,000 copies of its "Record," monthly. The Directors feel encouraged in their
> work, and will increase their efforts just as fast as funds are provided by friends
> of the Society. Your aid is respectfully solicited. (Weed, "Advertisement" 24)

A comparison of the March 1858 and January 1859 advertisements verifies its
commitment to large-scale publications. Within these nine months, the ARTBS
added three Sabbath school books, one tract on infidelity, three thousand copies
of the *Christian Press,* and one thousand pages of stereotyped plates.[43] This evidence of such extensive productivity establishes the ARTBS as anything but a
"special press."

Rather, the ARTBS appears as the most prolific publisher and champion of
women's abolitionist juvenile literature. In 1855[?], "a benevolent individual" who
recognized the need for additional abolitionist juvenile works authorized the
ARTBS to sponsor a contest that ultimately made audible a flurry of domestic
abolitionists' voices. The ARTBS offered a one hundred dollar premium "for the
best manuscript for a religious Anti-Slavery Sunday School book, showing [chil-
dren and youth] that American chattel slave-holding is a sin against God, and a
crime against man, and that it ought to be immediately repented of and abolished" (Frost, *Gospel* [v]). The one-hundred-dollar prize for a juvenile work that
blended religious and civic duty elicited forty-eight manuscripts.[44] The committee (H. Bushnell, John Jolliffe, and George L. Weed) awarded the premium to
Maria Goodell Frost's *Gospel Fruits; or, Bible Christianity Illustrated* (1856) (Figure 2) and recommended about fifteen others for publication (Frost, *Gospel* vi).
The gender of several authors whom the ARTBS published remains uncertain,
though the titles include: *The Child's Book on Slavery; or, Slavery Made Plain*
(1856), *A Tract for Sabbath Schools* (1857); and *Aunt Sally; or, The Cross, the Way of
Freedom* (1858). However, archival recovery work indicates that women penned
a majority of the works. Like Frost, other women submitted manuscripts: M. A.
F., from Troy, New York, sent *Gertrude Lee: or The Northern Cousin* (1856);[45] "A
Lady" sent *A Home in the South; or, Two Years at Uncle Warren's* ([c1857]); an

anonymous woman sent *Jemmy and His Mother, A Tale for Children* and *Lucy; or, the Slave Girl of Kentucky* (1858); Margaret Bayard Smith submitted *My Uncle's Family; or, Ten Months at the South* (1860); and "Lois" sent *Harriet and Ellen; or, The Orphan Girls* (1865). Many of these women may have concealed their identities because they lacked the backing of a renowned political figure (Frost had the support of her father, "the venerable Wm. Goodell" ([Advertisement, *Gertrude Lee* [np]). Although Frost did not gain her father's status, her juvenile

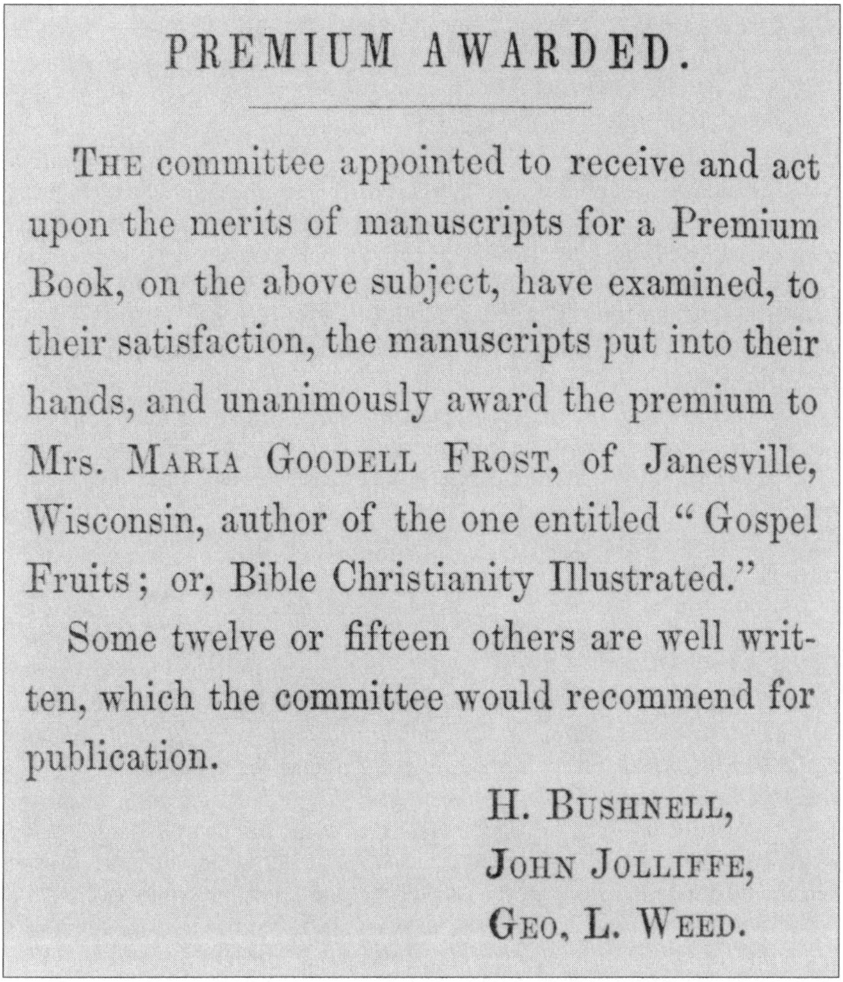

PREMIUM AWARDED.

THE committee appointed to receive and act upon the merits of manuscripts for a Premium Book, on the above subject, have examined, to their satisfaction, the manuscripts put into their hands, and unanimously award the premium to Mrs. MARIA GOODELL FROST, of Janesville, Wisconsin, author of the one entitled "Gospel Fruits; or, Bible Christianity Illustrated."

Some twelve or fifteen others are well written, which the committee would recommend for publication.

H. BUSHNELL,
JOHN JOLLIFFE,
GEO. L. WEED.

FIGURE 2. Award notice for Frost's *Gospel Fruits; or, Bible Christianity Illustrated. A Prize Essay* (courtesy of the American Antiquarian Society).

novel gained praise from reviewers as far as Connecticut and Boston.[46] It remains unclear whether each ARTBS domestic abolitionist gained similar praise; however, with the ARTBS's contest as license and its dedication to the power of words, each was probably insured a widespread audience.

The ARTBS's mission statement and publication history suggest that female contributors like Maria Goodell Frost could rely upon this staunch abolitionist message and commitment to widespread distribution. The ARTBS's voice had far-reaching resonance for two reasons. First, Cincinnati was such an important geographical point when it came to slavery "that only a hermit could have remained uninformed" (Adams 34). Second, as the largest publishing center in the west (Wroth 129), Cincinnati benefited from its status as a major city with many distribution options. According to John Scott, "When Harriet [B. Stowe] began to teach in the Western Female Institute in 1833, Cincinnati had become a town of twenty-five thousand and ranked among the biggest urban centers in the country" (40). The ARTBS itself recognized that its geographic position would facilitate distribution: "Its location is at Cincinnati, Ohio, the great heart of the west, is the focal point of the vast system of railroads and water communication, which enable it to distribute rapidly its publications, in every direction" (*Constitution* 11). Therefore, from 1853 to about 1863, the ARTBS established its offices and depository at 28 West Fourth Street,[47] just a few doors down from the Cincinnati branch of the American Sunday School Union, located at 41 West Fourth Street (Sutton 312). Location clearly did not impede circulation or distribution because the American Antiquarian Society's copy of M.A.F.'s *Gertrude Lee; or, The Northern Cousin* contains inscriptions by two Massachusetts women: Mrs. Maria Miller from Pittsfield and Mrs. Caroline R. Fisher from North Adams. The fact that these works traveled several hundred miles from Cincinnati to Massachusetts suggests that the juvenile novel had wide geographic circulation and also appealed to adult audiences.

In addition to its strategic geographical location, the ARTBS's extensive advertising and stereotyping techniques helped their contributors' voices reach progressively larger audiences. The back pages of many works contain advertisements for other publications, especially its juvenile series. For example, on the back pages of works like *Aunt Sally; Harriet and Ellen: or, The Orphan Girls;* and *Not a Minute to Spare,* readers found advertisements for *Gertrude Lee; or, The Northern Cousin; Gospel Fruits; or, Bible Christianity Illustrated;* and *The Child's Book on Slavery; or, Slavery Made Plain.* However, this extensive advertising would have been counterproductive if publication rates could not fulfill market demand. Confident in the works' popularity and need for republication, the ARTBS commissioned C. F. O'Driscoll, who conducted business in Cincinnati beginning in 1856,[48] to stereotype its publications. Hellmut Lehmann-Haupt argues that publishers stereotyped frequently reprinted books and very popular ones for which "a papier-maché mold [was] made from the type and metal plates [were] cast from this mold" (81). According to Papashvily:

> Under the old system, using a hand-set type, frames had to be broken and reset as a book progressed, since few printers owned enough spare type to set an entire volume. Consequently, a first edition often proved a last. The new cast plates (the stereotype and, later, the electrotype) not only permitted more impressions and hence more copies than hand-set type but, as an added advantage, might be stored for later printings. (36)

Stereotyping increased productivity as well as reduced manual labor and cost. Though the number of editions or reprints the ARTBS made of these women's books remains uncertain, the organization's use of advertising and technology suggests a response to consumer demand. Simultaneously, this widespread availability made these women's voices heard when "gendered expectations of bourgeois publicity" (Isenberg 61) would have preferred silence.

CONCLUSION

The biographical information and publication histories of Eliza Lee Cabot Follen, Elizabeth Margaret Chandler, Susan Paul, Hannah Townsend, and Maria Goodell Frost reveal a group of well-educated, northeastern and midwestern women who negotiated the tightrope between silence and political voice by writing abolitionist juvenile literature. Whether single, married, or widowed, they were politically active. These generic qualities help us to speculate that the more elusive Harriet Butts, Julia Colman, Matilda Thompson, "Cousin Ann," "Aunt Lizzie," M.A.F., and Lois most likely came from well-educated families in major metropolitan areas such as Boston, New York, or Philadelphia. Although it remains uncertain as to which women participated in regional female antislavery societies, each domestic abolitionist employed the "safe" and increasingly unique American genre to express subversive views about slavery that employed sentimental rhetoric, images of republican mothers, and/or fictional children who combat slavery. Through their partnerships with sectarian and commercial publishers, their widespread audiences witnessed nationalistic anxiety about and criticisms of America's inability to uphold the ideals voiced in the *Declaration of Independence*.

2

"Now, Caesar, say no more today; Your story makes me cry"

Sentimentalized Victims and Abolitionist Tears

One great reason why the people of this country have not thought and felt right on this subject, is that all our books, newspapers, almanacs and periodicals, have continued to represent the colored race as an inferior and degraded class, who never could be made good and useful citizens. Ridicule and reproach have been abundantly heaped upon them; but their virtues and their sufferings have found few historians.
—Lydia Maria Child, *Anti-Slavery Catechism* (1838)[1]

Compassion is a verb.
—Oprah Winfrey

POLITICIZING SENTIMENT

In her July 14, 1835, letter to the Lowell Female Anti-Slavery Society, Melissa Ammidon, of the Boston Female Anti-Slavery Society, exposes abolitionist women's attempt to elicit from children a private, sentimental response to a national problem. Ammidon informs female antislavery societies (FASS) from New York to Ohio of a commonplace, personal item imbued with complex politics:[2]

We have also published a pocket handkerchief for children, which will be ready for circulation in a short time, and we fervently pray, that the sad picture of human suffering these too *truly* portrayed may kindle in the breast of many a free born, happy child, a glow of heartfelt *sympathy*, and cause the *tears* to flow and the infant *offering* to arise to Heaven in behalf of those little injured down-trodden ones, to whom the blessed invitation of Jesus is alike addressed as to themselves to come to him but who by man are cruelly forbidden.[3]

The sympathy and tears the "truthful" handkerchief provokes would document the white child's ensuing empathy for the slave child. However, the strategy does not end with abolitionist tears for slaves whose "virtues and . . . sufferings have found few historians" (Child, *Anti-Slavery* 207), but with action: "offering" prayers for Divine intervention. By hybridizing sentiment and politics, female antislavery society members transferred a political subject to the most domestic space, the nursery, and instilled its occupants with power to recognize and battle oppression through politicized tears and prayers. In short, the FASS handkerchiefs instilled domestic objects with an activist agenda.

The various female antislavery societies' tactic of printing handkerchiefs with which children would dry their abolitionist tears parallels domestic abolitionists' attempts from the 1830s to the 1860s to print their messages on paper, which would record, not dry, the child's tears. Whether or not authors like E.T.C., "A Lady," "Grandmother," "Cousin Ann," Eliza Follen, Julia Colman, Matilda Thompson, Susan Paul, and Kate Barclay believed their works would attract a large readership, they used strategies that appealed to middle-class audiences. With an astute attention to literary trends and market demands, domestic abolitionists created the sentimental juvenile pseudo slave narrative, a hybrid genre that combined characteristics and strategies from three popular forms: the sentimental novel, the juvenile narrative, and the adult slave narrative. By hybridizing these narrative forms, these authors challenged contemporary juvenile literature that often evaded political discussions and thereby created a space from which to educate children about slavery and to inspire tears of compassion for its victims. Simultaneously, just as domestic fiction writers protested without appearing to endanger the status quo and true womanhood, domestic abolitionists' hybrid genre guaranteed them an entrée into the abolitionist debate. These authors carved out a "respectable" literary space from which they employed young victim's voices and experiences to express anxiety about slavery's destruction of childhood innocence, freedom, and family bonds: tropes for slavery's violation of the rights to life, liberty, and happiness.

Domestic abolitionists' hybrid creation counteracted the proslavery opinions that began to infiltrate the juvenile literary marketplace. Few proslavery children's works have surfaced during this recovery process, but those by Caroline Howard Gilman and Louisa Caroline Tuthill represent the attitude against which domestic abolitionists contended. Caroline Gilman published juvenile proslavery literature depicting contented slaves in *The Rose Bud; or, Youth's Gazette* (1832–1839), one of the earliest American magazines for children. According to Susan Sutton Smith, "Gilman's letters to her children after the Civil War show her still unchanged in the opinion that slavery had benefited the slaves" (129). Gilman voiced her proslavery views in works such as "The Planter's Son" and "The Plantation: A Ballad" published in *The Rose Bud Wreath* (1841), which characterize the Southern plantation as an ideal place with happy slaves. For example, in "The Plantation: A Ballad," she depicts contented slaves who sing, do not "repine alone" (I.76), happily weave baskets, and spend "careless" evenings after they return from the fields (I.92). Gilman's ideal pastoral society negates abolitionists' demand for intervention. She depoliticizes slavery further by instilling the story's "seeds of sorrow" (I.144) in the deaths of the overseer's two children, Anne and Francis. Consequently, she sustains proslavery sentiments and reinforces racial stereotypes rather than arousing compassion for slaves, the *living* "seeds of sorrow." Like Gilman, in *When Are We Happiest? or, the Little Camerons* (1848), Louisa Tuthill dismisses slavery's evils to establish the "happy slave" stereotype:

> "Are you talking about slaves?" my little readers ask, in some tone of surprise. To be sure, but we will not enter into any discussion about the evils of slavery. . . . The servants whom you will become acquainted with here are so kindly treated and so happy, that you will soon forget that they are not perfectly free. (3)

This nonchalant attitude continues as Tuthill encourages readers to accept the racist status quo:

> Have you [implied northern reader] a dislike to negroes? Ah, well! you will get over it before you have been long in the South, and it may be that you will begin to call some of those very black people "aunt" and "uncle"! You laugh at the very idea, but I can assure you that the little people to whom you are about to be introduced always call the old servants by these titles, and to them it does not seem at all strange. (2–3)

Turning fear into complacency and sorrow into happiness, Tuthill perpetuates an institution that violates principles of American democracy. Tuthill and Gilman's proslavery literature advocates that little, if anything, should arouse a young reader's anxiety about the peculiar institution's impact on America. Domestic abolitionists disagreed. Their hybrid narratives aimed to inform and lead readers to conversions that would ultimately change behavior.

In their efforts to challenge images of happy slaves, domestic abolitionists adopted and adapted strategies inherent to slave narratives, which Ephraim Peabody considered "'the most remarkable productions of the age'" (qtd. in MacKethan 55). Authentic slave narratives typically foreground a first-person narrator who recalls his/her early life, recognizes his/her disempowered status, resolves to ascertain freedom, and consequently rebels and attains freedom. Juvenile pseudo slave narratives foreground the African American perspective, but they vary from first to third person, usually focus on the slave's intense emotional experience related to one phase of the freedom quest, and often end unhappily. These modifications did not, however, alter the narratives' underlying values, which accounted for their widespread Northern circulation (Andrews 95). Domestic abolitionists realized that Americans like Ephraim Peabody "embraced and celebrated the fugitive slave as a kind of cultural-hero who exemplified the American romance of the unconquerable 'individual mind' steadily advancing toward freedom and independence" (98). These authors also fed the literary appetites for authentic slave narratives that exemplified "the cultivation of sensibility, the glorification of virtue, the preservation of family life, the revival of religion, and the achievement of a utopian society" (Foster 64). Like authentic slave narratives, the juvenile pseudo slave narratives demand that readers recognize how slavery threatens these ideals by exposing the slave child's lost innocence and the injustice of violated family life. Consequently, in these texts, establishing a utopian, American society entails viewing the slave child an "equal" rather than as an "other" (Fisher 99), ending childhood suffering, and restoring family bonds.

The domestic abolitionists' decision to add sentimental rhetoric to these already political adaptations further prevents labeling this hybrid form as apolitical, a judgment Ann Douglas passes on sentimental literature. In *The Feminization of American Culture* (1977), Douglas argues that dramatic economic and social changes during the early nineteenth century led to replacing intellectual and rational Calvinism with sentimental rhetoric; that is, "crude" examples of "anti-intellectualism" aimed at a "rationalization of the economic order" (12).[4] Romanticism "involves a genuinely political and historical spirit" (255); conversely, to Douglas, sentimentalism is apolitical: "the political sense obfuscated or gone rancid" (254). Douglas might argue that these domestic abolitionists merely capitalize on the appetite for slave narratives and the increasing mass consumerism to produce pabulum for young minds.[5] In actuality, domestic abolitionists directly and indirectly attempt to elicit abolitionist tears that would serve as springboards for activism, much like women's sentimental fiction, which critics such as Helen Waite Papashvily, Catherine E. O'Connell, and Jane Tompkins argue *embraced* gender, racial, and social politics. For Papashvily, the domestic novel provided women with a nonthreatening voice with which to "plead a special cause or share their convictions on a variety of controversial subjects" (xv). She states:

> No man . . . ever discovered that the domestic novels were handbooks of another kind of feminine revolt—that these pretty tales reflected and encouraged a pattern of feminine behavior so quietly ruthless, so subtly vicious that by comparison the ladies at Seneca appear angels of innocence. (xvii)

Just as some authors tactfully used this genre's rhetoric to voice their discontent about gender inequality, O'Connell contends that sentimental rhetoric gave authors a means to protest slavery: "Rather than representing retreat from public political discourse . . . the endorsement of the authority and authenticity of emotional experience . . . offers an alternative way *into* the political debate over slavery" (35). Clearly, domestic abolitionists recognized these strategies and employed them to educate children and to position their objections to proslavery sentiments in a respectable form.

ANXIETY OF LOST CHILDHOOD: EMPATHY'S FOUNDATION

Domestic abolitionists created this hybrid narrative to encode their anxiety about the child's (i.e., America's) fate under the corrupt political and economic system. By adopting the rhetoric of anxiety, they employed images which nineteenth-century scholars find inherent in the period's various art forms. Joy Kasson argues that nineteenth-century sculpture reveals anxiety that women might use their "social and sexual power" (3) to "triumph over their enslavers" (101). Similarly, Anne MacLeod considers children's literature "a source of social history" that "is useful for what it has to say directly about the values the authors hoped to teach children, and it is equally interesting for what it suggests about the fears, the anxieties, and the doubts of its creators" (11). But, most importantly, the rhetoric of anxiety pervaded women's sentimental novels, with which many domestic abolitionists were surely familiar. Jane Tompkins maintains that sentimental novels encode "some deeply felt national exigencies" (121) and offer solutions "at least as heroic as those put forward by the writers who said, 'No, in thunder'" (159–60). Similarly, Helen Papashvily, contends that these works "mirrored the fears and anxieties and frustrations, the plans and hopes and joys of those who read them so avidly" (xv) and Cathy Davidson stipulates that modern reader-critics trivialize the sentimental novel because they negate that "[t]he sentimental novel spoke more directly to the fears and expectations of its original readers than our retrospective readings generally acknowledge" (122). Recognizing the prevalence of anxiety in the period's art, children's literature, and adult fiction, domestic abolitionists, unsurprisingly, followed other artists' lead and encoded these national concerns in a palpable, gender-appropriate manner.

Through the sentimental rhetoric of anxiety, domestic abolitionists strategically inspire empathy for their new and most vulnerable political voices: slave children, traditionally marginalized in contemporary juvenile literature and adult slave narratives. According to MacLeod, conventional nineteenth-century juvenile literature often consisted of "tale[s] centered on a child in need of some moral correction; the correction of this or that fault then constituted the whole plot" ("Children's" 17).[6] Domestic abolitionists modified this expectation with stories about young victims who do not need moral reform but instead need rescue from an immoral institution. Furthermore, the rise of orphan and temperance literature urged young readers toward compassion for the less fortunate. For example, in

"Friendless and Homeless Children" (1857), Anne Wales Abbot narrates a story about poor white children and says, "A few facts will serve to give a perceptible reality to the gloomy picture, and quicken our sympathy for poor and parentless children" (97). She achieves these ends by emphasizing children's voices and stressing that "the want of sympathy grieved [children] more than the want of food, and clothing, and sport" (98). Via stories and pleas like Abbot's, domestic abolitionists endeavored to motivate privileged children to feel and eventually to act benevolently toward the less fortunate.

Creating a new cast of characters for juvenile fiction led these women to modify the typical protagonist in adult slave narratives. Frances Smith Foster contends that, except for chronicling the moment when the slave child shifts from innocence of his/her experience, "[t]here was little to be gained from extensive descriptions of early childhood; thus little space was devoted to this stage, and it is more appropriately considered prefatory to the mythic structure that dominates the work" (92). This argument seems valid in light of Frederick Douglass and Harriet A. Jacobs's works, in which childhood experiences constitute a very small part of their complex narratives. Yet, the portraits of violated childhood that give voice to the silenced victims suggest that domestic abolitionists *did* consider the slave child's experience unique and worthy of literary and political attention. Their narratives undermine Eugene Genovese's argument that slave children experienced a normal childhood and were better treated than children in European mills (503–504) and Foster's contention that slave children experienced a largely unthreatened childhood:

> Historical evidence supports what appears to have been the contemporary attitude that, on the whole, the slave child's story was the story of the poor and the working class, and although it could contribute to the overall antislavery theme, it was not sufficiently unique to justify the abolishment of slavery, the major emphasis of the slave narratives. (95)

In fact, the recovered texts reveal that domestic abolitionists documented, as contemporary historians have begun to recognize, that "enslaved children had virtually no childhood because they entered the work place early and were readily subjected to arbitrary plantation authority, punishments, and separations" (King xx).[7] Analogous to Frederick Douglass and his contemporaries' use of slave narratives to claim the freedoms inherent in the *Declaration of Independence*, domestic abolitionists used images of anxious young slaves to defend all children's right to Rousseauian doctrines of childhood innocence and happiness.

William L. Garrison's *Liberator* published two of the earliest examples that employ the slave child's voice to reveal anxiety over lost innocence and to pave the foundation for empathy. W.M.'s[8] "Address of a Little Slave Boy to His Master's Son" (1831) portrays a child who mourns the circumstances that deny him the same experiences as the white child:

> I wonder why should be
> Such differences betwixt you and me;
> For I'm as tall and strong as you,
> And many things as well can do,
> Have hands and feet, can run and walk,
> Can feel and see, can hear and talk. (3–8)

Despite his physical and linguistic similarities to the white child, the slave child identifies his forced inferiority: "[f]or me to labor, dig, and hoe, / Is all that I am like to know" (11–12). Acknowledging the absence of willing educators and the white child's inability to free him, he begs the white child to "befriend" him (18) and to "teach [him] part of what you know" (21) so that his "*mind* at least be free" (24, emphasis added). The slave child's two additional observations give him added leverage. First, he asks the white child to avoid hypocrisy and live out the Christian ethics his mother has taught him:

> She bid you fix it in your heart,
> Nor ever from its law depart:
> 'Be you to others kind and true,
> As you'd have others be to you. (27–30)

Second, he extends this religious belief to personal identification. The slave child states, "Now, dear young master, what would you, / Were our lots changed, wish me to do?" (37–38). Promising to respond empathetically to the white child, the slave child endeavors to elicit the same from the white child and "all of his [race]" (36).

Similarly, six months later the *Liberator* also published Philo Paidos's "Letter: The Little Slaves to the Sabbath School Children of New England" (March 17, 1832), another poem that asks the white child to imagine the slave child's lost innocence. The slave children state:

> O, favored, happy children, you
> Can never know what we pass through,
> Lest you yourselves should slaves become,
> And leave your parents, friends and home. (25–28)

Ironically, using the first-person plural, these slave children *do* let the white readers "know / All that we have to undergo" (1–2) as they expose slavery's horrors: the long hours of labor, the beatings they receive for stealing time to eat, the absence of secular or sacred education, and the deprivation of a mother's love. By graphically and poignantly establishing the difference between white and slave childhood experiences, Paidos insures a sentimental response, especially since her companion poem, "Answer to the Letter of the Little Slaves, by the Sabbath School Children," extends the least hopeful prospects of intervention.

The first identifiably female-authored juvenile work with designs to link slavery's violation of ideal childhood to America's future appears in Eliza Follen's *Hymns, Songs and Fables* (1846).[9] Follen raises consciousness about the slave child's plight by interspersing poems about slave children amid those about white children's innocence. Charles Follen, her husband, indirectly justifies this mixture, claiming;

> It may be objected to the book, that gay and serious pieces are bound up together; but so it is in human life and human nature, and it is essential to the healthful action of a child's mind that it should be so. The smile that overtakes its tears is as necessary to the child as the sun after a spring shower is to the young plant; and without it a blight would fall upon the opening blossom. (Preface iii–iv)

However, her mixture of "gay and serious" appears across different poems *and* within them. For example, Follen's poem "Children in Slavery"[10] recreates the nineteenth-century childhood experience as one of innocence, happiness, and uninhibited play. Given these conditions:

> Then earth and air seems fresh and fair,
>   All peace below, above;
> Life's flowers are there, and everywhere
>   Is innocence and love. (5–8)

The happy child's condition benefits all, beginning immediately with the reader's pleasant experience with the imagery. However, having established a middle-class, white child's experiences, Follen's second stanza disrupts this utopian vision with references to the slave child's mental distress. Follen utilizes the disquieting image of a fearful and tearful slave child to issue a warning about the interconnection between the child and the nation. She suggests that the child's seemingly insignificant sadness will have national and global implications. It threatens to plague America with blight and birds of prey (10–12), and to devastate the world:

> When young hearts weep as they go to sleep,
>   Then all the world seems sad;
> The flesh must creep, and woes are deep
>   When children are not glad. (13–16)

Follen's poem supports slavery's abolition, arguing that it will restore the slave child's right to childhood innocence and America's (and the world's) proper order and prosperity.

Like "Children in Slavery," Follen's "The Little Slave's Wish" (1846)[11] employs the slave child's voice to critique slavery for rupturing Romantic notions of childhood innocence and American declarations of each individual's *right* to happiness. Through a seemingly innocent child who wishes he were a bird, a brook, a butterfly, a wild deer, a cloud, or a savage beast, Follen constructs what Catherine O'Connell calls an "emotional analogy" (34), the moment when the white reader empathizes with the slave. White children realize that the slave child's desire does not seem extraordinary because many children voice such desires. For example, in Caroline Gilman's "Wishes," three children—Anna, Ellen, and Mary—wish they were a bird, a flower, and a goldfish, respectively. Similarly, Follen heightens the reader's empathy when she asserts that the slave child's wishes stem from a desire not to be "what I am, a slave" (24), thereby magnifying the moment in the typical slave narrative when the slave recognizes the internal war slavery wages in him. At this moment, Follen suggests lost Blakean innocence, or "the fullness of youthful glory before it has crossed the knife edge of difference between the thinking of the wholly young and the beginning of adult responsibility and knowledge" (Meigs 146). Having lost his innocence, the slave child's questions reveal a budding preoccupation that he caused or that God ordained his suffering. He asks:

> What wicked action have I done
>   That I should be a slave?"
>
> They tell me God is very good,
>   That his right arm can save;
> O, it is, can it, be his will
>   That I should be a slave? (27–32)

Rather than blame the truly culpable slavocracy, he almost blasphemes God by questioning His benevolence.[12] This slave child resembles Frado, the protagonist in Harriet Wilson's *Our Nig* (1859), who critiques a supposedly benevolent God and therefore "encourages the reader to sympathize with [her] rejection of a deity who knowingly subjects her to pain. For her such a deity is fraudulent and does not deserve her devotion" (Tate 45). By depicting a child questioning God's benevolence, Follen garners sympathy for slave children's violated innocence.

At the same moment that Follen employs the victimized slave child's voice to elicit empathy and sympathy, she also expresses anxiety about social and religious support structures—including God himself—that abandon the child rather than intercede to alleviate his/her suffering. In "The Little Slave's Wish," the child's final death wish rather than "to be what I am now,— / A little negro slave!" (35–36) suggests that he must rely on himself to alleviate his inner pain because others either create his suffering or abandon him to it. The revisions to this poem, however, for Julia Colman's "Little Lewis: The Story of a Slave Boy" reveals a shift from a quasi-blasphemous accusation to a request for intervention. Follen writes:

> I saw my little sister sold,
>   So will they do to me;
> My heavenly Father, let me die,
>   For then I shall be free. (29–32)

In the revised version, the child does not rely on a suicidal death wish, but calls to his *Father* to spare him from his sister's fate. Although still distressing, the prayer for divine intercession allows Follen to situate her criticism within the bounds of propriety and accents her critique against the American "fathers" (the political and judicial systems) who *fail* to intervene in the child's best interests. Follen possibly intended, therefore, that the young white readers express sympathy and subsequently work to ascertain his freedom, thereby rising above the adults who abandon the slave child to suffering.

Cousin Ann's Stories for Children includes the poem "Tom and Lucy: A Tale for Little Lizzie" (1849), which leads a white child first to empathize with slave children and then to sympathize with them by foregrounding the suffering that stems from failed intervention. Tom and Lucy Lee do not tell their own story as do the children in other juvenile narratives; however, hearing about their experience helps Lizzie recognize the similarities between the slave children and herself.[13] Cousin Ann awakens Lizzie's empathy by revealing that Tom and Lucy are "no bigger, dear, / Than cousin Charles and thee" (3–4) and that they behave just like Lizzie and other children:

> Long sunny days they played alone,
>   As little children play,
> But never hurt the butterflies,
>   Nor pelted frogs away.
>
> Sometimes they rambled in the wood,
>   Where moss and flowers grew,
> And little birds sang them to sleep,
>   As birds will often do. (13–20)

The parallel between Tom and Lucy's behavior and that of the white child transforms the slave children into "equals" rather than "others." Cousin Ann also insures identification and empathy by calling Lizzie's attention to the fact that Lucy is as precious as herself, and yet her skin color culminates in her punishment and sale "[j]ust like a calf" (17; see also 59). Through these repeated juxtapositions, Cousin Ann slowly dissolves racial differences by encouraging Lizzie and young readers like her to acknowledge the "other" as "self ."

Having constructed an "emotional analogy" (O'Connell 34) between the white reader and the slave, Cousin Ann raises the stakes for Lizzie/the reader by showing how slave children cope with slavery's violation of family bonds. Tom and Lucy's similarity to the white children foregrounds their need for protection, which

Lizzie and the white reader must realize slave children lack. At first, despite the daily separations from their mother, Tom and Lucy find comfort in her return and "with her, on the cabin floor, / They slept the night away" (12). Cousin Ann suggests that the security that their mother provides, if only at night, dissipates when,

> . . . one dark night their mother dear
> Stayed all the night away,
> And long they cried, and waited there,
> Until the break of day. (21–24)

After the children witness slave traders forcing their mother into a Floridian slave coffel, the children experience the high "emotional cost of family separation" (King 107) and their initial tears turn into "dreary days and dreary years" (Cousin Ann, "Tom and Lucy" 37). Without their mother's protection, these two forced orphans have "none to pity them" (41) and they encounter a master who readily whips them and orders them to work in the house, thereby destroying any remaining innocence. Cousin Ann's description of the violated family bond exposes slave children's powerlessness, confirming Wilma King's belief that "[c]hildren, because of their inability to protect themselves from devastation, suffer intensely" from slavery (xx).

The poetic description of Tom and Lucy's experiences after their ruptured family bond allows Cousin Ann to garner additional empathy for the children's suffering. Lacking their mother's protection (to the extent that a slave mother could protect her child) and experiencing a new life of work and suffering, Tom and Lucy initially cope by interceding on each other's behalf. Cousin Ann writes:

> They loved each other well,
> And love will always bring some joy,
> Wherever it may dwell.
>
> They said when they grew big and strong
> They both would run away,
> And, up in Pennsylvania, learn
> To read and write, each day. (42–48)

However, their attempt to empower themselves and to restore some sanctity to their violated bonds crumbles when a slave trader purchases Lucy for six hundred dollars (55). Unable to rescue his enchained mother, Tom attempts to prevent the separation from his sister through an act of resistance:

> Tom heard her scream, and ran to her;—
> To part they could not bear;
> He held her fast, and cursed the men,
> Who stood in wonder there. (61–64)

Tom's failed intervention reinforces the fact that these children fall prey to a system that will not intercede in the child's best interests. Awestruck by the possibility that Tom and Lucy actually love each other, the slave trader nevertheless perpetuates a system that sold "111,136 [children] . . . under nineteen years of age" between 1850 and 1860 (King 102) and that left them weeping like Lucy and brokenhearted like Tom.

Recontextualizing "Tom and Lucy" in her collection reveals that Cousin Ann hoped to shape the white child's political socialization. In her preface, Cousin Ann establishes the intent to socialize its audience when she states, "Dear Children . . . you will soon be men and women and I want you to grow wiser and better every day" ([2]). To accomplish this goal, she offers her readers didactic stories that define "good" children: temperate unlike "Johnny Vanline," honest and responsible unlike "Willy Way," independent like "Charles Clear," unselfish and kind like "Mary May," and moderate like Lila Lee in "Lola Lake and Lila Lee." In addition to anxieties of Americans becoming intemperate, dishonest, irresponsible, selfish, and immoderate, Cousin Ann fears the consequences of a proslavery society. Thus, "good" children would not only avoid alcohol and treat others kindly, but also express compassion for slaves who otherwise have "no one to pity them" (41). Cousin Ann's poem, like the texts by other domestic abolitionists, never depicts Lizzie expressing anything more than pity for the victimized slave children. However, just as adult slave narratives were designed to prompt readers to effect legal change, so too domestic abolitionists' hybrid genre elicited a private, compassionate response to anxiety-provoking images, the first step toward political intervention that would ultimately rescue powerless slave children and threatened democratic principles.

THE POWER OF ABOLITIONIST TEARS

Strategically, but cautiously, Eliza Follen, Cousin Ann, and an anonymous woman author give victimized slave children voices to generate both an anxious awareness of slavery's injustice and an empathetic response; but in each of their works, the white reader, though addressed, remains silent. However, another body of texts convey anxiety about the slave children's ruptured childhood, while simultaneously capturing the white listener's sympathetic response. E.T.C., "A Lady," "Grandmother," and Kate Barclay exemplify those authors who either depict a white child weeping or tell the reader to weep upon hearing a slave child's narrative. From the eyes of powerless fictional (and real) children, these private tears would seem to have a finite impact on a complex political system. Philip Fisher states, "[b]y limiting the goal of art to the revision of images rather than to the incitement to action, sentimentality assumes a healthy and modest account of the limited and interior consequences of art" (122). For Fisher, sentimentality could only incite private compassionate responses that effect little, if any, real change (108, 122).[14] However, these domestic abolitionists link private tears to public intervention. Nina Baym recognizes the genre's inherent power as she redefines sentimentality as a show of "public sympathy and benevolent fellow-feeling . . . [which spurs] philanthropy and benevolence" (*Women's Fiction* xxx). Like the tears shed for victimized women in sentimental novels, the tears shed for slave children extend beyond a concern for lost childhood or family bonds and plant seeds of activism. The white children in the sentimental juvenile pseudo slave narratives do not free any slaves or reunite slave children with their parents (as do the children discussed in chapter 4); however, like Little Eva from Stowe's *Uncle Tom's Cabin*, they cry upon recognizing the slave child's plight. The children in these recovered works do not abandon themselves to their emotions nor die (as does Eva); rather, their new empathy, prayers, and promises of activism encode attempts at intervention and reform.

E.T.C.'s "From an Infant Slave to the Child of Its Mistress, Both Born on the Same Day"[15] represents the earliest work to inspire intervention and reform by evoking tears of compassion and activism. In her poem, the slave child laments his lost innocence by contrasting his victimization and inequality to the white child's privileged naiveté. The slave infant questions their inequality because he discerns that he and the white child were both born on the same day and that "all things here beneath the sun. / To both are new" (11–12). In addition, he expresses an acute awareness that racism destroys fundamental parent-child bonds. The infant realizes that the white child's father rejoices in his son's birth while his own "groaned," mindful of his son's future enslavement (34). Similarly, although the white mother can love her son without fear, his mother must love him with the grief of knowing the child would live a life as degrading as her own. The child's lament accents these painful differences. Despite these differences, E.T.C ultimately employs anatomical references to emphasize the inherent similarities that would facilitate an emotional analogy:

> Beneath thy pale uncolored skin,
> As warm a heart may beat within,
>   As beats in me.
> Unjustly I will not forget,
> Souls are not colored white or jet,
>   In thee or me. (85–90)

Her repeated use of the warm, beating heart imagery has a double meaning: a literal organ and one capable of a sentimental response (being "warm hearted" or compassionate). Ironically, the slave child promises that if the white child were to face similar circumstances, he would act impartially and compassionately. Clearly, the companion poem, "The White Infant's Reply to the Little Slave," suggests that the slave child's plea for the white child to respond empathetically and sympathetically invokes the intended response. At least in the fictional world, mother and child respond with tears: "With many a smile and tear I read / Your pretty letter, dear. . . . My mother read your letter too,— / A tear fell from her eye" (1–2; 5–6). Yet, this poem also makes explicit the movement from sentimental to abolitionist tears. After the emotional response, the mother hopes that her child "might have the power to break / Your chain before I die" (7–8). Powerless to effect her own activism, the mother figure (and the author) must inspire and rely on the male child to effect slavery's abolition "when we both are men" (46). Although postponed, E.T.C. suggests that revolutionary action can surface from seemingly unimportant emotional responses.

E.T.C.'s work may have inspired abolitionist tears in the *Liberator*'s readers, but in 1854, a "Lady," perhaps Sarah Josepha Buell Hale, tried to effect the same response but on a larger scale by contracting with John P. Jewett to publish *The Lamplighter Picture Book,* a spin-off of Maria Susanna Cummins' best seller.[16] Susan S. Williams argues, "*The Lamplighter Picture Book* catered to the abolitionist market by giving *The Lamplighter* a more explicitly political agenda than was present in its original version: an agenda that promoted its 'extensive sale' not only to children, but also to their parents" (189). Scanty records prevent establishing how many copies were published and purchased;[17] however, children and parents expecting an abridged sentimental novel about a white orphan girl may have been surprised by a work that equates Gerty with slave children and Uncle True (the lamplighter) with the reader.[18]

Aligning the white, orphan girl with the slave's plight enables the audience to transfer their compassion from her to the oppressed African Americans. Within the sentimental prose narrative about young Gerty's plight, Hale [?] intersperses political poems about the suffering slave "who, alas! can seldom know / The joy of being freed" (Lady, "The Plaster Image" 19–20). As Susan Williams suggests, these poems compelled readers to transfer their compassion for Gerty, the suffering white orphan, to the slave, whom the author emblematizes with "the plaster cast of a bowing figure" kneeling in prayer (188).[19] To insure the transfer of a heartfelt response from Gerty to the slave, Hale [?] dictates the audience's expected behavior. In "Introductory Stanzas," Hale [?] writes:

> Ye who sigh as from these pages
>   Gerty's sorrows you may learn,
> Ne'er forget the bondman's sadness,
>   Never from his pleadings turn.
>
> Ye who weep o'er little Gerty,
>   Squalid, ragged, friendless, poor,
> Weep the more for slaves now mourning,
>   Oft with tyrant's lashes sore. (44–51)

The directive in each stanza's second half emphasizes the desired sentimental response (sighs and tears) and forces readers to politicize their tears. Notwithstanding, the "Lady" suggests that shedding tears of compassion does not suffice; the children must commit prayers of intercession:

> They [white children] need not ask for liberty
>   On them[selves] to be bestowed,
> Yet pray for those in slavery's chains,
>   Beneath a weary load. (Lady, "The Plaster Image" 29–32)

Through tears and prayers, the children can intervene on the slave's behalf. They must act like Uncle True (the lamplighter) who physically intervenes to save Gerty from Nan's physical and emotional abuse and like the "good people [who] often give / The fugitive a lodging" (Lady, "Little Gerty's Kitten" 21–22) even though they break the laws to do so.

Analogous to the *Lamplighter,* "Old Caesar," a narrative poem in *Grandmother's Stories for Children* (1854), focuses on how the compassion that ensues from hearing a slave's experiences about violated family bonds ultimately spurs prayers of intercession. In the only recovered work from a slave father's perspective and one that echoes the Uncle Tom and Eva relationship, "Old Caesar" sustains the authentic slave narratives' first-person and typical plot structure. When a young girl prompts Caesar to explain "[h]ow you your freedom won" (20) because she believes his tears represent a desire to return to slavery, he rectifies her assumption by narrating the stories of his family's separation, his escape to the bayou with two other slaves, and his eventual freedom. Caesar recalls that before the separation, he "had a happy home; / A good, kind wife and children dear" (29–30), fully aware that he "did not own myself or wife; My children,— they were not my own" (35–36). However, his master's death transforms Caesar's fear for his family's separation into a tragic and highly emotional reality:

> O, who can tell how sad our hearts,
>   With bitter grief and anguish torn?
> O woe the day!—the dreadful day!
>   I wished that I had ne'er been born.
>
> I had short time to say farewell
>   To children dear and wife so true:
> I loved my children, missy, dear,
>   Just as your own papa loves you. (53–60)

Debunking stereotypes, Caesar teaches his listener that African Americans love their families with the same affection as white Americans. However, he also emphasizes the slave's powerlessness over his children:

> With cruel blows their cries were hushed;
>   They dragged them from us one by one;
> With aching hearts we saw them sold,
>   Until at last we stood alone.
> . . . .
> My poor, sad, trembling wife and I
>   Drew closer to each other then;
> But all in vain. We, too alas!
>   Were parted by these cruel men. (73–76; 81–84)

Neither Caesar's nor his children's "anguished prayers" (65) effect a successful intervention. Thus, in contrast to the authentic slave narratives that celebrate the slave's fight to secure his freedom, "Grandmother" undercuts this convention by emphasizing Caesar's continued unhappiness: for Caesar, freedom only heightens the memory of his lost family and his inability to restore his violated domestic realm.[20] As Fisher would argue, the story's sentimentality stems from the fact the victims cannot change the fated action.

Fisher's argument about the limits to sentimental literature would prevail if Grandmother's narrative ended with the victim's tears; however, she advances that tears can spur action. First, Caesar's separation from his family leads him to flee slavery. Second, the child's new awareness of the reasons for Caesar's tears transforms her understanding of slavery. Caesar explains:

> And this is why the scalding tears
>   Roll down my withered cheeks like rain;
> I weep for those I dearly love
>   Yet never shall behold again (125–28)

His tears *do* effect change because they help the child shed tears and recognize slavery's "wickedness":

> Now, Caesar, say no more to day;
>   Your story makes me cry:
> O, what a wicked, wicked thing
>   Is human slavery! (129–32)

This new understanding subsequently incites the desire to act. The child wishes she were old and rich enough to exert the public influence necessary to liberate all the slaves, especially Caesar's family. Caesar rejects this possibility, stating that only his good works will reunite him and his family in heaven. The child then offers daily prayers for Caesar's wife and child to insure this reunion. These prayers differ from the "anguished prayers" (65) that Caesar and the children earlier offered to the slave traders because the child believes that her prayers will appease his tears and secure Divine intervention: God "[w]ill never turn his face from one / Who does his blessing humbly seek" (161–62). Domestic in its emphasis on the ruptured family and sentimental in its preponderance of tears, the poem derives its political nature by insinuating that prayer serve as an intermediary form of intervention until the child can exert public, political influence.

Kate Barclay's *Minnie May: With Other Rhymes and Stories* (1856) echoes "Grandmother's" poem in its progression from inspiring compassion to offering intercessory prayers. In "The Slave" (1856),[21] Barclay's rhetorical questions prescribe the behavior she expects from her young, white audience: "Whose heart does not bleed for the wrongs inflicted on Africa's sons? What eye can remain unmoistened at the recital of their woes" (31). Barclay compels the child to "feel for [the slaves'] condition" (31) with the story of an escaped slave woman who returns to her mistress because separation makes her "discontented and anxious for her children" (31) and her husband. This woman's love assumes heroic but tragic proportions when the mistress sells her to a North Carolina trader rather than allow a permanent family reunion. Barclay ends this woman's narrative with an explicit plea for emotional participation:

> Little children, pity the poor slaves—pity them with all your heart. How would you feel to be separated forever from your kind mother—to see her face no more—no more to see her smiling look of approbation—no more to receive the kiss of affection? I ask, how would you feel? Dear reader, you cannot imagine how much suffering is endured by the poor blacks. Husbands are separated from wives, children from parents, brothers from sisters. O, I do want you to feel for their condition, and, when you pray, ask God to bless *them*. (31–32)

Barclay forces young readers to identify with the slave's suffering by calling children to imagine *themselves* having their play restricted or being separated from a parent. Identification with an endangered existence stirs anxiety that may lead young readers, previously ignorant of the slave's plight, to express sympathy that prompts prayers of intercession. In case the slave woman's tragic story and the direct plea fail to stir readers' emotions, Barclay literally puts words into the mouths of these babes. She writes:

> I pity the poor little slave,
>   Who labors hard through all the day,
>   And has no one,
>   When day is done,
>   To teach his youthful heart to pray. (1–4)

Whether the child reads the poem silently or aloud, the first person pronoun forces him or her to adopt this political sentiment. S/he must confront the slave's forced solitude—no one to embrace, to love, or to comfort him/her daily. Furthermore, highlighting the absence of prayer in the slave child's experience reminds white readers to pray for the slaves. Thus, Barclay's emotional didacticism socializes readers into benevolent subjects by imparting specific images, words, and actions to arouse "right feelings" of compassion that reform the reader's conception of the "other" as human being rather than as object.

The American Reform Tract and Book Society's "Lucy; or, The Slave Girl of Kentucky" (1858)[22] represents one of the later narratives in which a slave child's anxious response to a forced separation from her mother leads a white child to move from ignorance, to compassion, to a promise of intercession. In this work, Arthur listens to Aunty's sentimental juvenile slave narrative that exposes a slave child's anxiety and suffering upon parental separation. When financial difficulties prompt the master to sell Lucy's mother to the slave traders despite his promise not to separate slave families, Lucy intervenes on her own behalf by shrieking so loudly and continuously that the trader sells her with her mother. Lucy's voice (scream) prevents the separation; however, it does not secure her happiness. Aunty's description of Lucy's physical appearance unmasks her psychological distress:

> I never saw such a picture of distress in a child . . . her hands clenched convulsively upon her sides, and even her little toes . . . were curled up tight as her fingers, and every few minutes her little body shook with convulsive sobs. . . . (49)

Recognizing that she has gained only a temporary reunion with her mother, Lucy considers death as the only means to achieve happiness and freedom. Noting that "Ebrybody'll be free an' equal when dey'se dead" (56), Lucy tries to starve herself because she "hopes [she'll] die afore dey has time to take me from mammy again; an' if I don't eat, specs I shall, an' den I'll be glad" (55). Like the child in Follen's poem who perceives that even God has abandoned him, Lucy discerns that since the forces oppose her, she must intervene on her own behalf, through death.

The sentimental narrative's focus on Lucy's internal struggle, however, acquires first a religious and then a political dimension when Aunty unveils an urgent need for intervention. Powerless to alleviate the child's suffering by purchasing Lucy and her mother, Aunty intervenes by making Lucy understand the possibility for freedom through faith. She tells Lucy that regardless of one's skin color, desiring death enslaves one to sin. Aunty may save Lucy's soul, but her intercession does not eliminate the threat to the mother-child bond, especially since the ambiguous ending depicts traders removing Lucy and her mother from the ship. The recurrent, external threats that limit her ability to end the child's emotional pain arouse "right feeling" in Aunty, who shares her "conversion" with her nephew. Arthur initially responds emotionally to the narrative he hears about Kentucky slavery. He states, "That's a right sad story, aunty" (68). Aunty acknowledges the sadness saying "but the saddest part of the story is, that it is *less* than what might be told of what passes every day in a slave country" (68). Therefore, she argues for ultimately moving beyond sentiment, especially when she claims, "Mrs. Stowe had not then told us Northerners what a horror the poor negroes have of being sold down the river . . ." (53–54). Aunty contends that since neither she nor the slaves have power, Arthur must acknowledge slavery's brutal reality and realize that as a sympathetic and politically astute older white male, he will have the political power necessary to intervene.

Anxious about the slave child's plight, the domestic abolitionists who focus on the impact the slave child's narrative has on white listeners draw attention to the link between shedding tears and interceding on slave children's behalf. While these white children do not literally free the slave children (as do the children in chapter 4), their promises of prayers set the groundwork for change. This suggests that the fictional white child who has listened to the story has recognized the slave's plight and seen him/her as an equal who needs help. A turn to activism would create the happy endings typical of authentic, adult slave narratives (Foster 55) and the common cultural or literary script well known to children through fairy tales and juvenile literature. Furthermore, such intercession would also function as a means to overturn racist stereotypes that threaten both children and America's basic democratic principles. Ironically, while these works oppose the slave child's lost innocence and depict individuals interceding to prevent the child's suffering, the domestic abolitionists nevertheless inflict lost innocence (through forced consciousness) onto the white child. *Reading* about slavery does not equal the slave child's actual experience; yet, it does rupture any preexisting innocence the white child may have possessed. By focusing on the negative consequences that slavery had on the black child, domestic abolitionists also revealed the threat to the white population, as did many adult slave narratives, all the further suggesting the need for abolitionist intervention.

MOTHERS AS INTERCESSORS

The recovered hybrid narratives discussed thus far reveal domestic abolitionists' anxiety about violating childhood innocence and about the absence of a formal system to intervene on the child's behalf. Other women plant seeds of intervention in young white characters who, inspired toward compassion, offer intercessory prayers and/or promises of activism. However, Eliza Follen, Harriet Beecher Stowe, "Grandmother," an anonymous woman, Matilda Thompson, and Julia Colman counteract images of powerless slave children and delayed intervention with sentimental juvenile pseudo slave narratives in which slave mothers intercede on their child's behalf to ease its anxiety and to restore a semblance of innocence and family. Ideally, white mothers countered the Industrial Revolution's corrupting forces to preserve their children's physical well-being and shape them into sound, moral citizens who would bring about America's glory. In the absence of a protective mother figure, nineteenth-century reformers coordinated efforts to work on children's behalf. For example, in 1834, Anna M. Shotwell and Mary Murray, two Quakers, opened the Colored Orphan Asylum in New York "for blacks were not accepted by the three other orphanages in the city" (Yee 81). Furthermore, in 1853, the Children's Aid Society was established in New York (Ginzberg 123–24; 127–28). By depicting slave women rescuing their children, domestic abolitionists added slave mothers to the catalogue of individuals and organizations who participated in the widespread political movement to safeguard childhood, the family, and America's future.

For the white community, death posed the most natural threat to both childhood and motherhood. Elizabeth Fox-Genovese claims, "Mothers had to expect to lose at least one child in infancy or early childhood, and frequently they lost two or more" (278). Sentimental fiction often includes mother figures weeping over dead children (Papashvily 194; O'Connell 29) to "offer solace to bereaved parents by confirming their belief that their children preceded them to heaven" (Hoffert 170). Recast in a positive light, the dead child was "remembered by the tiny rosebud, the golden curl, the crumbled shoe, the dented locket" (Papashvily 194). Hoffert contends that despite a sense of violated motherhood, the white mother could console herself in the belief that death preserved the child's innocence (180–82), served "as an occasion for demonstrating their willingness to submit to the will of God" (170), and foreshadowed a heavenly reunion (187).

While mothers and doctors remained powerless with respect to an infant's death, the judicial system shaped the most aggressive changes in the period's attempt to preserve childhood innocence. Michael Grossberg argues that three factors led courts to decide custody battles in the child's best interest: increased divorce rates, the slow shift away from colonial and republican beliefs that the child was the father's property, and the "new faith in women's innate proclivities for child rearing and in developmental notions of childhood" (235; see also Mason 53). Despite these increasingly progressive views of women and children, gaining custody did not come without complex judicial proceedings. As long as the father maintained good moral and religious standing, "paternal power reigned supreme" (Grossberg 236). White women could only gain custody or primary guardianship in cases—like *Prather v. Prather*—of adulterous, abusive, alcoholic, unfit, or deceased husbands (238–43). As Elizabeth Cady Stanton argued, woman was like a slave potentially "robbed of her property, 'stripped of her children,' and 'whipped and locked up by her lord'" (qtd. in Isenberg 107). While perhaps not a direct result to women's judicial plight, domestic abolitionists possibly encoded their objections to coverture rules in sentimental juvenile pseudo slave narratives depicting slave mothers "repossessing" and "kidnapping" their children when the judicial system denied them custody.

A child's death and familial custody disputes may have threatened white motherhood; however, for slave mothers the private threat to motherhood was secondary to the public, political threat. Slave mothers witnessed twice as many infant deaths as whites in 1850 (Jones 35).[23] But the greatest threat came from cruel slave masters who violated or threatened family bonds. Some masters kept families together, but Norrence T. Jones, Jr. asserts: "the threat of sale was the most effective long-term mechanism of control" that slave masters exploited to prevent or punish misbehavior (63). Nevertheless, King contends that many slave mothers successfully persuaded masters not to sell their children to a different plantation (104), or "[i]f forewarned about separations, slave parents groped for ways to prepare their children for parting. Some told stories about taking long journeys, while others tried to disrupt imminent separations" (103–104). Notwithstanding, most slave women had no legitimate recourse since the legal system safeguarded the slave master's, not the mother or the child's, best interests. As Nancy Isenberg demonstrates in *Sex and Citizenship in America*, "The plight of the slave mother and child nevertheless went to the heart of the dispute over birthright entitlements, primarily because the mother's natural entitlements to have children was declared null and void" (116). The debate over entitlement entered into literary conversations, such as in Maria Lowell's "The Slave Mother" (see page 60), as well as in legal cases such as the Boston Female Anti-Slavery Society's 1836 proceedings of *Commonwealth v. Aves* (or "little Med's case"):

> In the Aves case the theme of separation centered around the relationship between mother and daughter. The attorney for the slave-owner argued that the child Med was not the property but the ward of the master, and as her legal guardian the slaveowner gained custody that denied the mother any legal recourse to protect the child. Any "natural" entitlement to the child was "void," and the oath of the mother as to her parental status carried no legal standing, because mother and child were legally separated at birth. (Isenberg 114–15)

Subordinate even to orphans, slave children "were fully divested of their constitutional inheritance of birthrights" (115). Without legal protection, they were vulnerable to owners who cared little for the child's best interest.

With this historical background in mind, it is easy to see that domestic abolitionists transform sentimental scenes of threatened childhood into political displays of rebellion in which the slave mothers take custody matters "into their own hands" to individualize and humanize slavery's "dehumanizing tendencies of the materialism and individualism" (White, "Sentimentality" 105). In the absence of judges granting slave mothers custody when a father (in this case, the slavocracy and the American government) threatens the child's best interests, real slave mothers challenged and subverted the slavocracy, its masters, and the laws that denied them legal rights to claim and to protect their children. Some slave women forcefully attempted to reclaim and to preserve their children from

The Liberty Bell; By the Friends of Freedom
Boston: Massachusetts Anti-Slavery Fair
Portsmouth, New Hampshire, U.S.
1846

MARIA LOWELL, "THE SLAVE MOTHER"

Her new-born child she holdeth, but feels within her heart
It is not her's [sic], but his who can outbid her in the mart;
And, through the gloomy midnight, her prayer goes up on high,—
"God grant my little helpless one in helplessness may die!

"If she must live to womanhood, oh may she never know,
Uncheered by mother's happiness, the depth of mother's woe;
And may I lie within my grave, before that day I see,
When she sits, as I am sitting, with a slave-child on her knee!"

The little arms steal upward, and up upon her breast
She feels the brown and velvet hands that never are to rest;
No sense of joy they waken, but thrills of bitter pain,—
She thinks of him who counteth o'er the gold those hands shall gain.

Then on her face she looketh, but not as mother proud,
And seeth how her features, as from out a dusky cloud,
Are tenderly unfolding, far softer than her own,
And how, upon a rounded cheek, a fairer light is thrown;

And she trembles in her agony, and on her prophet heart
There drops a gloomy shadow down, that never will depart;
She cannot look upon that face, where in the child's pure bloom,
Is writ with such dread certainty the woman's loathsome doom.

She cannot bear to know her child must be as she hath been,
Yet she sees but one deliverance from infamy and sin,
And so she cries at midnight, with exceeding bitter cry,
"God grant my little helpless one in helplessness may die!"

Elmwood, Nov. 26, 1845

"death" through acts of resistance ranging from infanticide to flight.[24] For instance, citing Margaret Gardner's case, Isenberg writes, "Like the heroic Spartan or Roman mother, she decided that real death was better than civil death, and she took control of her destiny by refusing to surrender to the brutal system of slavery" (118). Domestic abolitionists reflect these contemporary events in hybrid narratives that depict slave mothers waiting neither for the judicial system to change nor for slavery's abolition to rescue their children. These rebellious slave mothers follow their own agendas of activism. Consequently, these portraits of interceding slave mothers (who often ascertain assistance from white women) shift the sentiment from anxiety over threatened American ideals, represented in images of violated childhood innocence and motherhood, to the "happy endings" of freedom and preserved familial bonds.

Domestic abolitionists whose narratives depict slave mothers intervening to save their children transform the slave mother stereotype from "breeder" and "mammy"[25] to "mommy." The authors' challenges to these racist images restored slave mothers to "an honorable status in African society" (King 2).[26] Furthermore, rebellious slave mothers defended their status as "mommy" by claiming a modified version of "the ideology of [white] motherhood [which] bestowed on childbearing women increasing responsibilities for the moral and political nature of childhood as well as for the stability of the family and the happiness of its members" (Hoffert 143). Having slave mothers share the dominant culture's value systems, these authors humanize characters whom Angela Davis argues "were practically anomalies" when juxtaposed to nineteenth-century ideals of womanhood (5). According to these authors, slavery did not eradicate love; rather, the constant threats strengthened it.[27]

"The Slave Mother,"[28] a poem based on a true infanticide story, represents the earliest, juvenile example of a slave mother's intervention. Recalling her personal suffering, this mother refuses to pass slavery's legacy to her children. She states:

> Oh, I have suffered much for you,
>   Nor will I live to see
> The dreadful evils come to you
>   Which long have come to me!
>
> When I was old as you, my son,
>   I can remember well,
> How I was brought across the sea,
>   With wicked men to dwell.
>
> They tore me from my mother's arms,
>   And brought me here to toil,
> And every day my tears and blood
>   Have stain'd this hated soil. (33–44)

The author uses this Kentucky slave mother's disquieting memories to justify the resistance she enacts in 1831 to preserve the threatened mother-child bonds. Like the white mother who rationalizes her grief by believing her child's death preserves its innocence and assures its place in heaven, the slave mother views drowning her six-year-old son and two younger daughters as deaths into freedom and innocence. Condemning all who might call "[t]hat mother cruel" (66), the author transforms infanticide into an act of intervention and archetypal mother love.

Whereas "The Slave Mother" offers young readers a harrowing scene of heroism, most of the juvenile pseudo slave narratives cast slave mothers as fugitives who heroically seek to save their children. For example, Eliza Lee Cabot Follen's juvenile novel, *Sequel to The Well-Spent Hour; or, The Birthday* (1832),[29] contains a chapter entitled "Conscience—The Runaway Negro." Follen frames a narrative about the disjunction between white and slave family security with the story of Catherine Nelson, who experiences a personal transition in class status when her father's financial difficulties necessitate auctioning the family's belongings and moving into a cottage. In this context, Follen reveals how white families often remain united despite economic crises whereas slave families must contest the slavocracy to restore and recreate idyllic domestic scenes.

Follen uses parental storytelling during a child's birthday celebration, symbolic of transition, as a strategy to awaken children's political consciousness. Mrs. Nelson apologizes for her didactic story that "has no interest, except what it derives from its truth, and from the moral it teaches" (Follen, *Sequel* 72). She speaks of a man whose guilty conscience leads him, after a twenty-year silence, to confess having kept five dollars mistakenly overpaid him after repairing a man's shoes. He states, "I was the father of a young family: I was very poor; I was tempted; and I received the money, knowing and feeling that it was dishonest" (74). Recognizing that "we are all" (75) like this man, the mother respects him, despite his low rank, because his confession reveals that he acted to preserve his family.

Mrs. Nelson's story about finances and guilt prepares her children for their father's narrative about a female slave who intercedes to preserve family bonds and affection. Mr. Nelson situates his narrative about slavery's oppression in light of family politics, an approach that parallels strategies in Harriet Jacob's *Incidents in the Life of a Slave Girl*. According to Claudia Tate,

> . . . rather than employ the abstract, polemical rhetoric of civil protest to mount an argument on slavery as an inhumane social institution that victimizes black and white people alike, as did Douglass, Jacobs feminized the presumably gender-free abolitionist polemics of the slave-narratives by situating her argument in the personal and individualized context of the sexually violated female slave and the morally outraged slave mother. (28)

Avoiding slavery's complex politics and trying "to imitate [the] mother's magnanimity," Mr. Nelson nevertheless transforms a child's fourteenth birthday celebration into a pivotal moment of increased political consciousness when he narrates a story about a North Carolina slave family. Mr. Nelson acknowledges the compassion he felt upon hearing how a slave woman, trying to remain close to her husband, flees with her two children and evades the slave catchers when her owner moves West. Mr. Nelson tells his children that the slave mother and sons live as fugitives for seven years as they wait for the father's escape.[30] During this time, the mother and children inhabit marshes, eat frogs, terrapins, snakes and mice, and make clothes from mice fur, stray wool, and cotton (Follen, *Sequel* 80). Their necessarily clandestine existence to evade slave catchers causes the two sons to develop deformed postures and low voices because they must squat and whisper for seven years (78–79). However, when the father does not appear—probably due to recapture—the mother surrenders. Ironically, her emergence from the marsh leads to their eventual freedom and the family's preservation because, upon hearing her story, her former master's son "in consideration of her sufferings, and from his grateful recollection of her kindness to him when a child, gave her and her boys their freedom" (82).

Follen's politicized sentiment not only arouses compassion for the victims, but also challenges conventional stereotypes that slave women fail to uphold nineteenth-century ideals of womanhood. She writes: Mr. Nelson's

> feelings . . . were divided between [his] compassion for this poor woman and her suffering children, and [his] admiration of the noble fortitude they had displayed during this long period of privation and misery, of their ingenuity, their self-denial, their self-control; but more than all [he] honored and admired the tender and faithful affection that had enabled a weak woman to endure with patience and constancy such evils from simple devoted love for her husband. The thought that she was deprived of this blessing, which had taken the place to her of all others, was more affecting to [him] than any part of her story. (81–82)

Mr. Nelson's admiration stems from recognizing that in the fight to preserve the family, the slave woman demonstrates the self-control and human affection that only the white middle class supposedly held. Furthermore, Mr. Nelson counteracts negative stereotypes as he aligns this woman with nineteenth-century true womanhood because of her willingness to sacrifice herself for her husband and children. Mr. Nelson's new respect functions to include her into nineteenth-century "institutions of womanhood, marriage, motherhood and family" as well as "all four institutions' social construction of female respectability" from which slave women were traditionally excluded (Tate 25). Thus, the sentimental story becomes a political springboard to help readers view the slave woman as a respectable wife and mother. This new status links the woman with the white constructions of family and gender because she has qualities that make her equal—if not superior—to middle-class white women.[31]

Finally, Follen intimates that "hearing" this story would produce a widespread cultural shift toward increasing support for enslaved African Americans. Mr. Nelson acknowledges that the story of suffering leads the master's son to act as a judge: he renounces his "property" and grants the mother custody of her children. Furthermore, although he conceals *his* feelings, Mr. Nelson believes the story will affect his children, stating:

> Numbers visited her and her children. I could not but hope that every one who saw her and heard her story, and who had ever failed to do honor to the immortal nature of the negro, or had been unfaithful in his own affections, might come away instructed and rebuked by the example of this humble, living martyr to affection. (Follen, *Sequel* 82)

Like Mrs. Nelson's protagonist who confesses his sin and gains a guilt-free conscience, so too can slavery's advocates examine their consciences to acknowledge their guilt for perpetuating slavery and realize that they fall short of the values/affections this ex-slave family exhibits. Consequently, Follen inverts black-white and rich-poor when she portrays the slave woman as a heroic model for white idea(l)s of fidelity and family. If a child reader does not adopt these sentiments or recognize the slave's true nature, then Follen implicates him/her in the institution that undermines America's cultural ideals.

Authors like Eliza Follen helped to create the portrait of the heroic slave mother, but Harriet Beecher Stowe's character, Eliza Harris, ultimately took center stage as a mother figure who willingly subverts the power structure in the child's best interest.[32] The novel's success led Jewett to publish *Pictures and Stories from Uncle Tom's Cabin* (1853), an adaptation of *Uncle Tom's Cabin* interspersed with poetry written especially for children. Like the adult version, *Pictures and Stories* immediately centers the reader's attention on the threatened child and Eliza's act of resistance to protect him.[33] For example, the illustrator focuses the reader's attention on Eliza's heroic Ohio River crossing by creating a book cover that centers and encircles the mother and child amid smaller scenes of working slaves. Furthermore, the large-font poems ("The Sale of Little Harry" and "Eliza Crossing the River") for younger readers also focus on the mother's heroic efforts to save the threatened slave child.[34] Echoing the original text, Stowe begins "The Sale of Little Harry" by depicting a little boy with whom readers can identify:

> Now Harry's hair was thick with curls
> And softly bright his eyes,
> And he could play such funny tricks
> And look so wondrous wise. (17–20)

Yet, the "emotional analogy" quickly subsides because Stowe depicts the "wicked trader" and "the rich man" threatening Harry's beauty and childhood security (23,

25). When Eliza overhears that "[t]o that hard-hearted evilman, / Her own sweet boy was sold" (39–40), the "poor mother . . . / With heart all sick and sore" (36–37), realizes she must intercede to save Harry from the corrupt politics and economics threatening his childhood. Believing that "mother knows best," Eliza's flight transforms a sentimental scene of violated motherhood and childhood into a political display of active resistance designed to preserve what the slavery dehumanizes. Unlike Eliza Follen's benevolent and converted master of *Sequel to The Well-Spent Hour,* Stowe makes God the final "judge" who grants the mother custody: "God did hear that mother's cry, / For never an ice-block sank" ("Eliza Crossing the River" 25–26). Albeit not a court of law, a benevolent God validates the slave mother's resistance by helping her act in the child's "best interest." By politicizing motherhood through the heroic slave mother, *Pictures and Stories* debunks the recurrent image of the slave child who lacks an authority figure to intercede on his/her behalf. In a letter to Eliza Follen on December 16, 1852, Stowe attributes her ability to empathize with slave mothers' loss of their children to her feelings after her child's death.[35] Stowe could not save her child, but she transforms an emotionally distraught Eliza into a heroic mother figure intent on saving Harry and the mother-child bond. Angela Davis views this characterization critically, stating

> Eliza is practically oblivious to the general injustices of slavery. Her feminine submissiveness has prompted her to surrender herself to her fate as a slave and to the will of her good, kind master and mistress. It is only when her maternal status is threatened that she finds the strength to stand up and fight. (18)

However, Davis overlooks the context of Stowe's characterization because both the adult and children's versions address readers who might have been equally oblivious to slavery's evils until a mother's struggle to keep her child engaged their sympathies. The nineteenth century placed mothers on a pedestal. Consequently, motherhood empowered women as children's guardians against the horrors plaguing America's burgeoning society. Davis may legitimately claim that the "source of [slave women's] strength was not some mystical power attached to motherhood, but rather their concrete experiences as slaves" (19). Yet, as a children's author, Stowe made the attack on slavery agreeable through the rebellious mother figure who challenges the collapse of American ideals of childhood, family, and democracy.

Harriet Beecher Stowe's success inspired many domestic abolitionists to politicize sentiment by adopting and adapting the heroic mother figure who subverts the power structure to save her child. For example, *Grandmother's Stories for Children* (1854) recreates Stowe's self-empowered slave mother whose rebellion liberates her child (see "Aunt Nelly" [14–20]). Interestingly, "Grandmother" may have endeavored to make the slave mother's actions more acceptable by situating Nelly's rebellious "custody dispute" in context of a white mother's similar attempt to preserve her children's innocence. Evidently, despite women's inability to claim custody unless the court found the father at fault, dying women elicited deathbed promises through which they seized judicial power. Grossberg cites *Chapsky v. Wood, U.S. v. Green,* and a third case from Georgia in which the courts upheld the mother's deathbed custody request when it favored the child's best interest (254–56). Similarly, in "Grandmother's" text, Mrs. Howard (on her deathbed) transfers custody from the father to the maternal grandparents asking that her three children, Lizzie and the twins (William and Charlie) "might be kept from ever being slaveholders, and brought up and educated at the north" (*Grandmother's* 6). Despite shifting the decision making from the court to an otherwise disenfranchised mother, the father submits to this instruction. He returns to his plantation but leaves the children with their Northern grandparents. Thus, through her death, Mrs. Howard intercedes to spare her children from firsthand experiences with slavery. Fulfilling her daughter's request, "Grandmother" protects her grandchildren from slavery's cruelties until Nelly (a former slave) exposes Lizzie to slavery's harsh reality (see "Aunt Nelly"). However, Grandmother assumes her intercessory role when Lizzie, on her tenth birthday (a transition to increased knowledge), asks her grandmother to narrate Nelly's story because: "I think grandmama, I shall not feel as bad to hear you relate it as I did when aunt Nelly's sorrowful face was before me" (9). Although emotionally painful for Lizzie to hear about slavery, she *must* listen because Nelly's story echoes her own mother's act of intercession and divulges a series of rebellious women who strive to preserve American ideals.

Lizzie and the young reader hear not only Nelly's sentimental narrative, but also several stories of free and enslaved women who undermine the status quo to abolish slavery's threat to childhood innocence and mother-child bonds. Grandmother initially shocks Lizzie when she reveals that Nelly rejoiced when her older child died because "its death was preferable to the service of a cruel master" (9). The white mistress, Mrs. Walberg, however, intervenes so that Nelly does not reexperience such suffering. At first, Mrs. Walberg protects Nelly by working within the system: she persuades her cruel husband, a relative of Lizzie's father, to make Nelly her maid during her trip North. Furthermore, Mrs. Walberg, who also has a two-year-old daughter, challenges the slavocracy when she waits until three days into their trip North before telling Mr. Walberg about having concealed Nelly's daughter (Juley) below the ship to prevent the mother-child separation. Ultimately, Mrs. Walberg's coup d'etat against the slavocracy occurs when she encourages Nelly to flee. Nelly almost loses Juley and her child's ally when, during a stop in Philadelphia, Mrs. Walberg's daughter dies from the typhoid or yellow fever epidemic. Mrs. Walberg seems to recover from the same illness, but she suffers a relapse after visiting her baby's grave. Having lost her own child, Mrs. Walberg empathizes with the slave mother's pain and consequently commands Nelly to "escape with her child before her master was summoned back" (11). Thus, Mrs. Howard's deathbed wish works *within* the status quo to prevent her husband from raising Lizzie, Charlie, and Willie on their Southern plantation; conversely, Mrs. Walberg's deathbed wish *challenges* the system because she prevents her husband from selling the mother and child to separate slave plantations. Thus, the deathbed becomes a site of rebellion where once again the female judicates a custody case.

"Grandmother" ultimately draws connections between these resistant white mother figures and slave mothers. While a nineteenth-century white woman's resistance could endanger her societal status since it undermines her expected submission, Nelly's resistance endangers her physically and emotionally. But it ironically elevates her above white women because she *can* save her child from "death." Once the Walberg child's death ends Nelly's status as "mammy," she undergoes considerable trials to reclaim her "mommy" status. Like Stowe's Eliza, Nelly wanders alone with her child until she reaches the frozen river, which she too crosses:

> God alone guided [Nelly]; for earthly guidance she had not. The Delaware was frozen over; and, thinking she should be more safe from pursuit on the opposite side, she crossed it. She met kind persons, who gave her milk for her child and food for herself, but asked her no questions. (13)

This heroic slave mother does everything possible to keep her daughter alive rather than rejoice in her death, as she had with her older child. In this divinely supported act of resistance, Nelly secures her own and her daughter's freedom because upon arriving in the North she meets Grandmother who, "determined to save her if I could" (13), conceals Nelly and Juley and deceives slave catchers until they terminate the search. When mothers (slave and free) cannot depend on the "Mr. Walbergs" or court justices to preserve the mother-child bond or the child's best interest, they intervene to safeguard what slavery threatens. Thus, these politically sentimental narratives depict empowered mothers assuming male roles and legal control to preserve childhood and family ideals.[36]

The anonymous female author of *Jemmy and His Mother* (1858) also creates a heroic, Stowe-like slave mother (Susan) whose anxiety about the threat to her child's innocence provokes her rebellion that awards her "custody." The author arouses readers' empathy by asking them to imagine white parents in the slave parent's position:

> My dear children, . . . kindly ask them [the slave holders] if they would think they were well treated if they had all they needed to eat and to wear, but were obliged to see their children one after another sold away from them, or put to work near them, where they could never help them if they saw them tired and sick. . . . (9–10)

Having created a basis for identification, she shifts from the hypothetical scenario describing the white parents' psychological distress and disempowerment to a fictional slave narrative about a slave mother's anxiety that "when her little boy was old enough to work he would be taken away from her, and perhaps be sold and carried away where she could never see him again" (5–6). Susan's distress over the violation of motherhood arouses the readers' sympathy and compassion.

This domestic abolitionist strengthens the basis for reader sympathy by shifting the mother's concern from anxieties of personal loss to fears about how a separation would threaten her child's best interest. Though she tries to conceal her emotional distress from herself and her mistress, Susan "would weep, and weep, and weep over him . . . and would wish that she could die, and her little boy could die too" rather than remain slaves or suffer separation (6). Her fears stem from her recognition that their separation would destroy his innocence: "Jemmy was a happy little slave boy . . . for he was too young to know what a dreadful thing it is to be a slave. He had never been bought or sold; and he had always lived at one place" (5). Her implicit acknowledgment that she has protected her child from the harsh realities intermingles with a critique of the slavocracy's ability to serve as a fit "father." Susan imagines Jemmy's new custodian as a negligent and abusive slavemaster-father who would undermine the child's physical and psychological needs. Without her, Jemmy would have no one to put him to bed or nurse him during an illness (6). Furthermore, he "would have to be driven and whipped if he did not do as much work as he was told to do, and no one would care whether he was tired or not" (7). But, Susan most deeply fears that no one would intervene to help her enslaved child, believing "if he should cry, as children are apt to do sometimes, she knows that no one would pity him, or say a word of comfort to him" (7). By depicting the mother's distress, the author establishes conditions to justify the slave mother's rebellion.

Like Stowe's Eliza and "Grandmother's" Nelly, Susan rises to heroic status when she challenges the slavocracy's claim to her role as mother and to her child's innocence. Susan aspires to ascertain experiences afforded white mothers and children by escaping to the "wonderful North . . . where loving mothers rock their little ones to sleep, night after night, without fear of any strange men coming and taking them away" (16). Susan does not face the immediate danger as does Eliza in *Uncle Tom's Cabin,* but her Eliza-like desire to reclaim her right to "own" and to protect her child motivates her night flight. As Eliza does for Harry, she gives Jemmy cake to appease his crying, collects berries for him and herself, and experiences troubled sleep; however, when Susan cannot cross the ice, she returns to the plantation to plan another escape rather than drown herself and Jemmy (25). The author's decision to have the slave mother reject suicide increases her acceptability to readers and also shifts the focus away from tragic sentiment to heroic, political action.

Circumventing suicide serves as a useful plot device to elevate the slave mother to the white woman's level and to license a white woman to subvert the law and undermine the status quo. Susan's return to the plantation advances freedom rather than separation because it provides a white woman with the opportunity to safeguard what the peculiar institution and the American government desecrate. When the mistress gives Jemmy "some old books—several picture books, and old spelling book, and part of an old Testament" (28), Susan realizes that learning to read will facilitate their escape. Therefore, she persuades Mrs. Harris, the children's governess, to teach her to read. Mrs. Harris does so fully mindful of Susan's intentions because Susan had "even ventured to tell her how she had tried to run away, and how much she wanted to get where she could always keep her child with her, and feel as if he were her own" (32). Mrs. Harris not only preserves Jemmy's innocence and the mother-child bond but also empowers Susan through literacy, just as underground railroad members undermine slavery's laws through their literal efforts to help Susan attain freedom. As lawbreaker, the fully knowledgeable white woman subverts a system from within and, like Mrs. Walberg and "Grandmother," helps a slave mother to regain the inherent right to raise and to nurture her child.

Although some domestic abolitionists focus predominantly on the child's voice and others concentrate on the slave mother's heroic intercession, Matilda Thompson and Julia Colman's sentimental, juvenile pseudo slave narratives heighten a powerlessness that causes emotional and psychological distress by presenting both the mother and the child's perspective. Urgency peaks in these narratives because slave children awaken to slavery's reality and the threat of separation before the distressed mothers can preserve their children's innocence. However, when the mothers *can* focus on the child's plight, they intervene predominately through verbal influence rather than physical flight. Furthermore, rather than the "happy endings" where a mother's heroism liberates the child and herself, these narratives contain muted happy endings which permit domestic abolitionists to encode sharp critiques of slavery's violation of human bonds and natural rights as well as to advance the need for abolitionist conversions and intervention.

Matilda G. Thompson's "Mark and Hasty; or, Slave Life in Missouri" (1859)[37] politicizes sentiment in the only recovered abolitionist juvenile work to depict a complete slave family: mother, father, and child. This slave family escapes violation until, ironically, the parents attempt to nurse their daughter. Fanny's illness with scarlet fever keeps her mother and father at her bedside throughout the night. Consequently, when Mark falls asleep the next morning while feeding the horses, his infuriated master, Mr. Nelson, says: "[Mark] had *no right* to sit up if it was gwine to interfere wid his work" (71, emphasis added). Mark's daring claim to parental rights equal to Mr. Nelson's results in his sale "down the river way down South" (72). Consequently, Mark's inability to protect his daughter prompts an emotional narrative about Hasty's psychological distress and their child's awakening to her enslavement. However, this family's tragedy also arouses one slave mistress' grief and compassion that spurs her to renounce slavery and to intervene.

Thompson politicizes sentiment in a narrative where the threat to the familial bond arouses anxiety, then tears of compassion, and ultimately intervention. Unlike the slave women in earlier juvenile narratives, Hasty does not subversively challenge the system that claims her husband. Rather, when she discovers Mark's fate, Hasty seeks her mistress' assistance. The fear that arises when Mrs. Jennings imagines herself as a slave woman threatened with losing her husband and child awakens her sympathy and compassion. Thompson describes the "emotional analogy" (O'Connell 34), stating:

> [Mrs. Jennings] thought of Hasty's grief, as poignant as would have been her own, had her husband been in Mark's place. . . . She thought of the father torn from his wife and child; of the child fatherless, though not an orphan; of that child's future; and as it presented itself to her, she clasped her own little girl closer to her heart, almost fearing that it was to share that future. Ah! she was putting her "soul in the slave soul's stead." (73)

Unlike Fisher, who maintains that sentiment arouses emotion and little else, Thompson suggests that sympathy can prompt intervention: Mrs. Jennings willingly postpones her vacation East to "do all in my power to prevent [Mark] from going" (73). Initially, the mistress' power rests in her husband, whom she asks to purchase Mark from the slave trader, M'Affee. The resistance and failure that Mr. Jennings encounters awakens Mrs. Jennings's deeper resentment of the peculiar institution. Even though Mrs. Jennings recognizes some slave owners' cruelty, "here was a case which outraged every womanly feeling in her breast, a case of suffering and wrong, occurring to persons in whom she was personally interested, and she was aroused to the wickedness of the system which allowed such oppression" (77). Consequently, the mixture of heartfelt sentiment with newfound opposition spurs activism independent from her husband's. She attempts to speak to *Mr.* Nelson because she believes "[I] shall feel less conscience stricken than if I had remained at home, knowing that I have done all in my power to prevent his going" (79). Thompson exposes the limits of intervention through the meeting between Mrs. Jennings and *Mrs.* Nelson, who argues "we wives can do nothing, however great our repugnance may be to it" (81).

The absolutist tone in Mrs. Nelson's defeatist statement about women's powerlessness initially gathers validity as the white woman can neither save Mark nor mediate Hasty's despair and psychological decline. Unable to prevent the separation, Hasty experiences a mental decline after her shipside separation from Mark. Thompson accentuates Hasty's powerlessness by contrasting how white husbands and wives can separate at shipside because of the promise of reunion whereas the slave's deportation undermines this hope (86). As Jacqueline Jones asserts in *Labor of Love, Labor of Sorrow*, "[t]he reality or threat of separation from their families . . . caused some women to descend into madness" (36). Hasty's reaction approaches madness: she loses her "elastic step" (90), becomes "downhearted" (91), and experiences "troubled slumber" (92). When she awakens and realizes what has transpired, she lets out "a moan of agony [and] . . . [sinks] insensible upon the bed" (95). Her "shattered nerves" (95) restrict her to "a kind of stupor" (96) for several days. Mrs. Jennings can only express "[shock] at the ravages that mental and bodily suffering had made on the once handsome woman" (102), a reaction that encodes Thompson's critique of slavery's perpetuation rather than alleviation of psychological distress imposed upon slave women. Consequently, the separation both destroys a marital relationship and leads to a mother's psychological decline that prevents her from rising above the law, as do the slave mothers in the other texts, to preserve the mother-child bond and the child's innocence.

Thompson's careful attention to details illustrating an adult woman's powerlessness in the face of slavery elevates the anxiety about the child's powerlessness. Scarlet fever keeps Fanny oblivious to the family's tragedy, thereby preserving her innocence. However, when her fever breaks, so does her innocence and with this awakening, Thompson captures one stage in the typical slave narrative:

> When Fanny was fully recovered she learned the fate of her father. She did not weep, or sob, or complain, but for the first time she realized the shadow that slavery had cast over her; and the change was instantaneous, from the mirthful, happy child, to the anxious, watchful slave girl. Hereafter there was to be no trusting confidence, no careless gayety, but this consciousness of slavery must mingle with every thought, with every action. (96–97)

Fanny's transformation highlights the violation of the period's ideals for children and consequently adds both a sentimental and political dimension to her plight. Mrs. Jennings, a reader surrogate, expresses compassion for the child's anxiety upon losing her protective father. Yet, Thompson's portrait of Fanny's reaction to her mother's death intensifies the compassionate response. Upon Hasty's death, Fanny's vulnerability surfaces: "Hasty's spirit was released, and she was *free*. Fanny gave herself up to a child's grief, and refused to be comforted. To the slave, the affections are the bright spots in his wilderness of sorrow and care" (102). To Thompson, the peculiar institution's power to violate Fanny's emotional attachments, as it does her mother's, justifies slavery's abolition.

Losing both parents could cause Fanny to experience the extensive psychological distress that Hasty experiences when her owner sells Mark; however, before dying, Hasty tempers Fanny's suffering by ensuring her daughter's freedom, thereby rupturing slavery's legacy. Echoing the *Commonwealth v. Aves* (or "little Med's") case, Thompson attacks the system that prevents a mother from protecting her child: "Yet what is a slave mother's protection to her child? What blow can she arrest? What temptations avert? None. Even a mother's claim is unrecognized, and the child's affection unregarded" (101). Just as the judicial system overruled many white women's custody decisions under coverture laws, the slavocracy, Thompson stresses, disregards the slave mother's claims to her children, evident when the slave mistress, Mrs. Le Rue, expresses no compassion for Hasty's distress. Indeed, she threatens to make Fanny pay through labor what Hasty owes her. Having lost her husband, the potential threat to her child ultimately kills Hasty; but before her death, she persuades Mrs. Jennings to purchase Fanny and to keep her "beyond the reach of a slave girl's perils" (102). Hasty makes a deathbed wish that ultimately asserts her claim to Fanny and frees her daughter in ways she could not effect with her husband. Echoing instances of dying white mothers who decide their child's custody, Hasty ensures Fanny's freedom through a verbal promise with her mistress.[38] Their verbal agreement functions like the binding legal document that Stowe's Ophelia ascertains from St. Clare to ensure Topsy's freedom and that judges granted to mothers in real custody disputes.

Mrs. Jennings upholds this verbal "adoption" contract because, as Thompson suggests, she has undergone a slow conversion from proslavery to abolitionist sentiments. Notwithstanding her earlier failed attempts at intervention, Mrs. Jennings protects Fanny by relocating the entire family to Chicago, "where she is an active worker among antislavery women in that liberty-loving city" (103). Unlike Mrs. Nelson, who claims women can do nothing and Mrs. Le Rue to whom "[t]he idea of commiserating with Hasty's condition as a human being, as a sister, never for a moment occurred to her" (98), Mrs. Jennings rejects powerlessness and hardheartedness. Instead, her abolitionist tears inspire activism. In turn, Thompson may have hoped that upon hearing this family's tragic narrative, her readers, like Mrs. Jennings, would awaken to slavery's destructive nature and undergo similar conversions from apathy, to compassion, to action.

Published alongside Thompson's "Mark and Hasty," Julia Colman's "Little Lewis: The Story of a Slave Boy" (1859)[39] represents the most complex, hybrid text that politicizes sentiment. Colman discusses the interconnection between a slave mother's suffering, her child's awakening to his enslaved condition, and the subsequent attempts to ascertain freedom. However, Colman replaces images of women engaged in acts of physical resistance with the portrait of a violated slave mother who defends her child's best interest by encouraging him to use deceit to ascertain an education and freedom. Nancy's words steer Lewis toward freedom's path and a white woman's conversion leads to subversive activism that completes the process.

Like her foremothers, Colman expresses anxiety for Lewis, the slave child, who "[found] himself a friendless orphan, in a cold world with a cruel master" (31). As a slave "orphan," Lewis literally has no one to alleviate his suffering or to intervene on his behalf. Almost as white as "massa Harry" (21), his white father-master deprives him of access to a typical white childhood. Nor can Lewis achieve inclusion in the children's games because the white children abuse the slave boy whom they view as property. For example, Dick, an older white boy, physically abuses Lewis and takes his primer: "the young tyrant, giving the boy a vigorous kick or two as he rose, stuffed the book into his own pocket, and walked off" (24). Similarly, Hal could escalate his learned cruelty toward Lewis since "if he had been at home he would have had some little fear of breaking the child's back, for his father was more careful of his *property* than Uncle Stamford was" (23). Even Katy, the most benevolent white child, is a "frolicsome, romping witch" (22). Nor do the other slaves console him. Aunt Sally, who "sometimes scolded, and sometimes listened" (24), provides Lewis with little comfort. Through these images of cruelty and disregard, Colman creates an air of anxiety with respect to the child's life experiences and his best interest.

No one intervenes in this slave child's behalf because the slavocracy displaces the mother and denies her access to a judicial system that safeguarded the child's best interests. Lewis's mother is separated from her husband and is "sold quite a distance away to a very bad man who used her cruelly" (28). But Colman indicates that Nancy's greatest suffering stems from her violated maternity. Nancy's sons (Tom and Sam) and her daughter Nelly "were all taken off in one day by one of the ugliest negro drivers that ever scared a little slave boy's dreams" (26). Nancy considers her second's daughter's death not "half so sad" (27) and wishes the other children had died as well. The narrator counteracts a negative reaction to Nancy's desire by asking readers to identify and to sympathize with the slave mother: "How would you feel if all you loved best were carried off by a cruel slave driver, and you had *no hope* of hearing from them again in this world?" (35). Through such identification, Colman inspires compassion for Nancy's violated maternity, especially since, unlike her white counterparts, "she could not have the privilege of ministering to the least of [her children's] wants, of soothing one of their sorrows, or even dropping a silent tear beside them" (35). Colman further increases empathy by suggesting that the forced separation from her children drives Nancy mad. Her master permits Nancy to visit her children only when episodes of insanity make her useless at work (36–37). Given the opportunity to see her children, Nancy "would hold their hands lovingly in hers . . . would lay her hand gently on the heads of one and the other, and her eyes would wander lovingly over their faces, and then fill with tears" (39). Aware that she cannot "reclaim" her children, Nancy attempts to kill Lewis to spare him from "growi[ing] up and suffer[ing] what she had" (27; see also 36). The white community would have viewed infanticide as a violation of ideal motherhood; yet, Colman instills this attempt with heroic qualities. Unable to kill her son during their brief reunion, Nancy attempts suicide, which the community also prevents (34).

Circumventing the infanticide and the suicide not only serves as a plot device to expose Nancy's debilitating suffering, but also allows for the words of intervention that ultimately free Lewis. Not an Eliza-like mother who commits heroic feats to free her children, Nancy intercedes for Lewis by exposing slavery's unspeakable brutalities. Colman writes:

> [Nancy] showed [Lewis] her wrists where they had been worn by the irons, and her back scarred by the whip, and she told him of cruelties that we may not repeat here. She talked with him as if he were a man, and not a child; and as he listened his heart and mind seemed to reach forward, and he became almost a man in thought. (39)

During this meeting, Lewis recognizes his enslavement:

> It was here that the fearful fact dawned upon him as it never had before. *He was a slave!* He had no control over his own person or actions, but he belonged soul and body to another man, who had power to control him in everything. And this would not have been so irksome had it been a person that he loved, but Master Stamford he hated. (39)

This awakening to powerlessness could debilitate Lewis; however, his mother's words initiate transformation and eventual freedom. In contrast to white mothers who teach obedience to parent, God, and country, Nancy teaches Lewis about subversive resistance that "implants in his heart an early love for knowledge" (42) thereby giving her child hope and a potential future. As the narrative progresses, Lewis repeatedly expresses a desire for an education and he tries to learn his ABCs from a "ragged primer" (2) because he imagines himself as "a fine man . . . when he had learned to read" (21). Aunt Sally mocks his desire for literacy and the white children abuse him for it, but Nancy insists that freedom depends upon literacy, obtainable only through deceit and quiet rebellion against the slave laws that deny him an education.

Lewis's awakening to his enslaved state and his mother's insistence on education motivate his freedom quest. The visit with his mother "[h]ad fixed a purpose within, which was helping him to work out his destiny" (42). Just as Frederick Douglass tricks the children into teaching him his letters, Lewis gains his education through deceit. Rather than ascertain permission to attend the Sunday school on the Pond plantation, Lewis goes secretly. His deceit proves justified because when he asks his master's permission, Mr. Stamford whips him for wanting an education and then whips him even harder for having already attended school. Nevertheless, determined to learn to read, Lewis convinces Sam Tyler to teach him letters at night or in his master's absence. Despite his persistence and diligence, Lewis makes slow progress and when his book disappears from its hiding place, "by degrees he settled down into a state of despondency and indifference" (48). As in adult slave narratives, Lewis overcomes these temporary setbacks to win a second chance at education and freedom. When Mr. Stamford auctions his slaves, Lewis gains a new incentive. Like Frederick Douglass, Lewis realizes, "Ah, I have a *mind* and it's my mind that they have sold," he added with a sudden gleam of thought. "And what have I of my own? Nothing! They buy and sell, and control soul and mind and body" (50). Yet, Lewis's sale ultimately liberates him body, mind, and soul because his new master, Mr. Johns, lives near Ohio and makes Lewis do gardening (51). Unlike Frederick Douglass who documents Colonel Lloyd's violent efforts to "[keep] the slaves out of his garden" (33), Lewis's entrance into the Edenic space results in emancipatory knowledge. Through gardening, Lewis gains access to Miss Ford, the children's Northern governess, and he convinces her to give him reading lessons at sunrise (55). Unlike Eve, who causes Adam's fall, Miss Ford takes Nancy's place as educator and offers Lewis the knowledge his mother assured him would secure his freedom.

Like her foremothers, Colman depicts how a white woman's nascent compassion inspires activism. Initially, Miss Ford views Lewis disdainfully. Echoing Mr. Auld's reprimand to his wife for teaching Frederick Douglass the alphabet, Mr. Johns grows angry at Miss Ford; however, she appeases him by defending her enterprise as intellectual play: "'Surely, now, you would not deprive me of such an innocent amusement' said she, with mock lamentation" (56). Her amusement takes a serious turn because upon hearing stories about Lewis's childhood and his mother's experiences, Miss Ford undergoes a conversion and adopts abolitionist principles. She slowly realizes slavery's evils: "that even she herself was not at liberty to speak out her sentiments about it. But she could think, and she did" (58), and that

> [t]hese poor creatures had a right to their own personal freedom, and she thought it would be doing God and humanity a service if she could help them to obtain that freedom. She did not know that in doing thus she would be sinning against the laws of her country, (!) and perhaps she would not have cared much if she had, for she was one of those independent souls that dare to acknowledge the law of right. (58)

Consequently, the newly converted abolitionist and surrogate mother figure joins forces with Mr. Dean, "the worst abolitionist in the neighborhood" (59), ascertains Lewis's freedom, but must go to jail and pay fines for aiding a slave (61). Thus, Lewis gains his freedom not through a physical battle with a "Mister Covey," but through verbal persuasion that inspires an outsider's intervention.

"Little Lewis: The Story of a Slave Boy" represents the only recovered text whose ending echoes traditional slave narratives. Frances Smith Foster contends that traditional slave narratives regularly remain silent about the details concerning the course of freedom, but often relate the ex-slave's integration into the community (122). Similarly, Colman offers no particulars about Lewis's flight to freedom, stating only that with "face and hands dyed, and his clothes changed, [Lewis] was to go with Mr. Dean in the capacity of a servant to Cincinnati, and he should then run his own chances of escape" (59). However, she does depict Lewis as a productive society member: he marries, has three children, teaches in Boston, and devotes himself to Christianity (61).

In conclusion, the hybridized sentimental, juvenile pseudo slave narrative represents one strategy that domestic abolitionists used to make a complex, political issue accessible to children (and perhaps their mothers). Through the rhetoric of politicized sentiment infused with anxiety, these women authors create a new space from which to voice their abolitionist views and to critique slavery's destruction of childhood innocence and the family unit. "Grandmother," "Cousin Ann," Eliza Follen, Julia Colman, and Matilda Thompson encode their agendas of activism in a rhetoric that inspires empathy and abolitionist tears, thereby validating emotional appeals as a means to arouse identification and to effect change. These domestic abolitionists encourage boys and girls to listen to stories about innocent but violated children and to respond from the "heart" by enacting private, benevolent activism. In "How Shall Children Do Good?" (1844), Eliza Follen argues that despite their young age and financial dependence, children can effect positive change because "[l]ove flows from the heart of a little child as purely, and as freely, as from the heart of the profoundest philosopher" (110). To Follen, a child who acts from true love and concern makes the poor and suffering feel like less of an outcast and more like a brother (111). Using slavery as an example of the work children can do, she asks:

> [I]s it not work enough for a child, to learn that these unhappy beings, are all the children of God; that they have a claim upon him as their brothers and sisters, and that they are calling for help from every Christian heart? Is it not work enough for the child, in his early days, so to study the perfect law of love and liberty, that when his reason is strong, and his highest faculties are matured, he shall be prepared to live a life of self-denial and self-devotion, and to consecrate himself to the cause of humanity, to the service of his suffering brethren? (111–12)

She implies that teaching a child about Christian empathy and American principles can ultimately remedy American's religious and political corruption. Thus, she enjoins children to:

> Seek daily and hourly to be good. When you are called upon to make any little sacrifice for the good of another, make it cheerfully, freely. Do what you can; and complain not if it is but little.... Cherish the desire to bless others, and the holy work shall ere long be given you to do. Learn to look upon every human being as equally with yourself the child of God, however degraded he may be, however the world may cast him off. So that when the ministry of your life begins . . . you may be ready to stretch forth the arms of your love towards all your fellow men. (113)

Follen suggests that the preparation for future work outweighs the concern that children can do little actively now. Rather, she advocates a "virtue ethics" that places emphasis on sympathy and empathy. Like temperance and other nineteenth-century reform movements, this type of abolitionism stressed "right feeling" as the basis for private acts of resistance that would ultimately restore domestic principles and American ideals. In this light, women and children would intervene, assume power, and act in the best interest of the children, the slaves, and America.

3

Seditious Histories

The Abolitionist Mother-Historian

The women could talk freely *within* their all-female organizations; they were not allowed to address a mixed audience. This objection to women as public speakers ("public" referring to a mixture of male and female listeners) persisted—indeed increased.... For a woman to fight slavery in the pages of a periodical, then *was* daring for these times.
                                                                        —Mary Patricia Jones 26

In March 1845, *Godey's Lady's Book* published "Maternal Instruction" (Figure 3), an engraving that encapsulated the nineteenth century's conviction in a mother's responsibility for her children's education. Patricia Okker suggests that this engraving limits the woman to the maternal role and to a small, domestic space, but it also associates her with reading and education, intellectual activities that transcend the domestic sphere (119–20). What is this woman reading to her daughters? Contemporary viewers may have assumed that this ideal mother transmitted sentimental, patriotic, or morally correct information.[1] However, what if that assumption proves false? The engraving does not reveal titles of spellers, grammars, or sentimental novels. What if "Maternal Instruction," actually depicts an abolitionist mother reading seditious political works to her daughters? The question poses a real possibility. Domestic abolitionists embraced the ambiguity inherent in *Godey's* "Maternal Instruction." Many authors, like Kate Barclay, Matilda Thompson, Elizabeth Margaret Chandler, Eliza Follen, Jane Elizabeth Jones, S.C.C., and Harriet Butts, created juvenile, abolitionist historical fiction and a new protagonist: the *abolitionist mother-historian*.[2] Rather than employ the victim's perspective intrinsic to sentimental juvenile pseudo slave narratives (see chapter 2), this maternal voice educates her children about abolitionist politics by narrating histories that otherwise "found few historians" (qtd. in Dudley 207). Situating this mother-historian in the safety of the nursery or schoolroom and having her do legitimate work allowed authors to support gen-

FIGURE 3. "Maternal Instruction" from Godey's *Lady's Book* (March 1845)
(from the copy in the Rare Book Collection, the University
of North Carolina at Chapel Hill).

der paradigms and to placate the stigma against women's public dissention. However, this figure's revisionist histories employ everything from sentimental rhetoric to an increasingly radical, legalistic, and quasi-seditious rhetoric. Thus, domestic abolitionists cleverly empowered women's voices in the act of documenting a threatened and preferably forgotten history.

Contemporary nineteenth-century audiences often saw women as transmitters of knowledge to American children. In *The Mother at Home; or, the Principles of Maternal Duty* (1834), John S. C. Abbott argues that God endowed mothers, not educational institutions, with the power to serve as educators who could reform America's ills before the millennium. He states:

> O mothers! reflect upon the power your Maker has placed in your hands. There is no earthly influence to be compared with yours. There is no combination of causes so powerful, in promoting the happiness in the misery of our race, as the instructions of home. (167)

Furthermore, he aligns women's superior moral status to America's political climate: "When our land is filled with virtuous and patriotic mothers, then will it be filled with virtuous and patriotic men" (166). Like Abbott, Reverends Daniel Wise and Theodore Cuyler affirmed the beneficial power of a mother's influence (Douglas 97, 99). Not surprisingly, contemporary women also supported the mother-educator. For example, in *Letters to Mothers*, Lydia Sigourney espoused "the omnipotent quality of maternal influence" (Douglas 74) and Lydia Maria Child dedicated *The Mother's Book* "[t]o American [m]others on whose intelligence and discretion the safety and prosperity of our republic must depend" (v). Finally, in *Woman in America: Her Work and Her Behavior* (1850), Maria Jane McIntosh suggests that women, to whom "important work has been committed" (29), could facilitate America's reformation from their private spheres.[3] She states:

> But while all the outward machinery of government, the body, the thews and sinews of society, are man's, woman, if true to her own not less important or less sacred mission, controls the vital principle. Unseen herself, working, like nature, in secret, she regulates its pulsations, and sends forth from its heart, in pure and temperate flow, the life-giving current. It is hers to warm into life the earliest germs of thought and feeling in the infant mind, to watch the first dawning of light upon the awakening soul, to aid the first faint struggles of clay-encumbered spirit to grasp the beautiful realities which here and there present themselves amid the glittering falsities of earth, and to guide its first tottering steps into the paths of peace. (25)[4]

Thus, notwithstanding their primary relegation to the home, women would use their superior moral status as mothers "to stabilize society by generating and regenerating moral character" (Cott 97) and thereby theoretically shape America's success or failure (Cott 84, 200; Tompkins 143–45).[5] As Ann Douglas argues:

The cult of motherhood . . . was an essential precondition to flattery [which] American women were trained to demand in place of justice and equality. It offered them . . . a very genuine basis for self-respect. It gave them, moreover, an innate, unassailable, untestable claim to charismatic authority and prestige, a sanction for subjectivity and self-love. The theories of motherhood promulgated by women like Sigourney generated important programs of child-raising, but they also found wide use and justification for conventionally unmaternal pursuits. American women over the course of the nineteenth century were able to exonerate almost any action performed in the sacred name of motherhood. (75)

Thus, motherhood could empower women intellectually, religiously, and civicly.

Clearly, when criticism thwarted all but the most outspoken women from public speaking and publishing their antislavery sentiments in arenas like *The Liberty Bell* or various abolitionist newspapers, domestic abolitionists turned to the power in motherhood. Women engaged in fireside politics may have found their deliverance when the Anti-Slavery Convention of American Women adopted two resolutions that used motherhood to foster women's abolitionist efforts. In May 1837, liberal and conservative female abolitionists at the convention gave women an entrée into the abolitionist debate by politicizing woman's most traditional role (Swerdlow 14–15; 41).[6] Abby Ann Cox and Rebecca Spring's resolution argued:

That there is no class of women to whom the antislavery cause makes so direct and powerful an appeal as *mothers,* and they are solemnly urged by all the blessings of their own and their children's freedom and by all the contrasted bitterness of the slave-mother's condition, to lift up their hearts to God on behalf of the captive. (qtd. in Swerdlow, *AS* 41)

Affirming the ideologies about women's morals and virtues as well as their responsibilities as mothers, the Cox-Spring motherhood resolution intertwined the public and private spheres to encourage women's antislavery activism and to grant them political power.[7] Through politically motivated prayer, women and God would work together to save America.

The belief that "No one could vote against motherhood" (Swerdlow 41) may have also prompted Sarah Grimké's "motherhood resolution," which urged mothers to *educate* children about slavery rather than guard them from its reality (Bogin and Yellin 14–15; *Proceedings . . . 1837* 8–12). This resolution perpetuated the nineteenth-century concept Linda Kerber calls post-Revolutionary "republican motherhood":[8]

In the years of the early Republic a consensus developed around the idea that a mother, committed to the service of her family and to the state, might serve a political purpose. Those who opposed women in politics had to meet the proposal that women could—and should—play a political role through the raising of a patriotic child. The Republican Mother was to encourage in her *sons* civic interest and participation. She was to educate her children and guide them in paths of morality and virtue. But she was not to tell her male relatives for whom to vote. She was a citizen but not really a constituent. (283, emphasis added)

Just as late-eighteenth-century mothers ascertained a voice in the country's political future, Grimké's 1837 resolution empowered mothers because it upheld, rather than challenged, America's cult of motherhood. Thus, when female antislavery factions from New York to Boston reemphasized child rearing's political dimension, they expanded women's domestic power to include current public issues. The resolution gave mothers a national responsibility. If mothers did not teach this reformist consciousness, establish the historical reality, and create a new understanding of the "other,"⁹ their child's subsequent ignorance would perpetuate slavery's inherent evils and further threaten America's future.

Beginning with the 1837 female antislavery societies' resolutions and lasting throughout the antebellum period, mothers could instill this reformist consciousness in their children either through indirect modeling or direct instruction. Children could imitate mothers who "lift[ed] up their hearts" for the slaves and who modeled Christian behavior (Swerdlow 41). Moreover, a child could undergo deliberate socialization as Elizabeth Lloyd advocates in "An Appeal for the Bondwoman, to Her Own Sex" (1846):

> Mother! [the slaves] invoke thy aid!
> Not to bear the battle blade,
> Aim a spear, or break a lance,
> For the slave's deliverance,
> But to train thy little child,
> 'Ere the world shall have *beguiled*
> From thy side the precious trust,
> For the armies of the just. (31–38, emphasis added)

This mother must not wage war on a public battlefield. Rather, from her private lectern, she must enlist as a warrior-mother whose role as educator situates her as an arbitrator between the powerless slave, the young child, and the unjust proslavery forces. The mother exerts extensive influence because her "faintest tone / Lives upon the inward ear / Like no other sound we hear" (124–26). However, like the mother's gendered space, her instruction maintains gender stereotypes as it inscribes boys and girls into traditional spheres. The mother must teach her little boys, fascinated with battles, knights, and chivalry (88–90), about the abolitionists who fight the South, "Truth's defyer to lay low" (102). Conversely, to the little girl "of softer mold" (106) the mother must

> In a gentle voice and mild
> Tell her of the Captive's child;
> Whose tiny form is uncarressed,

> Whose lip in love is rarely pressed,
> Who sits neglected day by day,
> And wears its little life away,
> With none to cherish, no one near,
> To hush the wail or wipe the tear. (115–22)

Unlike her brother, this young female must not learn about the abolitionists' battles, but about the victims, especially the children. Ironically, though Lloyd depicts mothers whose lessons sustain gender differences, *her* commands accent a politically conscious voice that ruptures imposed gender limitations in its demand for women's activism.

More specifically, in "To Mothers in the Free States" (1855), Eliza Follen transfers the eighteenth-century ideology of "republican motherhood" to nineteenth-century abolitionist motherhood. She calls mothers to "come to the rescue of this land" (4) by rekindling their foremothers' achievements:

> In the early days of our country we had such [heroic and moral] mothers; and they had such sons. Let them of the present day emulate their example. Let them so consecrate themselves, so dedicate their children; and ere long, the chains will fall from our three millions [sic] of captives, and the jubilee be heard in our land. (3)

Follen urges mothers to achieve these ends by adopting the role of abolitionist storytellers whose lessons about the "other" would initiate children's transformation into adults who advocate a new morality and sanction civically responsible political action. She states:

> When [the children] are of an age to understand and hear the sad story, she [the mother] will tell them of the wrongs done by the white man to the poor slave. She has kindled in the hearts of her children a love of justice, a hatred of tyranny, a passionate desire to take the part of the oppressed, which shall enlist them for life as the champions of their sorely injured, down trodden, colored brethren. Such a mother is as an abiding inspiration to her children. Her son will not vote for the Fugitive Slave Law or the Nebraska Bill, nor become a kidnapping United States Commissioner! (3)

Follen clearly links a mother's stories with the capacity to shape increasingly benevolent and democratic American children, who would ultimately influence adult political decisions.[10] Like eighteenth-century republican mothers who "did not vote, . . . [but] took pride in their ability to mold voting citizens" (Kerber 285), these abolitionist mothers crafted a political outlet *within* a traditional role. Thus, affirmed by the 1837 resolution, Follen's rhetoric reinforces the acceptability of storytelling by abolitionist mothers acting not for political self-interest but for a desire to fashion a generation that would rescue America's endangered democratic principles.

Notwithstanding the new power the "motherhood resolutions" extended, the emphasis on abolitionist mothers as storytellers continued to confine women to private, domestic circles. However, the decision to publish abolitionist juvenile historical fiction shows how these domestic abolitionists used appropriate female roles to move the *privatized* political discourse into the *public* realm. In *American Women Writers of the Work of History, 1790–1860,* Baym recovers over 150 women historians among whom she finds that "[b]etween 1790 and 1860 at least twenty published history textbooks designed for school and/or home use" as well as "historical texts for family reading" (35). She documents how these women, given cultural authorization to study history, "absorbed the writing of history from the start" (31) because "[i]n the home . . . were formed the beings whose virtue or vice, civic patriotism or self-interest, would preserve or destroy the republic" (12). Furthermore, Baym argues that women penned histories to demonstrate their intellect and to "express political and public opinion" (40). She identifies women like Sarah Hall, Lydia Maria Child, and Anne Tuttle Bullard who used the "mother or woman teacher as mouthpiece for tendentious political or religious views" (37). However, by overlooking women's abolitionist histories for children, Baym ignores the authors who redefined women not only as teachers or historical commentators, but also as political activists who made current policy their province.[11] Writing histories for children and/or appearing as maternal historians within the texts may have helped cast women as intellectuals "comfortable with book-learning and a range of public discourses" (Baym, *American* 45), especially contemporary political, religious, and cultural theories. In the name of shaping American children's historical and political consciousness, the mother-historian emerged as an activist who encouraged children to speak and act against the state, a step the republican mother seemingly did not take.

In addition to reenvisioning the maternal figure and expanding women's political voice, domestic abolitionists challenged traditional history curricula by refusing to perpetuate the incomplete or biased American histories. For example, the publication of "The Slave Poet" (1845) in *The Child's Friend* suggests that Eliza Follen recognized the importance of offering children biographies of African Americans like George Moses Horton, the North Carolinian who sold his poetry to purchase his freedom. Such biographies added new faces to the catalogue of typical American heroes and patriots who filled children's histories like Lydia Sigourney's, *Evening Readings in History* (1833), Priscilla Wakefield's *A Brief Memoir of the Life of William Penn: Compiled for the Use of Young Persons* (1821), and Lydia Maria Child's *Biographical Sketches of Great and Good Men for Children* (1828).[12] Such standard children's histories had various designs. Lydia Maria Child's biographies of William Penn, Benjamin Franklin, Captain John Smith, General Israel Putnam, Christopher Columbus, John Ledyard, and Sir Benjamin West were

> presented to the youthful reader with the hope that he may be induced by
> exhibitions of goodness to strive to be good, and by example of eminence

attained by virtuous exertion, prudence and industry, to follow those paths which, in our republic surely lead to honorable independence, if not enviable distinction. (Advertisement)

Other authors claimed less lofty goals. For example, in "Independence Day," the author explains, "We are sorry to find . . . that so many children, and large children too, are ignorant of the most common facts in our own history. Every child of eight or nine years old ought to know why Independence is kept; and to what great man, under God's blessing, we owe it" (35). Ironically, although the author narrates America's battle against the British, s/he never mentions how slavery replicates the revolutionaries' charges against the British.[13] Baym recognizes a comparable silence in work by Elizabeth Peabody, who "simply declined to address slavery in her United States history: 'A book intended for public schools of all the United States, is not the place for the discussion of a subject so vital to the interests of the Union as the slavery question'" (*American* 62).[14] Similarly, once Eliza Follen ended her tenure (1844–1849) as editor of *The Child's Friend,* her successor(s) no longer published stories about slavery that challenged the practice of teaching children historical distortions.

Sarah Hale represents a woman who questioned whether children should recognize the falsehoods their history lessons led them to believe. Patricia Okker states, "Hale's own position [on slavery] reveals her division: although she opposed slavery, she rejected the abolition movement as too partisan. In keeping with her association of women with morality, Hale did not remain silent on the subject" (80). While she worked for Godey, who censored politics in his magazine (Okker 76; Finley 176), Hale published two adult novels about slavery's immorality (Okker 81): *Northwood, A Tale of New England* (1827 and revised in 1852) and *Liberia; or, Mr. Peyton's Experiments* (1855), which advocates recolonization. Nevertheless, she excluded such discussions about slavery from her prolific children's publications, thereby undermining her otherwise progressive views of childhood education (Okker 41). The prefatory remark in *Poems for Our Children: Designed for Families, Sabbath Schools, and Infant Schools: Written to Inculcate Moral Truths and Virtuous Sentiments* (1830) reveals Hale as "an ardent patriot" (Schilpp & Murphy 38)[15] and a teacher who bridges familial, religious, and civic ideals. Addressing "All Good Children in the United States," she writes:

> I intended, when I began to write this book, to furnish you with a few pretty songs and poems which would teach you truths, and, I hope, induce you to love truth and goodness. Children who love their parents and their home, can soon teach their hearts to love their God and their country. (5)

As she shifts from the private love of parents, home, and God to the public love of country, she intertwines familial, religious, and nationalistic politics but never challenges the status quo.

Archival recovery work has lead to identifying only two children's texts that reveal this patriotic woman teeter-tottering between whether or not to expose children to the untruths of American history. For example, "My Country" clearly espouses Hale's patriotic idealism:

> America! my own dear land,—
> O, 'tis a lovely land to me;
> I thank my God that I was born
>   Where man is *free!*
>
> Our land—it is a glorious land—
> And wide it spreads from sea to sea—
> And sister States in Union join
>   And all are *free.**
> . . . .
> You hear the sounds of healthful toil,
> And youth's gay shout and childhood's glee,
> And everyone in safety dwells
>   And all are *free.*
>
> We're brothers all from South to North,
> One bond will draw us to agree—
> We love this country of our birth—
>   We love the *free,*
> . . . .
> My land, my own dear native Land,
> Thou art a lovely land to me;
> I bless my God that I was born
>   Where man is *free!*

(1–8; 17–24; 29–32)

Hale's absolutist rhetoric praises America's majestic landscape, security, union, personal empowerment, and freedom. The reality of African Americans' enslavement appears only in an asterisk (after line 8) that points readers to a footnote: "All but two millions." But how many children read or understood the footnote? Hale may have explained it to her students during her seven years as a teacher (Okker 41); however, how many parents explained this statistic and thereby transformed the child's understanding of "my country"? Putting aside Hale's progressive, educational principles, the collision between absolute patriotism and the almost hidden critique suggests her refusal or reluctance to document racist American politics in her children's literature. Hale never undergoes the complete transformation from a republican to an abolitionist mother.

The ambiguity in Hale's poem, "Independence," further divulges her battle over presenting an idyllic or historically accurate view of American democracy in *The School Song Book* (1834). Hale's first stanza celebrates the forefathers who gained America's freedom during the Revolution. She writes:

> We come with hearts of gladness,
>   To breathe our songs of praise,—
> Let not a note of sadness
>   Be blended in the lays;
> For 'tis a hallowed story,
>   The theme of Freedom's birth
> Our *father's* deeds of glory
>   Are echoed round the earth. (1–8)

However, this seemingly conventional praise for the "liberty and justice for all" mentality subsequently acquires a strained tone when Hale shifts from the past to the future. She writes:

> The sound is waxing stronger,
>   And thrones and nations hear;
> "Man may not triumph longer,
>   For God, the Lord is near—"
> And He will crush oppression,
>   And raise the humble mind,
> And give the earth's possession
>   Among the good and kind.
>
> And then shall sink the mountains,
>   Where pride and power were crowned;
> And peace, like gentle fountains,
>   Shall shed its pureness round—
> And then the world will hear us,
>   And join our glorious la[y],
> And songs of millions cheer us,
>   On this our Nation's Day.
>
> Soon Freedom's loud hosannas,
>   Shall burst from every voice,
> Till mountains and Savannas
>   Rock back and sound—"Rejoice!"
> To God, the king of heaven,
>   Then consecrate the strain;—
> Earth's fetters will be driven;
>   And God the Lord will reign[.] (9–32)

The emphasis on America's future redemption obfuscates Hale's intent. Does Hale refer to the day when God will intercede to break the slaves' fetters so all may truly sing "[f]reedom's loud hosannas" (25)? Her ambiguity and inability to redefine patriotism in terms of historical accuracy perpetuates an inaccurate understanding of American freedom and accentuates the sadness that the narrator asks the celebrants to deny.

Hale, Peabody, and the post-Follen editors of *The Child's Friend* exemplify those who evaded discussing slavery in juvenile literature; however, the decision to silence its reality did not gain absolute consensus. Recovered abolitionist juvenile historical fiction reveals that many domestic abolitionists responded to the "motherhood resolutions" and to Lydia Maria Child's complaint in her *Anti-Slavery Catechism* (1838) that the slave's experience had "found few historians" (qtd. in Dudley 207). Domestic abolitionists, like the author of "The Slave Poet," implicitly assert: "When, without uttering a falsehood, [may we] say, 'Go and tell the world America is free'? Children as well as grown people should think of these things" (257). While some employ the sentimental rhetoric and strategies intrinsic to juvenile pseudo slave narratives, most abolitionist mother-historians engage in discussions about slavery that do not betray any confusion about what to tell children, for they silence neither information nor themselves in their often seditious challenges to traditional American history lessons.

American women may have looked across the Atlantic to their British foremothers who wrote slave histories for children. Eliza Weaver Bradburn's *Pity Poor Africa: Three Dialogues, for Children* (1831) represents the earliest instance of a mother documenting the history of slavery for children. This British woman affirms that children should learn about slavery from their mother; yet she so unobtrusively shapes the image of the abolitionist mother-historian that she defuses the text's politically subversive overtones. Rather than allow the mother figure to dominate the text, Bradburn's first two dialogues foreground the children's voices as Eliza and William establish their understanding of slavery.[16] In the first mother-daughter dialogue, Eliza tells her mother what she learned about missionaries' attempts to convert Africans. Pitying the "heathens recognizing the persuasive, educational, and reformative power of books," Eliza vows to make a box in which to save money for the missionaries (13). Furthermore, she desires to write books for children "about Missionaries, and slavery, and idolaters. I dare say some children would be induced by them to give their money" (14). Similarly, in Dialogue II, the mother asks why the children have remained indoors with "three Bibles, a Concordance, and writing materials" (18). William reveals that Eliza's newly acquired knowledge about slavery spurred them to assemble a religious history of Bible passages that condemn slavery, which he, Emily, and Eliza then present to their mother, cast as the listener-learner.

Having postponed sharing her knowledge about slavery until "tomorrow" (20), in Dialogue III the mother figure gains a powerful voice as slavery's historian.

Bradburn's abolitionist mother figure justifies teaching children about slavery because she believes knowledge outweighs the damaging repercussions of ignorance. She says:

> I have read old accounts which would not only shock your affectionate hearts exceedingly, but would, in all probability, excite anger, hatred, and revenge, towards the perpetuators of such cruelty. At the same time I am aware that, without some information on the subject of slavery, we do not sufficiently estimate the blessings of freedom; nor can you, my dear children, set a proper value on every effort to abolish this bondage so disgraceful to human nature. (19)

Striving to help the children create for others the freedom they themselves may not value, this mother figure supplements the stories Eliza has reported and the Biblical history the children have reconstructed with an increasingly complex history of slavery from its origins, to British participation, and its spread to America. She recalls facts and reads excerpts from various reference books: geographies, pamphlets, anecdotes, missionary reports, and other histories. The mother's ability to utilize historical resources adds a new dimension to children's knowledge and understanding. The children trust their mother's teachings and eagerly embrace the new perspective, evident when William says, "And little have we thought when looking at [maps] how many thousands of inhabitants would be carried away as slaves. Poor things! I shall always think of [slaves] when learning any thing about Africa" (29). Ultimately, Bradburn suggests that via a mother's knowledge, both fictional and real children can affect change when they transmit to future generations these new perceptions of the "other."[17]

In comparison to their British counterparts, American women's publications depicting abolitionist mother-historians appear more often and in a greater variety. Like Bradburn's first two dialogues in *Pity Poor Africa*, Kate Barclay's "The Ride" (1856) and "The Sale" (1856) foreground mothers listening to their children's recognition of the paradox inherent in American democratic principles that permit slavery or acting as a spokesperson for abolitionist principles, respectively. In "The Ride," Barclay depicts a mother noting her daughter's sad expression upon her return from a pony ride with Henry, her "gallant young friend" (18). The daughter confides that unlike her companion whose residence in the South leaves him unaffected, her "*heart* grew sore at the sight of [the slaves]" (29) sold in the slave market. Her emotional distress, evident in the desire to return to her utopian North, "our own sweet home . . . where free banners wave" (45–46), reveals how the "eyewitness history" (Baym, *American* 96) transforms her experience. She states:

> But, mother, that sight from my mind ne'er will pass;
>   And my free spirit droops 'neath the power
> Of slavery's deeds, which appear to me now
>   To deepen and darken each hour. (37–40)

Therefore, in "The Ride," Barclay recalls Bradburn's portrait of the mother who listens to a child's historical report; however, this mother serves only as a confidant to whom the child voices her new consciousness of and opposition against slavery. Conversely, in "The Sale," Barclay gives the mother an increasingly active role in her child's reeducation. Whereas Bradburn's mother figure refers to historical texts that document slavery's past, Barclay's character responds to a first-hand, public encounter with slavery. She writes:

> "'SALE at twelve o'clock!' Now, what does it mean?
> Dear mother, do just look at that!
> See that girl standing there, with her head bent down,
> By that man in a beaver hat!
>
> "And that one behind, with his hand on her arm,
> Seems pushing or pulling her back:
> I wonder if that is a slave being sold;
> She don't look to me very black."
>
> "Yes, Johnny; this is a slave auction, you see;
> There's the auctioneer standing up there,
> With mallet in hand, crying, 'What will you bid?'
> And the purchasers stand down there.
>
> "How my very heart fills with sadness and grief
> As I think of that poor girl's fate!—
> Not a friend to protect or shield her from crime,
> Nor lift from her spirit the weight." (1–16)

Albeit Johnny (much like the daughter in "The Ride") expresses grief and sympathy for the quadroon rather than dedicating himself to abolitionism, his grief gives his mother the opportunity to affirm his observations and to explain the scene objectively rather than to conceal or mitigate its painful reality. Therefore, unlike "The Ride's" more passive mother, this mother figure's explanation of the public event extends the child's knowledge and imparts a new consciousness that may later lead to action, rather than escapism.

Published in the same year as Barclay's poems, Matilda Thompson's "Aunt Judy's Story: A Story from Real Life" (1859),[18] contrasts a father and a mother's transmission of early American history and antebellum slavery history, respectively, to highlight how women simultaneously seized and reenvisioned their roles as American historians. Thompson's short story includes a father figure, Mr. Ford, who acknowledges the Native Americans' unjust loss of land and the violence they suffered from white settlers. However, he also supplants his children's perception of Native Americans as victims who suffered more than slaves when he depicts them as oppressors, a "war-like and treacherous race" (119), undeserving of the compassion Alfred wishes to extend to them. Mr. Ford never hesitates to make broad claims about colonial history, nor does he support them with references to secondary sources, as does the mother in Bradburn's *Pity Poor Africa.* Instead, Mr. Ford has the last word in this father-child debate and his history lesson ends with Alfred laughing and "willingly surrender[ing]" (120) to his father.

Conversely, Thompson's mother figure uses a very different strategy to collect and to transmit history. Unwilling to generalize or speculate, she initially refuses to tell the children Aunt Judy's history because "it is not in my power to do so, as I am not very well acquainted with their history" (114). Handling history more mindfully, Mrs. Ford obtains a firsthand account from the ex-slave woman's experience. Only when a snow storm prevents Aunt Judy from leaving her home to narrate her story does Mrs. Ford tell the children about Aunt Judy's attempts to remain with her husband (who dies after being violently beaten and sold), the forceful separation from her children, and her reenslavement (despite her free papers). Affirming the victim's perspective, this maternal historian establishes this microcosmic narrative as grounds for a revised account of American slavery.

Despite this new approach, Thompson limits this mother-historian's subversiveness by having her narrate a domestic history and having the listeners respond with tears. In contrast to the nationalist history Mr. Ford narrates, Mrs. Ford casts the war between the free and the enslaved as a domestic one, which Cornelia (the daughter) emphasizes with her recognition that slave owners separated mothers and children (113). Furthermore, Thompson contrasts the response the two historians elicit from the children. Mr. Ford's lesson ends in laughter, not new compassion for Native Americans. Conversely, Mrs. Ford asks Alfred, Cornelia, and Harry to imagine the suffering stemming from the intimate narrative about violated bonds and brutal experiences. At the narrative's conclusion, "Mrs. Ford ceased, her *tears* falling fast, and the children were sobbing around her" (153). Mrs. Ford's experience with the slave woman's "herstory" changes her children's and supposedly the readers' experience. With their new sympathy for and consciousness of the "other," mother and children must reconsider America's past without laughter because the history of slavery was serious business. Through the domestic imagery and sentimental rhetoric, Thompson (like Barclay) tempers women's opposition to slavery but simultaneously challenges how the "Mr. Fords" teach history,

Just as Thompson limited the subversiveness of the fictional mother figure by never explicitly challenging the patriarchal powers inherent in a figure like Mr. Ford, in *Ralph; or, I Wish He Wasn't Black* (1855), Harriet Butts narrates a politicized history with mother figures, white *and* African American, who employ seemingly nonsubversive religious rhetoric to document and to counteract a hypocritical community's racism. Just as Thompson carefully enables Mrs. Ford to document a silenced history, clearly Butts has Mrs. Medford and Mrs. Willard address what the educational system evades. For example, during a lesson, the Sunday school teacher asks her students to consider the question of their creation. When Ralph Medford and the other white children fall silent, Tommy Willard, the slave child, states:

> I expect God makes all the white folks, but don't know 'zactly who makes the black ones, 'less as Topsy says they all growed; but I don't b'leve this, for I b'leve some would grow white as well as black. I can't tell how it is if God did make the black boys, as well as the white boys, why He lets wicked men sell little black boys' fathers, when he always lets the white boys' father stay at home. I can't tell—I don't know; I wish you would tell. (23–24)

Rather than explain Tommy's confusion about religious principles and secular politics, the Sunday school teacher, endowed with the responsibility of educating, sidesteps Tommy's question stating she "would explain this matter to him when he was 'old enough to understand it'" (24). Yet, Tommy and Ralph's discussions with their mothers reveal that the children *are* "old enough to understand." Through the political and unequivocal mother-educator figure who intertwines sentiment with criticism, Butts records a microcosmic history of racially inspired religious corruption.

In a narrative lacking effective Sunday school teachers and adult male characters, Butts charges mothers to document the historical conflict between religion and proslavery politics. Mrs. Medford assumes her role as educator when her son Ralph begs her to ask Tommy Willard and "Aunt Molly" *not* to sit in the Medford family's church pew notwithstanding their long, bias-free friendship with Tommy. Ralph's request arises after he overhears young and old church members' racist gossip and encounters peers who taunt him for being a "little abolitionist" who plays with Tommy. The "bullies" also announce that their mothers cannot understand why Mrs. Medford, a woman with "such influence in society" (5), would associate with fugitive slaves. This mother figure intervenes because the ridicule threatens Ralph's friendship with Tommy and his religious training. Mrs. Medford had

> early impress[ed] on the plastic mind of her little boy, truths lofty and pure, simplified to his youthful comprehension.—The religion that she taught him was void of that mysticism, which so often confounds the childish head. It was a natural as well as revealed religion, and so loving did God appear in charaeter [sic] with which she clothed Him, that Ralph early learned to associate everything that was pure with the "Good Father" as he very appropriately called Him. (13)

Thus, Butts creates an auspicious mother figure who softens, but does *not* dismiss, the political dimension she adds to Ralph's religious instruction. After affirming Ralph's love for Tommy and Aunt Molly and determining that his prejudicial demands stem from peer pressure rather than racism, Mrs. Medford offers religious instruction that counteracts prejudice. Rather than critique American's violation of the principles inherent to the Declaration of Independence, Mrs. Medford reminds Ralph that God made all people free and equal, Christ's teachings require treating all equally (4, 8, 24), and "[i]t was man's wickedness which caused this misery in our world" (24). Mrs. Medford calmly and lovingly reinforces Biblical principles and offers little commentary or elaboration about "man's wickedness." Since Butts never permits the mother figure to attack Mrs. Scornful, Mrs. Pride, and the young George Pride (three community members whose racist and classist distinctions violate Biblical doctrines), she remains a devout and moral figure rather than an outspoken and possibly threatening abolitionist woman.

Butts extends the image of the temperate abolitionist by having Mrs. Medford share her identity as a moral, mother-educator with Tommy's mother. Mrs. Willard, the African American fugitive mother, teaches her son about the difference between God-given and human laws. Spurred by the Sunday school teacher's evasion, Tommy expresses his own understanding of racial prejudice and reveals his discontentment with his self-image:

> I wish I was a little white boy, like Ralph. Everybody seems to love him; all the boys run up to him after school, and I know they would not have done so if he had been black like me. Mother, can't you wash off the black nohow? Take some strong soap suds and scour my face, mother, and see if I look any whiter. When I was coming from school one of he boys ran up to me and put his finger on my face and rubbed hard, and then he looked to see if the black did not rub off at all. Do you see any white mark on my face, mother? (25)

Like Mrs. Medford, Mrs. Willard sidesteps denouncing the white boys who attempt to remove Tommy's darkness. Rather, she employs religion to encourage him to love himself. She states:

> God who gave your friend Ralph such beautiful skin, and formed his features so regularly, also gave my little Tommy the skin which he is destined to wear. God does not look at the *skin*, my son, but at the *heart*. If you try to do well, and love to be a good boy, God will love you as well as He possibly can the most beautiful child, graced with the fairest features and vieing with the lily in whiteness. (25–26)

Yet, Tommy's astuteness questions this religious lesson: "Mother, if you think God will love me as well as he does beautiful white children I will not care so much if I am black, for I do want God to love me. But why did God take away my dear father? He lets Ralph's father live here with him!" (26). Again, Mrs. Willard could voice a harsh political critique against those who stole her husband back into slavery under the Fugitive Slave Law (1850); however, Butts muffles the mother figure's political stance and revisionist history with religious sentiments:

> [Mrs. Willard] explained to him how man had framed laws, in opposition to God's laws, and how selfish man had become; and then she talked with him about the beautiful sprit land—told him his father had gone to live where color ceases to be a crime; that in a little while they would all be in Heaven. (26)

Mrs. Willard verses her son in the reality, but she does not linger on the seditious political statements that attack the slave drivers, the "manmade" laws, or the government responsible for such laws. Instead she moves to the religious, quasi-sentimental image of a heavenly reunion.

Despite this seemingly nonthreatening narrative, Butts's mother figure nevertheless betrays a glimmer of defiance when Mrs. Medford defends nonconformity and critiques the Fugitive Slave Law. Unlike Mrs. Pride who teaches her son George to disdain those who allow fugitive slaves to share a supper table with a white family (5), Mrs. Medford teaches Ralph about equality, rather than "otherness." She urges Ralph to use his religious training as the basis for nonconformist behavior:

> My son, try, and from this hour discard the feeling which is already so common, that the colored people are only fit to do our drudgery. Try, too, and rise above the false theories which men in their blindness have set as parting walls between the laboring classes and those who think themselves too good to labor. (8)

Through the soft-spoken and motherly Mrs. Medford, Butts argues that men's "false theories" must surrender to women's ethical ones if children like Ralph are to mature into true democrats rather than elitist hypocrits. In doing so, her lesson offers the possibility to change American history by reforming the next generation.

In addition to encouraging nonconformity, Butts frames her sharpest attacks against those who support the Fugitive Slave Law. In a tangential comment that the young reader could potentially forget in his/her haste to return to the narrative, Butts writes:

> Yes, the Fugitive Slave Law, more infamous than any law ever framed in *heathen* lands, is the law of our "*Christian* America," and is sanctioned by those who profess to love liberty and equality—ah, more than this, even those who profess to love and follow the liberty-loving Savior. (16)

This statement openly attacks those who hypocritically uphold American legal ideals that undermine basic religious principles. Butts extends this attack in what appears as a sentimental narrative about how slavery violated the Willard's family bonds:

> Yes! The Fugitive Slave Law has reached our worthy friend Thomas. It found him happy in his own home surrounded with peace and plenty, together with love pure as an angel's breath! O, ye who coldly and deliberately stood up in our

Congress halls using all the eloquence which wit and intellect could possibly call to your aid, could you but look upon this heart-stricken family and see that strong man bowed in sorrow . . . could ye have *seen* all this, methinks the love of fame, ambition, power, would have sunk into nothingness, and ye would have spurned the idea of adding another fetter to the bondsman's limbs, or causing another sigh, another groan to be wrung from the bosom of the enslaved. Ye cannot form the *faintest* idea of the anguish which has come like a thunderbolt from a clear sky. See that wife clinging with devotion to him she loved, as well perhaps, as those who have skins a few shades whiter than her own. See our little Tommy with his arms fondly entwined about his father's neck, begging the officers of *(in)* justice, not to take away his dear papa. But tears and lamentations are of no avail; affection, devotion, parental love and connubial happiness are trampled low in the dust, and made subservient to tyranny, ambition and power. The colored man is now powerless in the hands of his tormentors. He is taken, bound hand and foot, and driven away from his own peaceful home to return no more. (16–20)

By embedding the history of America's religious and political hypocrisy within a sentimental narrative of a family's personal history, she appears to muffle the critique against immoral and prejudicial white laws. Ironically, the direct address to "ye" (the Congressmen) and the commands to "see" the consequences of their actions amplifies her critique, which instills a seemingly sentimental narrative with elements of a quasi-seditious revisionary history.

In contrast to Barclay, Thompson, and Butts's revisionary sentimental and religious histories, other domestic abolitionists rewrite history through increasingly political mother-historians. Rather than uphold false utopias manifest in traditional histories for children, these figures voice seditious sentiments that challenge patriotic American definitions of freedom and equality. For example, through a mother-child dialogue, Elizabeth Margaret Chandler's juvenile abolitionist poem "What Is a Slave, Mother?" (1831) establishes the mother as educator and revolutionary. The poem's inquisitive child looks to the mother to refute the existence of cruelly treated, uneducated slave children forcefully separated from their mothers. However, in each stanza's last half line,[19] Chandler's mother-figure delineates an increasingly barbarous portrait of the slave's and/or slave child's experience. In the last stanza, the child's statement, "Oh surely the land where such deeds are done / Must be a most savage and wicked one?" (43–44), suggests disbelief and a budding understanding of a nondemocratic and oppressive culture. The mother's abolitionist, antipatriotic response, "It is this, my child" (45), politically socializes the child as it indicts slave-holding America. Thus, unlike the mother in Barclay's "The Ride" who does not question her daughter's desire to escape the reality of slavery by returning to her utopian, Northern home, Chandler's abolitionist figure imparts to the child a nonutopian, political awareness of America's supposedly democratic government.

Chandler's abolitionist sentiments and her belief that women should participate in the movement (M. Jones 2; 100–101; Dillon, *Notable* 319) may have
spurred her repeated use of the abolitionist mother-historian figure. In "Looking
at the Soldiers" (1832), a child's fascination with a parade of marching soldiers
sparks a mother-child dialogue that critiques American politics. Thrilled by spec-
tacle and costumes, the child believes he has learned a patriotic lesson about
American independence. The child states:

> This, mother, you know, is a glorious day,
> And Americans all should be joyous and gay;
> For the Fourth of July saw our country set free;
> But you look not delighted, dear mother, like me![20] (9–12)

The mother attributes her unhappiness both to the bayonets that herald brutal
bloodshed and to America's willingness to perpetuate slavery: "For less guilt
would be hers [America], were her own fetter'd hand / Unable to loosen her
slaves from their band" (23–24). Chandler, therefore, does not endorse an ideal
republican mother who stresses patriotism, but an abolitionist mother who questions it and exposes a hypocritical America celebrating its independence while
enchaining millions:

> Even 'midst these triumphant rejoicing, to-day,
> The slave-mother weeps for her babes, torn away,
> 'Midst the echoing burst of these shouts, to be sold,
> Human forms as they are, for a pittance of gold!
>
> Can you wonder, then, love, that your mother is sad,
> Though yon show is so gay, and the crowd is so glad?
> Or will not my boy turn with me from the sight,
> To think of those slaves sunk in sorrow and night! (29–36)

Thus, as in her adult protest poems, here Chandler "transform[s] an initial trope
of historical patriotic affiliation into antislavery commentary" (Baym, *American*
76). Furthermore, by asking the child to align himself with her as she turns her
back on the scene that masks America's wrongs, this abolitionist mother-historian encourages the rising generation to resist this hypocrisy. This radical, though
private, act of turning away to support the slave fosters a new civic virtue that
reforms the child's behavior and perception of American history.

"Fourth of July Address to Children," a poem included in *Aunt Lizzie's Stories* (1863), also employs the trope of the abolitionist mother-historian overturn-
ing simplified American history. Asa Bullard obfuscates the gender of the poem's
narrative voice in this edited collection. However, positioning this poem in its
original place—as part of Matilda Thompson's "Mark and Hasty" (1859)[21]—
establishes its seditious female voice. In "Mark and Hasty," a firsthand encounter

with slavery leads Mrs. Jennings, the mother figure, to sell the family's St. Louis farm and to move to Chicago, where she joins a female antislavery society. Inspired by her abolitionist efforts, Mrs. Jennings "instilled the principles of freedom for all men into the minds of her children, and recently wrote the following verses for them on the occasion of the Celebration of the Fourth of July" (103). "Fourth of July Address to Children" thereby challenges children's knowledge of American history by placing patriotism and slavery in a dialectical relationship. She writes:

> Little children, when you see
>   High your country's banner wave,
> Let your thoughts a moment be
>   Turned in pity on the slave.
>
> When with pride you count the stars,
>   When your heart grows strong and brave,
> Think with pity of the scars
>   Borne in sorrow by the slave.
>
> Not for him is Freedom's sound;
>   Not for him the banners wave;
> For, in hopeless bondage bound,
>   Toils the sad and weary slave. (1–12)

The children can no longer embrace a history, as Sarah Hale may have desired, defined by a patriotic call of "freedom and justice for all" and a waving flag. Rather, the abolitionist mother calls them to consider the slaves (3–4) as well as an otherwise distorted and silenced past and present. This redefinition of American political history forces a newfound consciousness that also critiques the exclusionary side to America's supposedly inclusive principles.

Similarly, Eliza Follen's collection, *Liberty Cap* (1837, 1840, and 1846), exemplifies the increasingly vocal and subversive abolitionist mother. Like Elizabeth Chandler's poems, Follen wrote "Dialogue," a story in which international politics serve as the springboard from which a mother gives her child more accurate historical and political information about slavery. In this work, Robert informs his mother of stories he has heard about Russians oppressing the Polish (23). The mother figure, however, gives oppression immediacy when she engages in an act of historical revisioning. Although she admittedly attempts to arouse sympathy for the victims and withholds information about some atrocities to protect Robert, the mother exposes the existence of a

> nation as wicked and cruel as the Russians that you perhaps have not read any complete history of, and which you ought to know something about, and in

many respects I think them worse than the emperor of Russia. No correct history has yet been written of this people, for their historians are afraid to tell the truth of them because they fear the people would be angry and not read their books. Shame on them for their mean cowardice and want of principle! (24)

Through her powerful statement, "I think," Follen's mother figure (like Biddy, the Irish servant in Jones's work) exposes the silenced history and simultaneously condemns the government that allows slavery as well as violence against abolitionists "even here in the free States" (30). She tells Robert about slave children separated from parents and "defrauded of all rights of intellectual and immortal beings" (29), as well as about the violence inflicted on fugitives when they escape from the "savages" (27). She even implies that owners sexually violate slave girls (26). Ultimately, the mother says:

> You are living in [this country], my son; you are one of its citizens; your father pays taxes to support the government which sanctions and defends these crimes against innocent beings. This country is now at war, as you know, with Mexico who has abolished slavery, for the purpose of making this infamous system more secure and extending it further. (28)

By implicating the American government, the child, and the child's father, the mother's final statement destroys the possibility of sustained childhood innocence. Her confidence and adamancy lead Robert, who "never knew it was so bad" (29), and readers to revise their notions of cruel Russians, kind Americans, and benevolent fathers and then situate him/herself as a citizen of a less than ideal community.

Notwithstanding this abolitionist mother-historian's confident and persuasive voice, Follen hints at how opponents may have responded to such subversive, revisionist histories. The mother states: "Whoever . . . dares to tell the whole truth about slavery, and says he will have nothing more to do with it in any way, is an exile from that part of our country where these wicked things are done" (29). Does this abolitionist mother-historian divulge her status as an exiled abolitionist in her own community because her seditious comments overstep the boundaries of women's "proper" sphere? Or, may this comment have revealed Follen's own anxiety about "tell[ing] the whole truth about slavery"? Just as abolitionists and this mother figure risked exile from the South or from the Northern communities that prized "true womanhood," so too Eliza Follen may have experienced criticism about the publication of her abolitionist juvenile historical fiction. Yet, unlike Hale, Follen and others like her did not mince words, not even for children.

If Eliza Follen felt anxious about the criticism that "Dialogue" might elicit, Jane Elizabeth Jones, who experienced much censure for her vocal abolitionism, must have also feared censure for publishing *The Young Abolitionist; or, Conversations on Slavery* (1848), which depicts a mother-educator whose political frankness challenges the limits of woman's sphere. Jones suggests the opposition she and other women may have encountered through a fictional parental dispute over educating children about slavery. Mr. Selden dissuades his wife from her adopted political mission as child consciousness raiser claiming that he "could not bear the thought that the joyousness of their young spirits should be checked by the contemplation of such terrible cruelties" (20). However, Mrs. Selden disagrees with her husband and defends her intentions by arguing that children's involvement in the temperance movement sobered many fathers because children "are effective preachers of righteousness; and their freedom from guile, and clearness of vision, render them powerful agents for good when properly instructed" (21). She also claims parental duty,

> remind[ing] her husband that their children would be learning these sad stories from one and another, and it was best for parents to instruct them in regard to slavery and other evils, that the proper impression might be made—that they might have a just abhorrence of wrong and enlightened views of the course to be pursued toward the wrong-doer. (21)

She justifies her actions further, asserting that the children have already expressed curiosity: "[Charlie] frequently asked his father questions about the slaves; but Mr. Selden did not say much to him on this subject, so he generally preferred talking with his mother" (59; see also 9). Ultimately, Mr. Selden leaves this job to his wife (23), who candidly addresses her children's inquiries.[22] Thus, through Mrs. Selden, Jones offers the most thorough redefinition of American history for juvenile readers and the most complex example of a seditious abolitionist mother-historian.

Refusing to create an exclusively sentimental storyteller, Jones crafts the portrait of a knowledgeable and politically savvy woman who challenges existing ideologies of gender and patriotism. Like Abbot's narrator in "A Massachusetts Slave" and Follen's mother figure in "Dialogue," Mrs. Selden insists on communicating the silenced past. She recognizes her children's biased historical education when she states "I wish the injustice of America as well as that of England had been taught [to] you also" (69). She assumes responsibility for correcting their misconceptions about slavery and "wishes to make a lasting impression upon the minds of her children" (47), but does so "by giving them a few facts only at a time" (47). Her history begins with extensive descriptions of plantation and house servants and the abuse by slave owners who "regar[d] [the slaves] as inferior beings, and kept only for the master's use" (12). She compares the slave's experience to the criminal's imprisonment and argues that criminals have more comforts since owners give slave men, women, and even children (10) insufficient food and clothing, force them to work long hours, deprive them of education, physically abuse them, and rupture family bonds. As Moser suggests, "maintaining a slave society inevitably corrupts slaveholders" (17). However, Mrs. Selden's critique also exposes Southern women who inflict violence with whips and hot irons:

I am sorry, my son, to state this dreadful fact about women, who are supposed to be more gentle and kind than men; but slavery renders all hearts hard and flinty that have anything to do with it; it transforms them into unfeeling tyrants, and makes them commit deeds we blush to think of. (42–43)

By disclosing the mistress' brutality, this mother-historian challenges the senti-mental ideal Southern matron as the innocent, devoted, and submissive "paragon of virtue" (A. Scott 6). Mrs. Selden insists (as does Jones) that her children recog-nize how slavery sullies everyone: Southern womanhood, slave owners, and slaves.

Jones does not limit her criticism to the South; rather, she overturns her chil-dren's belief that all Northerners oppose slavery. She reveals that "both by *word* and by *deed* do [Northerners] encourage the slave-holder to continue his wicked course" (61). This mother figure exposes Northern antislavery sentiments when she states "No, my son, there is no freedom *here* for the slave" (63) because many Northerners "[r]aise no voice against it—they utter no protest" (60). Foreshadowing the Fugitive Slave Law's passage, she unabashedly blames America's laws for granting slave own-ers the right to retrieve their "property" (77). Furthermore, like Follen's mother fig-ure, Mrs. Selden critiques America's political foundations when she divulges that slave holders hypocritically signed the Declaration of Independence (70) and authored both the American Constitution and laws supporting slavery (75–79). The children's disbelief upon learning that their hero, George Washington (72–73), and many Northerners (except those from Massachusetts)[23] (75) held slaves highlights the children's previous idealism and misinformation. Believing "[no country] had ever so shamefully trampled these principles [of freedom and equality] in the dust" (65), Mrs. Selden leads them to critique America, evident when Charlie states "I should think the government of *Canada was better,* as it does not let one man hold another in bondage" (65, emphasis added). By challenging patriotism based on dis-torted truths, Mrs. Selden epitomizes the abolitionist mother figure who possesses a facility with history and willingness to unveil its lies.

Yes, slavery sullies its victims, slave owners, Southern women, heroic forefa-thers, and even Northerners; but Jones also warns that without abolishing the peculiar institution, its corruption will violate every citizens' rights, especially free speech. Mrs. Selden records the histories of Southerners who threaten outspoken abolitionists such as Charles T. Torrey, William Lloyd Garrison (102), Calvin Fairbanks, and Jonathan Walker of Massachusetts. Yet again, she argues that such oppression has even permeated the North—thereby undermining the child's perception that "here in the North we can say what we please about slavery, and do as much as we like to help fugitives" (105). She denounces Northerners like Mr. Wilmot, who "would sacrifice his life in order to maintain the system" (109) and documents how Northern mob violence injured and drove abolitionists groups and persons like Elijah P. Lovejoy (120)[24] from burning lecture halls like Pennsylvania Hall (120–21). This new perspective clearly transforms the child's understanding of citizens' rights:

"It seems to me there is no safety in this country for anybody who tries to do right," observed Charlie. "For keeping fugitives they can be fined or imprisoned, when holding meetings they are mobbed, their property destroyed, their public houses burned, and they themselves beaten, and tarred, and killed, and all because they want to make the slaves free, and stop men from robbing them and selling away their children. Why, mother, it is horrible! I should think that such things would not be allowed, even among savages, who are very ignorant and wicked." (122–23)

Charlie also notes, "'Every time we talk about the slaves, mother, you make their case worse and worse" (110–11). Mrs. Selden completely discards the role of republican mother who shapes a submissive, patriotic child and assumes the voice of an abolitionist mother-historian whose discussion of slavery's threat to America's political and social principles molds informed, political nonconformists.

Jones, however, does *not* create an "all talk and no action" abolitionist mother figure. Rather, she depicts a woman who acts on her moral principles, theoretical abolitionism, and civil disobedience. In her husband's absence, Mrs. Selden shelters "*non*-threatening compassionate fugitive slave characters with whom white readers can sympathize" (Moser 21). Furthermore, when slave catchers forcefully attempt to enter the Selden home,

Mrs. Selden, feeling indignant at the manner and the request, replied—
I told you they were not here; but if they were, do you think I would lead a rapacious man-hunter to their hiding place! Do you think I would betray them into the hands of the base miscreant before me! Go home, and seek some more honorable employment than hunting out the stricken and famishing children of oppression, and dragging them back into the vile den of slavery. Begone! unmerciful wretch! let not my threshold be disgraced by contact with such pollution. (89)

Thus, the children witness their mother confronting the intruders, reclaiming her free speech despite their demands, and engaging in an civilly disobedient act. Without Mrs. Selden's words and actions, Mr. Selden could not have facilitated, upon his return, the fugitive family's flight to Canada via the Underground Railroad. Thus, Jones affirms that relegation to the home does not exclude women from politics; in actuality, the rhetoric woman develops while socializing her children about slavery fortifies her activism and civil disobedience.

Jones further illustrates how Mrs. Selden does not mince words by creating a foil in Biddy O'Flannagan, the family's Irish servant. As she listens to Mrs. Selden tell the children about slavery, Biddy heightens the criticism claiming that American slavery exceeds the oppressive conditions in Ireland. She supports slaves who rebel against their masters but condemns the physical violence inflicted on revolting slaves: "It's a purty law though you've made in this *free* country . . . to kill one bekase he won't peaceably submit to be beaten to death with a poker! A purty law surely, and its a purty country I've come to!" (45).

When she learns of the slave hunts, Biddy says, "Sure, it's better to be free to die of famine in Ireland, than to have the freedom of a nager slave in Ameriky" (51). Shocked that slave owners sell children like pigs, Biddy condemns insensitive Americans: "Sure, but the landlords are cruel in Ireland . . . but the'd niver be thinkin of taking away the darlint babe from the mother of it, at all at all" (14). Biddy recalls powerless Irish parents who witness their children starve, yet "there's not one of them . . . would have been willing to have a childer made a slave ti save *it* from starvation" (36). Spoken by a woman who has witnessed cultural oppression, Biddy's emotionally high-pitched comparative history counteracts Mrs. Selden's rational gentility; simultaneously, it masterfully intensifies Mrs. Selden's portrait of American slavery's barbarity.

Jane Elizabeth Jones forcefully replaces the ideal of republican motherhood with an abolitionist mother-historian who utters quasi-seditious rhetoric and engages in civil disobedience. Taking Jones one step further, in *Louisa in Her New Home* (1854), S.C.C.[25] uses the abolitionist mother-historian not only to inculcate a daughter with a new consciousness of abolitionist ideas and civil disobedience, but also to express overt abolitionist and feminist politics. With a peculiar absence of male characters, the mother-daughter discussion about slavery stems from the family's financial difficulties that require them to sell their new house, surrender some comforts, and dismiss most of their servants. Before the financial difficulties, Louisa's mother initially resembles *Mr.* Selden from *The Young Abolitionist* because she shields Louisa from knowing that the family housed a fugitive slave, Mary, whose light skin conceals her enslavement and escape. However, the father's financial difficulties cause a transition from a wealthy to a modest existence and from ignorance to knowledge. Faced with the impending move, the mother states, "I will not put off what I dreaded to tell you, for it will make your heart ache when you know all" (14). In the process of divulging Mary's history and the family's participation in her "passing," the mother utters politically charged criticisms that initiate Louisa into a troubling world of political consciousness and social activism.

S.C.C. transforms a mother figure's sentimental narrative of a slave mother and child's separation into an opportunity to condemn those who legislate such violations. As her mother narrates an emotion-filled account of Mary's willingness to commit suicide upon losing her child, Louisa reenvisions Mary as a violated mother rather than merely the family's servant. However, the abolitionist mother counteracts a domestic history about slavery's victims who would make Louisa's heart "ache when [she] know[s] all" (14) with an denunciation of Southern mistresses who violate maternal bonds. Louisa's mother states:

> Poor Mary was miserable, and so angry with the woman who could do such a cruelly wicked thing, that she determined to run away from her, even though she knew that she might starve before she found any one to give her shelter or help her on her long and perilous journey; for after her baby was taken from her she

did not care to live, and would have been glad to die at any moment. She hated
the woman who could do so wicked a thing as to take her baby from her arms
and sell it to another person. She knew the baby came from God, and that it was
hers, and no one had a right to it but herself and its father, her husband. (16–17)

Like Mrs. Selden in *The Young Abolitionist*, Louisa's mother rewrites Southern
history as she challenges the widespread view of the Southern matron as a
"paragon of virtue" (A. Scott 6). Louisa accepts Mary's hatred and escape when
she understands that the slave-holding Southern mistress violates a sacred,
maternal bond. Louisa also hears about how her mother challenged the status
quo by nursing, educating, employing, housing, and showing compassion toward
Mary as well as by allowing Mary to mother her daughters, Louisa and Lucy.
Through the abolitionist mother's ability to overturn misconceptions and accu-
rately document Mary's history, Louisa moves from ignorance to political knowledge necessary to sustain women's supposedly inherent moral predilection, which
slavery threatens.

S.C.C. launches an even harsher attack against slavery by implicating not
just one Southern mistress but all Northerners and the legal system that advocates the Fugitive Slave Law. Proslavery Northerners' advocacy of the Fugitive
Slave Law provokes the mother's condemnation:

> If we were better at the North than at the South, where they own slaves, we
> should never have made a law to help them get back their slaves that had
> escaped to us. No, I am afraid the reason many do not hold slaves here is, that
> at the present time the laws of the Northern States forbid their doing it. (30)

S.C.C., however, differentiates this abolitionist mother from those she condemns
by casting her as one who deliberately violates the "terrible law" (26) with her
plan to send Mary to live with a Canadian relative. Upon Louisa's objection to
the separation, her mother states: 'Would you not rather have me send her away
to a safe place than have any one come after her and carry her away by main force
back into slavery?" (19). Through the contrast between "me" and "them," Louisa's
mother heightens the negative perception of racist, proslavery actions because as
Dana Nelson suggests, "[w]hether one regards the . . . Other as a second person
and immediate presence, or as a third person, absence can profoundly affect the
possible actions conceptually available toward the Other" (198). Ultimately, this
question forces Louisa either to advocate slavery (become one of "them") or serve
as an accessory to her mother's *crime:* harboring a fugitive. S.C.C. suggests that
if Louisa supports her mother, it would require changing the "me" to "us," thereby
marking a challenge to the "normal" course of history and the onset of an abolitionist women's coalition.

The possibility of a mother-daughter coalition suggests S.C.C.'s determi-
nation to write a history of self-empowered, politically active women. Given the

option to do nothing, Louisa adopts her mother's politics and supports Mary. However, S.C.C. advances that the shift from acting as an oppressor to a liberator and law breaker requires action *and* empathy. The mother challenges Louisa's desire to maintain a purely sentimental approach stating, "I should be sorry if you did not [feel so badly]; but we must act as well as feel; and as soon as you begin to do something you will bear better the knowledge of that painful truth" (21). Louisa quickly adopts the mother's balanced approach and after "mourning" for Mary, she plans to use her savings to buy Mary a new Bible and to make her a needle case (23). However, the mother then posits that action includes both benevolent deeds and civil disobedience. She defends activism of voice and deed stating, "The only thing to be done, at present, is for those who disapprove of them to say so everywhere, and not to obey the wicked law made to please the powerful, without a desire to protect the weak and helpless" (26). Although she reveals the limitation she feels in her ability to assist the "many other poor runaway slaves beside Mary, who have no friends to think and act for them" (26), as an adamant supporter of civil disobedience, the mother admonishes Louisa when she expresses a wish to leave the South (28). Claiming that escapism and laziness perpetuate slavery, the mother gives her daughter instructions in activism: Louisa must reject silence, claim free speech, and act both through her words and deeds. Through their decision to defy the laws, S.C.C. affirms women who claim their voice and participate in public politics, thereby writing a new chapter of women's activism.

The mother's abolitionist sentiments complicate Louisa's understanding of activism, but her feminism compels her daughter to rethink the potential for political influence that transcends the "separate sphere." Even at her young age, Louisa voices her conviction that gender, not age, hinders political activity:

> "I wish I was a man, mother, and I would do nothing else but show how wicked and mean I thought it [slavery] was."
>
> "It is not necessary to be a man for this."
>
> "But women and girls can't do anything about making laws, mother, and if men choose to make such laws I don't see how we can help it."
>
> "We can show what we feel and think about it. All of us have either fathers, or husbands, or brothers, or cousins, or friends that we may try to lead to do right. If a young girl is going to engage herself to be married, she can let her lover know that if he thinks nothing about such a great sin as slavery is, and cares nothing about it, she can't continue to care much about him. Such a girl may well fear, when she is married, her husband may wish to make a slave of her, and she may be sure there can be no love that will last if people are thinking more of each other than of what is right." (26–27)

The mother's feminist stance spurs her daughter to reject silence and to use her right to free speech within the domestic sphere to effect national change. Moreover, she furthers this empowerment by stating: "there are many good men and women who write against slavery, and some who devote much time and money to show the evils of slavery " (27–28). By acknowledging women's abolitionist publications and fundraising, she undermines the separate-sphere ideology and offers Louisa the opportunity for both private and public resistance and activism.

Kate Barclay, Matilda Thompson, Harriet Butts, Elizabeth Chandler, Eliza Follen, Jane Elizabeth Jones, and S.C.C. reject the image of women as non-threatening republican mothers presented in *Godey's* "Maternal Instruction." Instead, each portrays abolitionist mother-historians voicing sentimental and seditious rhetoric to stir their fictive children into adopting an abolitionist mind-set. Without apology, these women question the impropriety of informing children about slavery and advocate women and children's activism and civil disobedience. These works of historical redefinition and overt critique create a space to bridge the gap between private and public influence so that women might publicly advocate slavery's abolition. Interestingly, just as the mothers in this literature walk a tightrope to correct their children's knowledge of America history, the recovered records of juvenile antislavery societies suggest that real mothers may have done the same.

4

"We boys [and girls] had better see what we can do, for it is too wicked"

The Juvenile Abolitionists

George Shelby:

> [My parents] never sent for me, nor sent any word [that Tom had been sold], and, if it hadn't been for Tom Lincon, I shouldn't have heard it. I tell you, I blew 'em up well, all of 'em, at home! . . .
>
> But there [Tom], now button your coat tight over [the dollar coin], and keep it, and remember, every time you see it, that I'll come down after you, and bring you back. Aunt Chloe and I have been talking about it. I told her not to fear; I'll see to it, and I'll tease father's life out, if he don't do it. . . .
>
> I'm ashamed this day, that I'm a Kentuckian. I was always proud of it before.
>
> —*Uncle Tom's Cabin* 86–88

Eva St. Clare:

> O, that's what troubles me, papa. You want me to live so happy, and never to have any pain,—never suffer anything,—not even hear a sad story, when other poor creatures have nothing but pain and sorrow, all their lives;—it seems selfish. I ought to know such things, I ought to feel about them! Such things always sunk into my heart; they went down deep; I've thought and thought about them. Papa, isn't there any way to have all slaves made free?
>
> —*Uncle Tom's Cabin* 241

Whatcan I do to end slavery? represents a fundamental question that abolitionists repeatedly asked themselves and Americans. Women did not hesitate to pose this question in female antislavery societies and then in print,[1] and some women encouraged children to ask the same question. Interestingly, by mid 1840, several domestic abolitionists like Harriet Beecher Stowe, Jane Elizabeth Jones, Eliza Lee Cabot Follen, and Maria Goodell Frost, among others, published juvenile literature in which they posed the question, What can I do to end slavery? which proponents of juvenile abolitionism started asking in the late 1830s. Juvenile antislavery society advocates believed that children could effect change through activities ranging from liberal, public activism to private, familial, and/or individual reflection in America's meeting rooms, on America's streets, and in America's homes. By establishing an ideology and avenue of action, organizers hoped children's accumulated efforts would help the cause and shape children into active, politicized adults who could effect definite change. Female authors like Stowe, Jones, Follen, and Frost adopted these questions and strategies and infused them into their juvenile works that cast children, with an increasing emphasis on girls, in abolitionist roles.

THE RISE OF JUVENILE ABOLITIONISM

Domestic abolitionists did not create purely imaginative tales with abolitionist children protagonists; instead they constructed them from their cultural moment. The late 1830s witnessed the formation of juvenile antislavery societies, which represented the most direct, politically charged, and public means for organizing children's abolitionist efforts. The editor of the *Slave's Friend*[2] suggests that the paper's widespread circulation and its ability to stimulate interest in the slaves' plight inspired the creation of juvenile abolitionists groups. Consequently, to "show [other potential] young abolitionists how they can go to work to form societies, and thus act out the principles they have read in these little books" (*SF* 2.5 (1837): [66]), the *Slave's Friend* devotes an entire issue to the formation of the Chatham Street Chapel[3] Juvenile Anti-Slavery Society, an "Auxiliary to the New York City Anti-Slavery Society" (71). In August 14, 1836, Lewis Tappan,[4] a New York businessman who served on the executive committee of the American Anti-Slavery Society, addressed the audience in attendance at the first Chatham Street Chapel Juvenile Anti-Slavery Society meeting. Bertram Wyatt-Brown describes the scene, stating: "Solemn parents sat in rows of chairs against one wall of the lecture hall; young wives loosened their bonnet strings; husbands perspired in bulky suits. Opposite them were their girls and boys, none over fourteen, squirming in stiff-backed seats" (172). Defending the legitimacy of such societies, Tappan states:

> Does any one [sic] doubt the propriety of children associating to form Anti-Slavery Societies? There are already Juvenile Temperance, Missionary,[5] and I

believe Peace Societies. . . . If it is a duty for children to form other moral societies, can any one doubt that it is their duty to form Anti-Slavery Societies? Is
not slavery as bad as intemperance? . . . For one, I hope all the children in our
Sabbath schools will come out against every sin, be young moral reformers
indeed, and say of all kinds of wickedness—*Touch not, taste not, handle not.* (*SF*
2.5 (1837): [67–68])

Wyatt-Brown argues that Tappan thought "[i]t was particularly important . . . to
reach the Sunday-school-age children and to instill in them a perfect hatred of
southern slavery and all other forms of wrong doing. They might be called upon
to complete what their fathers had only begun" (173). Tappan's insistence on
informing children about slavery and encouraging their involvement represents
an early attempt to break the sociopolitical silence enveloping children. Socializing the next generation to carry their fathers' abolitionist efforts would hasten
Tappan's belief in America's glorious millennium.

Socializing America's future, however, would require reaching beyond a few
Sunday school children from lower Manhattan. While scanty record keeping
hinders recovering information about each juvenile antislavery society, children
organized in several states. The *Slave's Friend* records the establishment of such
societies in Richmond, Ohio; Pawtucket, Rhode Island; Portland, Maine; as well
as in Newark, Patterson, and Whippany, New Jersey. New York City had several
juvenile antislavery societies: Reverend T. S. Wright's Church, the Chatham
Street Chapel, and the Juvenile Phoenix Anti-Slavery Society.[6] In a letter to
William Lloyd Garrison, Henry C. Wright recalls lecturing to over one hundred
young New Yorkers. The *Journal of Commerce*[7] supported children's reformist
movements and the *National Anti-Slavery Standard* regularly published the date
and time of the Junior Anti-Slavery Society of Philadelphia's monthly meetings
as well those for the group in Longwood [Pennsylvania]. Finally, records held at
the Massachusetts Historical Society reveal that twenty-five girls formed a Juvenile Anti-Slavery Society in Boston.[8] The geographical spread in the northeast
suggests that these juvenile societies transcended Lewis Tappan's original sphere
of influence.

Although juvenile antislavery societies appeared to have flourished, children's participation in the movement often elicited conflicting responses. Some
critics questioned the appropriateness of children's efforts and the impact children could actually effect.[9] For example, on August 11, 1837, the *Liberator's* editorial section included a letter from Lydia Maria Child critiquing children's political activities. She says:

Your paper of the 14th ult. contains a notice of Children's Petitions to
Congress, and an exhortation to abolitionist parents to encourage their circulation. I regret this measure exceedingly, and cannot but hope that it will not be
carried into effect. I consider it an error of judgment, because the inevitable tendency will be to throw contempt on *all* our petitions; and it seems to be

improper, because children are of necessity guided by others, and because this step is involved with questions evidently above juvenile capacities. Abolitionist parents ought thoroughly to prepare the hearts and minds of their children for the conscientious discharge of duties that will come with their riper years, but this haste to invest them with the attributes of citizenship appears premature, and almost ridiculous. I have not as yet conversed with an abolitionist who did not view the subject in the same light. (qtd. in Meltzer 68–69)

Furthermore, on November 12, 1840, the *National Anti-Slavery Standard* reports that "leading politicians, in Congress and out, and the newspapers generally" (90) ridiculed children's participation in antislavery politics because they "thought it to be very improper for any person, who had not arrived at the grave age of twenty-one, to meddle with a matter so closely connected with the politics of the country, and so vitally affecting its welfare" (90). However, this author admonishes these critics and asks "that hereafter the politicians of that city [Boston] at least . . . refrain from sneering at the [children's efforts for the] antislavery cause on account of the large proportion of children who are devoting to it their just and holiest sympathies, and who are thus giving token of present integrity and future usefulness" (90). In contrast to this criticism, the Juvenile Female Anti-Slavery Society records include Robert Bartlett's[10] January 19, 1838, letter praising the society's female membership:

It is a solemn and deeply interesting sight—to contemplate hearts like yours banded together for such an object. The withering [,] depraving influences of this present evil world have as yet hardly begun to harm the simplicity the uprightness of your youthful and generous feelings: and, because you have not yet been exposed to such fiery trials, your hearts are far purer than those of your elder brethren and sisters of the generation that is passing off before you; and, because you are purer, you are warmer and stronger. It is not in the old, hardened with prejudices and follies and sins[,] but in the growing generation of which you and I are a part that the hopes of the crushed slave and of the race rest: and if this be so [,] what high and peaceful responsibilities are ours. Let us even now before the night cometh hasten [sic] to fulfill our work. Much shall be required at our hands to whom so much is given. Let us strengthen to perform it that the wronged slave may become free and a Christian and that the guilty master may be forgiven and turned to righteousness.[11]

Bartlett's rhetoric critiques American adults' racial prejudices and sinfulness that perpetuate slavery. He calls these young female abolitionists to use their uncorrupted spirit and morals to effect the slave's political freedom as well as the slave and white master's religious (re)education. While Lydia Maria Child and others opposed children's abolitionist efforts, Bartlett reveals his faith in and encouragement of the young girls' efforts to reform America's moral and political decline.

Many abolitionist women also supported juvenile abolitionism perhaps because nurturing children recalled women's "proper" work. In June (either 1837 or 1838), an unidentified juvenile antislavery meeting in Boston received a visit from Sarah and Angelina Grimké, who told the audience stories about children sold into slavery and separated from their parents. However, women exerted even more widespread influence than their limited visits could accomplish through their writings. For example, the *Slave's Friend* reports, "A committee was appointed by the Anti-Slavery Convention of American Women, in May last, in this city, to write to you [the children of a juvenile antislavery society]" (3.2 [1838]: [23]). This announcement may refer to the decision at the May, 1837, Anti-Slavery Convention of American Women's Committee of Arrangements to appoint Sarah Pugh, Juliana A. Tappan, and Anna Hopper to write a letter to juvenile antislavery societies (*Proceedings . . . 1837* 6–7, 17). Furthermore, at the 1839 Anti-Slavery Convention of American Women in Philadelphia, women adopted Eliza Barny's motion that

> . . . we view, with particular satisfaction, the efforts of young people to promote the abolition of slavery, not only because they have a tendency to improve the moral condition of mankind, but also are a stimulus to the exercise of those mighty energies of mind, which, for want of being employed on proper objects, either lie dormant, or are used to minister to the vices which degrade, instead of the virtues which ennoble mankind. (*Proceedings . . .* 1839 10)

Like Tappan and Bartlett, who praised children's abolitionist efforts because such reform would effect national reform, Barny and the entire Anti-Slavery Convention of American Women supported children's engagement in abolitionist activities, arguing that the children's efforts would not only help the slaves but also reduce their own sinfulness. The latter, in turn, would improve America's general moral condition (*SF* 2.12 [183?]: 28–30).

Yet, having established these organized groups and their civic goals, the question remained: What could children do? Organizers advocated various activities that echoed adult abolitionist strategies. The board and members of the Juvenile Anti-Slavery Society of Chatham Street Chapel developed a constitution[12] to outline appropriate activities. Its constitution states that children "under fourteen years of age, who contribute at least a cent a month" (*SF* 72) would strive "to collect money for the Anti-Slavery cause, to read and circulate the *Slave's Friend*[13] [and other tracts], to do all in [their] power to have the free colored people respected and well-treated, and the enslaved set at liberty" (*SF* 2.5 (1837): [71–72]).[14] Shirley Samuels posits that the *Slave's Friend* expected that children who looked at images of a slave being whipped and who read about slavery would defend its abolition. She writes:

> Reading operates here not merely as a means to correct thinking but also as a mode of correct thinking: namely, the refusal to reduce meanings to bodies or to merely physical surfaces (skin color for instance), and the insistence on thinking and feeling as antidotes to identifying with nothing more than the body. ("Identity" 163)[15]

In addition to encouraging children to learn about the slave's experience, the society's resolutions also included boycotting sugar products made by slave labor, refraining from calling slaves vulgar names (79), encouraging other children to form similar societies (76), and imitating abolitionist parents even though opponents "called [them] fanatics, incendiaries and enemies of their country, for being abolitionists" (79). Finally, children's activism paralleled adult activism when children led "two great political processions in Boston"[16] and when in 183?, Henry C. Wright, the appointed children's antislavery agent,[17] urged children to sign and to send the "Petitions for Minors," which the Boston Juvenile Anti-Slavery Society published and circulated, to the Senate and the House of Representatives (Ruchames 112–13).

While these recovered documents paint a gender-neutral approach, at least two juvenile antislavery societies had a gender-determined membership that shaped behavior. As an auxiliary to the Pennsylvania State Anti-Slavery Society, the Junior Anti-Slavery Society of Philadelphia's (JASSP) constitution and preamble (1836?) reveal an exclusively male membership whose statements and actions echo adults' politically charged statesmanship. The first constitution (1836?) establishes the membership age at fifteen while the second (n.d.) specifies that members must be age twenty-one and under. These young men, who recognized how slavery violated the Declaration of Independence, argued that "it therefore becomes our duty as Americans [and] as Christians to use every honorable means to affect its speedy overthrow" (*Constitution and Preamble* [1]). The group's *Minute Book* (1836–1846), which establishes it as a formal organization, reveals that the young men spent their early meetings electing club officials and writing/revising a preamble and a constitution, activities resembling those of adult politicians who attempted to remedy the religious and national errors of America's ways. However, in their desire to act as proper Christians, JASSP members formed a highly structured and politically conscious organization. The detailed minutes between 1836 and 1846 reveal that the young men began each meeting by reading the minutes; engaged in lively debates about abolition; discussed how they would eradicate slavery through acts such as boycotting products not made by free hands (*Minute Book* [11]); and voted on motions, committees, and resolutions. For example, on December 16, 1836, the society appointed George D. Jones, George D. Parish, George Tauerman, and Israel H. Johnson to a committee that by June 6, 1837, had successfully opened a school in Clarkson Hall for free African Americans. When finances allowed, the JASSP printed and circulated antislavery publications and, on one occasion, asked children to make donations to fund the publication of the constitution "to prove that the young are not asleep, but are doing what they can—if that be but little—to advance that, which they believe to be the cause of practical Liberty" ([18]). In May 1838 the group published a statement condemning the mob who murdered Elijah P. Lovejoy while he exercised his constitutional right to free speech. The Lovejoy incident incensed the young abolitionists so much that in addition to collecting

money for Lovejoy's widow, in May 1838 they "'Resolved:—That we will plead
the cause of the suffering slave, and assert the duty of immediate emancipation
undeterred by any threat or conduct of our opposers, until 'Liberty shall be pro-
claimed throughout all the land, unto all the inhabitants thereof'" ([19]). Furthermore, the fact that members circulated a petition,[18] which they sent to the
Senate and the House of Representatives, represents the clearest indication that
their participation represents an early education in statescraft. However, this
sophisticated statesmanship may have hampered membership because in 1842
the minutes reveal a plan to restructure meetings so "that they should be rendered
interesting and attractive, as to induce our citizens to attend, and more particularly the younger classes of the community for whose benefit this Society was
specially formed" ([117]).

Like their Philadelphian "brothers," Bostonian girls formally organized
their own juvenile antislavery society, whose records reveal their interest in
education, intellectual debates, and self-improvement. During their weekly
meetings held at varying members' homes, the girls occasionally invited guest
speakers like Mr. Inglas, Mr. Channing, and Mr. Robert Bartlett[19] or remained
current on abolitionist opinions by reading *The Youth's Cabinet*[20] and *The
Oasis.*[21] Like the boys, they too discussed political and moral issues: on September 13, 1837, they debated the right to kill others and on October 6, 1837,
they discussed the fugitive slaves' plight.[22] However, while the boys talked of
boycotting goods, the girls phrased the issue in more acceptably "feminine"
terms by calling it self-denial: they "had quite a discussion on self-denial and
on the use of sugar and butter and at last came to the conclusion that we would
deny ourselves of something so as to contribute one cent weekly to the society"
(August 22, 1837). Therefore while the boys boycotted slave-made products,
the girls both "boycotted" and raised funds. Furthermore, the girls' frequent
references to religious and domestic activities also reveal a modeling on adult
female antislavery societies. Similar to their "mothers," who began each session
of the Anti-Slavery Conventions of Women by reading parts of scripture and
by offering a prayer, these girls had religious inclinations. They sang hymns
such as "Missionary Hymn," "Dismission," "O Lord While Angels Praise
Thee," "See the Rain Is Falling," "From Greenland's Icy Mountains,"[23] and
Elizabeth Margaret Chandler's, "Peace of Berry."[24] These girls also had a clearly
domestic agenda similar to the adult female abolitionist group's sewing circles
and fundraising antislavery fairs. They regularly collected donations ranging
from 12.5 to 80 cents, a portion of which probably came from their "sewing
patch work needle books pincushions kniting [sic] garters suspenders and
stocking" (September 6, 1837). Despite the seemingly more "feminine" nature
of this girls' juvenile abolitionist society, these young women were developing
the benevolent and political organizational skills that they would need to
understand and participate in the intense slavery debate of the 1850s, when
they would probably be in their thirties.

The recovered information about juvenile abolitionist societies (whether in the form of minutes, constitutions, diaries, or published records in otherwise little-known publications like the *Slave's Friend*) adds an interesting dimension to our growing understanding of American abolitionism. Despite the criticism such societies may have received, they shaped their young members' understanding of an economic system that threatened fundamental American ideals. Although the recovered records do not make it possible to determine how many children participated in juvenile abolitionist societies, they do reveal that asking children to formulate answers to the question, What can I do to end slavery? was a real and growing enterprise.

FICTIONAL JUVENILE ABOLITIONISTS: THE PRE-STOWE YEARS

Advocates of juvenile abolitionism spent the 1830s and 1840s including children in a range of public and private abolitionist activities and offering them publications such as the *Slave's Friend* and *Juvenile Poems for the Use of Free American Children of Every Complexion* (1835), a collection of several works printed in the "Juvenile Department" of Garrison's *Liberator*. However, the 1840s and 1850s witnessed domestic abolitionists creating exemplary fictional, abolitionist children on which their young readers could model themselves and facilitate their quest "to do something." In "To Mothers in the Free States" (1855), Eliza Lee Cabot Follen argues that a mother should instill

> a passionate desire to take the part of the oppressed, which shall enlist them for life as the champions of their sorely injured, down trodden, colored brethren. . . . Her son will not vote for the Fugitive Slave Law or the Nebraska Bill, nor become a kidnapping United States Commissioner! (3)

Domestic abolitionists before and after Follen advocated these sentiments and constructed a fictional idea of abolitionist children for others to emulate. Hence, children's literature played a direct and effective role in abolitionist activism, one in which women could participate without conflict or criticism on a gender basis.

In "The Child's Evening Hymn,"[25] Elizabeth Margaret Chandler represents one of the first to create a fictional white child who pleads for white masters to undergo a change of heart. Chandler's narrator addresses the "Father" and thanks God for his parents' love and protection. However, the shift in the third stanza to the child's prayer for the slave reveals an awareness of the suffering other. The child states:

> Yet while 'neath the evening skies,
> Thus we bid our thanks arise,

Father! still we think of those,
Who are bow'd with many woes,
Whom no earthly parent's arm
Can protect from wrong and harm;
      The poor slaves, Father.

Ah! while we are richly blest,
They are wretched and distrest!
Outcasts in their native land,
Crush'd beneath oppression's hand,
Scarcely knowing even thee,
Mighty Lord of earth and sea!
      Oh, save them, Father!

Touch the flinty hearts, that long
Have, remorseless, done them wrong;
Ope thy eyes that long have been
Blind to every guilty scene;
That the slave—a slave no more—
Grateful thanks to thee may pour,
      And bless thee, Father. (15–35)

The white child calls on God's help to save them and to change the slave hold-ers' views. While "The Child's Evening Hymn" does not proffer public activism, the image of the child's private activism reflects those who supported prayer as one means for children's participation in abolitionist politics.

Chandler's poems, "Christmas," "The Sugarplums," and "Oh Press Me Not to Taste Again" (1832), posit that in addition to prayer (see chapter 2), children could combat slavery by refusing to eat slave-made products.[26] As a member of the Ladies Free Produce Society (M. Jones 6), Chandler

advocated the free-produce movement, an enterprise especially favored by the Quakers, as a means by which women could make their influence felt most effectively; since women more than men controlled the purchasing of food, clothing, and household supplies, they could refuse to buy goods produced by slave labor. (Dillon, *Notable* 319)

She transferred her personal sentiments and actions into her juvenile poems depicting women and children working together. For example, in "Christmas" (1834), a child asks her mother to boycott sweets during the holidays despite the pleasure she obtains from them. The child rejects the sweets:

I have learn'd, dear mother,
      That the poor and wretched slave

> Must toil to win their sweetness,
>   From the cradle to the grave.
>
> And when he faints with weariness
>   Beneath the torrid sun,
> The keen lash urges on his toil,
>   Until the day is done. (9–16)

Having attained this knowledge, the child's compassion prompts her to deprive herself rather than to inflict pain upon another. She questions Christian principles and wonders about the Christian ideas of "peace and love to men" if men can sell humans as animals (33). She concludes:

> And 't is because of all this sin, my mother,
>   That I shun
> To taste the tempting sweets for which,
>   Such wickedness is done.
>
> If men to men will be unjust, if slavery must be,
> Mother, the chain must not be worn; the scourge
>   be plied for me. (41–46)

The child's actions, stemming from a belief in slavery's sinfulness, exemplify an individual's ability to renounce the slavocracy. Similarly, Chandler offers young readers another role model of juvenile resistance in Fanny from "The Sugarplums" (1832).[27] Although the sugarplums that grandmother sends entice Fanny, she refuses them, stating "I want no slave toiling for me in the sun, / Driven on with the whip, till the long day is done" (7–8). She extends her personal boycott to include all food that is a by-product of violence as she imagines the young field slave being flogged as his mother watched. Thus, she addresses her grandmother, stating:

> So grandma, I thank you for being so kind,
> But your present, to-day, is not much to my mind;
> Though I love you so dearly, I choose not to eat
> Even what you have sent me by slavery made sweet. (13–16)

The word "choose" implies that Fanny's political consciousness allows her deliberately to situate the slave above her family bond. This echoes Lydia Maria Child's recommendation in the *Anti-Slavery Catechism* (1839) that individuals must examine their prejudices and "If, after conscientious examination, you believe it right, cherish it; but do not adhere to it merely because your neighbors do. Look it in the face—apply the golden rule—and judge for yourself (qtd. in Dudley 207). Through her outspoken, young protagonists, Chandler gives young readers images of how even a child's private act can have public ramifications.

Perhaps following the lead of her good friend Elizabeth Margaret Chandler, Hannah Townsend published *The Anti-Slavery Alphabet* (1846 and 1847),[28] another early work encouraging juvenile abolitionism. Mary Lystad argues that between 1836 and 1875, instruction in both social behavior and school subjects drove the children's publishing industry (*From Dr. Mather* 84, 85). Townsend cleverly integrated the publishing trend with her belief in encouraging children's abolitionist efforts. In *The Anti-Slavery Alphabet*, Townsend addresses "Our Little Readers" affirming that "there's much that [children] can do" to end slavery (4). To her, the ideal abolitionist child "plead[s]" with slave masters because his/her entreaty may be more effective than the adults' petition (5; 9–10); discusses "the slave child's fate" (13) with other children on their way home from school; and boycotts "[c]andy, sweet-meat, pie or cake" (16) because "the slave shall not work for me" (18). This indoctrination into activism occurs before the children even begin to read the highly politicized alphabet that exposes Townsend's anxiety about American politics, economics, religion, and the family. This atypical alphabet does not teach children that "a" is for apple or that "x" is for xylophone. Rather, Townsend's alphabet educates a child about various aspects of slavery and abolitionism with the intent to effect behavioral change. Townsend reinforces the need for children's activism through the final heroic images:

> Y is for Youth—the time for all
> Bravely to war with sin;
> And think not it can never be
> Too early to begin.
>
> Z is a Zealous man, sincere,
> Faithful, and just, and true,
> An earnest pleader for the slave—
> Will you not be so too?

By leaving readers with this image of the heroic child, Townsend's final rhetorical question almost compels participation.

After Townsend, women authors offered children more concrete and developed images of child abolitionists. For example, in Jane Elizabeth Jones's *The Young Abolitionist* (1848), Mrs. Selden offers her children a history of the difficulties and successes that adult abolitionists encountered.[29] After engaging in complex and extensive discussions about slavery and abolitionist principles, Mrs. Selden's eldest son's states that, as a man, he "[s]hall do all [he] can for the slave" (150). However, although Jones never gives readers a view of a boy's abolitionist activities, she does depict young female activism. Mrs. Selden encourages self-sacrifice and compassion when she permits her daughter, Janie, to sell her favorite new apron to "purchase an antislavery book," which would theoretically change her slave-holding uncle's ideas about slavery (25). Interestingly, Janie transforms a domestic tool—her apron—into an economic tool for altering a male's political views. Despite this single-gendered incident, Mrs. Selden encourages all her children, sons and daughters, to join other children who have already made efforts to abolish slavery (129).

Eliza Follen perhaps offers some of the most exciting creations of pre-Stowe abolitionist children in her short stories and poetry collections. In her collection entitled *The Liberty Cap* (1846),[30] Follen captures the first moment of a child's abolitionist mindset in her epistolary short story "Picnic at Dedham,"[31] in which the child protagonist, Hal, differentiates himself from his parents' political views by adopting an abolitionist stance. After a long hiatus of not writing home during his stay with his relatives, on August 3, 1843, Hal enthusiastically reports attending a picnic where approximately 1,500 people celebrated slavery's abolition in the West Indies (12). Having acquired new information from the banners, poems, hymns, and political speeches given by freedmen and ex-slaves at the August first picnic, Hal argues, "every boy ought to know what American slavery is" (18). Clearly his parents have offered a different perspective, evident when he states, "I never heard you or father speak of the 1st of August" (12) and when he refers to their antiabolitionist sentiments: "When you and father speak of the fanaticism of the abolitionist, you can't mean this, I'm sure" (13). Challenging his parent's views, Hal adopts a newfound, abolitionist stance from his firsthand experience at the antislavery picnic. First, he utters a passive wish "that the time might come when we might be thanking God that our slaves were all free" (16). However, later he desires to participate in the abolitionist process: "I think that if the men don't all do something about slavery soon, we boys had better see what we can do, for it is too wicked" (17). Hal's "we"—though gendered—not only affirms children's active role in the abolitionist movement, but also serves as a declaration of independence from oppressive ("wicked") values, whether paternalistic or nationalistic.

In addition to her prose character, Hal, Eliza Follen also peppers her poetry with images of abolitionist children, but unlike Hal, children who perpetuate oppressive values suffer much criticism. In the poem-fable "Billy Rabbit to Mary" (1846), Follen begins with a headnote that suggests a harmless situation—a boy catches a little rabbit named Billy and gives it to a little girl who tries to make him happy. However, Follen instills the poem with political overtones when she permits Billy Rabbit to state, "To him who a hole or a palace inhabits, / To all sorts of beings, to men and to rabbits, / Ah! dear to us all is sweet Liberty" (19–21). This seemingly frivolous poetic epistle from a bunny to its owner[32] assumes abolitionist overtones when it admonishes a young girl who carries out proslavery behavior. Billy Rabbit states:

> You thought, my dear Mary, you had Billy fast,
> But I tried very hard, and escaped you at last;
> The chance was so tempting, I thought I would *nab* it,—
> It was not very naughty, I'm sure, in a rabbit. (1–4)

By casting himself as a clever fugitive from Mary's hold, Billy transforms Mary from a pet owner into a Southern slave-owning mistress. As trickster-rhetorician,[33] he gains supremacy over his young oppressor by rendering his freedom quest normal and excusable. He empowers himself through his escape, but disempowers and silences Mary with his reprimand. He traps her further when he asks her to "think what a joy it is to be free" (6) and then defines freedom by referring to things she, as a child, would find enjoyable, such as playing in the fresh air, running in the fields, and exploring the woods. Follen suggests that by enslaving Billy, Mary not only prevents his unhindered childlike capers, but also severs his bond to family and community. Follen rouses the reader's sympathy with a scene in which Billy is reunited with his family and the larger community. Billy states:

> O, how glad they all were to see me come back,
> And everyone wanted to give me a smack.
> Dick knocked over Brownie, and jumped over Bun,
> And the neighbors came in to witness the fun.
> My father said something, but could not be heard;
> My mother looked at me, but spoke not a word;
> And while she was looking, her eyes became pink,
> And she shed a few tears, I verily think. (11–18)

The comic and celebratory tone inherent in the words "smack," "knocked over," "jumped over," and "fun," give way to the more sentimental image of a speechless father and a tearful mother. Yet, both the comic and the sentimental celebratory responses stress the strength of the rabbit (slave) family and community's bond, a bond that Mary hindered. Finally, Follen suggests that the jubilant atmosphere that comes with liberation does not overshadow the ex-slave's resentment of his former owner. Mary, the former slave mistress, must recognize that, while Billy begins the letter with "my dear Mary" (1) and signs the letter "your devoted, affectionate BILLY" (26), this fugitive ex-slave has less than genial feelings for his former mistress. When the reader recalls that Billy Rabbit "sealed [the letter] with a thorn" (headnote), rather than a kiss, the violent undertones undermine the idea of a happy slave and confirm that this trickster feels differently.[34] In this less than flattering portrait of Mary, Follen may have helped children to challenge those who perpetuated the fallacy of benevolent masters and contented slaves.

Whereas Eliza Follen's "Billy Rabbit to Mary" condemns children who perpetuate slavery, her "Soliloquy: Of Ellen's Squirrel and His Liberty;—Overheard by a Lover of Nature and a Friend of Ellen" (1846) and Cousin Ann's poem "Howard and His Squirrel" (1849) praise children who participate in slavery's abolition. Like "Billy Rabbit to Mary," these poems also establish parallels between pet ownership and the master-slave relationship. Follen's "Soliloquy" gives readers another ex-slave squirrel with a voice that celebrates the ability to "taste of the joys that still are dear" (4) and "make [a] winter's nest again" (8). Unlike Mary in "Billy Rabbit to Mary," Follen attributes the squirrel's freedom to young Ellen's desire to establish equality: that the squirrel "skip and dance like [her]" (22). The squirrel suggests that because of Ellen's "best gift,—sweet Liberty!" (16), he gains what was previously denied to him but allowed to her. He tells Ellen:

> Oft in your gayest, happiest hour,
>   When all your youthful heart beats high,
> And, hastening on from flower to flower,
>   You taste the sweets of Liberty (17–20)

Thus, Follen's squirrel teaches Ellen to appreciate her own freedom as well as to celebrate her decision to bestow it upon another creature. Unlike Mary who encounters geniality that hides the violent undertones, upon liberating her squirrel, Ellen receives sincere thanks, "a pure a joy as e'er you knew" (24). Similarly, Cousin Ann's poem, "Howard and His Squirrel," celebrates the child as emancipator. Initially, Howard loves his pet squirrel, which he confines to a "wiry cage, / And there it had to stay" (3–4); but once he experiences slavery through his pet and realizes "she should not like / A little slave to be" (9–10), Howard frees the squirrel because "God had made the nimble squirrel, / To run, and climb the tree" (11–12). "Cousin Ann" offers a final didactic statement:

> A bird or squirrel in a cage
>   It makes me sad to see;
> It seems so cruel to confine
>   The creatures made so free. (17–20)

Praised for their benevolence, Ellen and Howard heroically restore each animal's God-given freedom as well as each American's inalienable rights established by their forefathers. In doing so, they represent characters whom the respective authors wish other young potential abolitionists to emulate.

FICTIONAL JUVENILE ABOLITIONISTS: HARRIET BEECHER STOWE'S LITTLE EVA

In the 1840s, young readers of works by authors like Townsend, Jones, Follen, and Cousin Ann had access to images of young children who engage in abolitionist activities. Follen creates male voices in "Picnic at Dedham," "Billy Rabbit to Mary," and "Soliloquy: Of Ellen's Squirrel and His Liberty;—Overheard by a Lover of Nature and a Friend of Ellen" and Cousin Ann celebrates the male, child protagonist in "Howard and His Squirrel." Girls, however, are silent: Jones's mother figure talks *about* Janie's actions in *The Young Abolitionist* and Billy Rabbit and Ellen's squirrel critique and praise, respectively, young girls. By the 1850s,[35] the recovered literature reveals a shift in thinking as fictional abolitionist children—predominantly girls—liberate slaves rather than rabbits and squirrels, as they face the real dilemma of slavery and the desire to "see what we can do." Furthermore, in the process of liberating the slaves, these fictional post–Seneca Falls girls liberate themselves as they combat being silenced in voice or in action. Interestingly, their transition from giving the *slave* a voice to giving *themselves* a voice parallels the fact that the abolitionist movement inspired women's battle for a public voice.[36] For example, responding to a pastoral letter from Theodore Weld, Angelina Grimké rejects silencing women's political voices. Grimké writes:

> Could they not see that the clergy, in attacking their right to lecture, were trying to prevent people from hearing what they had to say? "If we surrender the right to *speak* to the public this year, we must surrender the right to petition the next year and the right to *write* the year after and so on. What *then* can *woman* do for the slave when she is herself under the feet of man and shamed into *silence?*" (qtd. in Lerner 201)

Just as Grimké defends women's political voice and activism, so too Harriet Beecher Stowe's *Uncle Tom's Cabin* (1852), Aunt Mary's *The Edinburgh Doll* (1854), M.A.F.'s *Gertrude Lee; or, the Northern Cousin* (1856), Maria Goodell Frost's *Gospel Fruits* (1856), and Anna H. Richardson's *Little Laura, the Kentucky Abolitionist* (1859) contain fictional girls who likewise combat silence. These domestic abolitionists do not depict the girls negatively as nonconformists, but approvingly as heroines.

Using her literary foremothers and her belief that women assert their political voice,[37] Harriet Beecher Stowe creates, in *Uncle Tom's Cabin*, the first girl to articulate abolitionist principles. Eva has fictional "cousins" in the earlier abolitionist juvenile fiction and in George Shelby, but she is the first female who takes center stage, talks, and tries to abolish slavery. While I acknowledge Eva's evangelical nature, critics who have limited their discussions to evangelicalism have "silenced" Eva's abolitionist voice.[38] Gay Schwartz Herzberg argues that Stowe uses angelic girls "as ministers of a religion of love and testimonials to female perfection" (99). Anne Trensky calls Eva a quintessential saintly child, "sent here to convert sinners and help those sinned against" (392). Similarly, Jane Tompkins aligns Eva's Christlike death to a "cultural myth" that endows Eva, the "innocent victim," with the power to change people's minds about slavery (130). Tompkins writes, "in the system of belief that undergirds Stowe's enterprise, dying is the supreme form of heroism" (127).[39] However, situating Eva's behavior, while she is *alive*, in the context of the recovered juvenile abolitionist society records and texts that depict fictional abolitionist children requires analyzing her attempt to abolish slavery from a purely political perspective. In other words, we must pay attention to when and how Stowe replaces Eva's religious rhetoric with abolitionist rhetoric and behavior. Denying these moments silences a significant portion of her character, just as Stowe would argue in "Appeal to the Women of the Free States" (1854) that "there have been many things tending to fetter our hands, to perplex our efforts, and to silence our voice" (qtd. in Ammons 427). Consequently, focusing on Eva's living moments reveals that she embodies not only a sentimentalized, "salvific," though dead angel (Tompkins 129), but also the first, young, Southern, abolitionist girl, like her historical foremother Angelina Grimké,[40] and her fictional foremothers: Mrs. Selden, Mrs. Bird, and Miss Ophelia.

Stowe's characterization of the novel's adult female activists offers a starting point for establishing Eva's abolitionism. Speaking of Stowe's character, Rachel Halliday, Jane Tompkins argues:

> The brilliance of [Stowe's] strategy is that it puts the central affirmation of a culture into the service of a vision that would destroy the present economic and social institutions; by resting her case, absolutely, in the saving power of Christian love and on the sanctity of motherhood and the family, Stowe relocates the center of power in American life, placing it not in the government, nor in the courts of law, nor in the factories, nor in the marketplace, but in the kitchen. (145)

However, while Tompkins marks Rachel Halliday as an archetype of women's ability to reform American economic and social ills, she overlooks the struggle the female characters in *Uncle Tom's Cabin* (including Eva) undergo to carry out their antislavery beliefs. Unlike Rachel Halliday, who "can do almost everything" (122), the women in Stowe's novel do not live in idyllic, quasi-utopian, Quaker communities on the threshold between slavery and freedom. Rather, situated in less than ideal, slave-holding communities, Mrs. Shelby and Mrs. Bird encounter male cynicism, evident when their husbands criticize them for expressing abolitionist views. For example, when Mrs. Shelby voices her anger upon learning that her husband has sold Tom, Mr. Shelby responds mockingly: "Why, wife, you are getting to be an abolitionist, quite" (Stowe, *Uncle* 29). Mr. Shelby continues to criticize his wife's opinions when he states that she "talk[s] like a fool" (35) for rejoicing in Eliza's escape. Similarly, when Mrs. Bird voices knowledge of and dissatisfaction with the passage of the Fugitive Slave Law, Senator Bird jokes, "Why, Mary, you are getting to be a politician, all at once" (68). He adds to his criticism by calling her "my fair politician" (69) once she realizes he voted for the law. Mr. Bird and Mr. Selden imply that politics, especially abolitionist politics, should remain outside women's realm. The men attempt to limit these women to their proper, nonpolitical sphere and thus recall Theodore Weld's argument that women not speak publicly about slavery. However, just as Grimké rejects Weld's attempt to silence women, Mrs. Selden and Mrs. Bird refuse to stand back, remain silent, and do nothing. As Bardes and Gossett suggest, Mrs. Selden and Mrs. Bird's experiences exemplify "the uselessness of speech . . . and efficacy of action" (54). Though unable to speak their political minds, they refuse to remain in their apolitical roles and therefore risk criticism when they participate in abolitionist activities to help Eliza attain her own and Harry's freedom.

Whereas Mrs. Selden and Mrs. Bird take "covert action [when] words are not enough" (Bardes and Gossett 54), Ophelia embodies one of Stowe's few female characters, whom as Bardes and Gossett suggest, does not "just talk, powerlessly and inconsequentially" (54). Initially, the interchanges between Augustine St. Clare and Ophelia reiterate both the male's disdain for female politicians and the women's rejection of this view. For example, when Ophelia, "with a tide of zeal that had been gaining strength in her mind all morning," defends educating the slaves, Augustine St. Clare dismisses her by playing the piano "piece after piece" (Stowe, *Uncle* 153) and then "whistled a tune" (153). Later he tests Ophelia's true dedication to her philosophy of educating the slaves by jokingly giving her Topsy, "a present of a fresh-caught specimen" (207–208). Furthermore, when Ophelia tries to argue that individuals like Augustine prolong slavery because they do nothing, he responds:

> "O, now, cousin," said Augustine, sitting down on the floor, and laying his head back in her lap, "don't take on so awfully serious! You know what a good-for-nothing, saucy boy I always was. I love to poke you up,—that's all,—just to see you get earnest. I do think you are desperately, distressingly good; it tires me to death to think of it."
>
> "But this is a serious subject, my boy, Auguste," said Miss Ophelia, laying her head on his forehead.
>
> "Dismally so," said he; "and I——well, I never want to talk seriously in hot weather. What with mosquitoes and all, a fellow can't get himself up to any very sublime moral flights; and I believe," said St. Clare suddenly rousing himself up, "there's a theory, now! I understand now why northern nations are always more virtuous than southern ones,—I see into that whole subject." (192–93).

Augustine's implicit statement that cold weather accounts for Northern action trivializes and silences Ophelia's argument. While she eventually persuades him to take her argument seriously, he blames his passivity on Southern heat and mosquitoes, and implicitly wishes that Ophelia would stop behaving like a pesky insect.

However, when Ophelia demands that Augustine give her legal rights to Topsy, the two engage in an extended, heated debate, which reveals that Ophelia learns, with practice, to assert her opinions in the face of condescension. Stowe writes:

"I want her to be mine legally," said Miss Ophelia.

"Whew! cousin," said Augustine, *"What will the Abolition Society think? They'll have a day of fasting appointed for this backsliding, if you become a slave-holder!"*

"O, nonsense! I want her mine, that I may have a right to take her to the free States, and give her her liberty, that all I am trying to do be not undone."

"O, cousin, what an awful 'doing evil that good may come'! I can't encourage it!

"I don't want you to joke, but to reason," said Miss Ophelia.

. . . .

"Well, well," said St. Clare, "I will;" and he sat down, and *unfolded a newspaper to read.*

"But I want it done now," said Miss Ophelia.

"What's your hurry?"

"Because now is the only time there ever is to do a thing in," said Miss Ophelia. "Come, now, here's paper, pen, and ink; just write a paper."

. . . .

"Why, what's the matter?" said he. *"Can't you take my word? One would think you had taken lessons of the Jews, coming at a fellow so!"*

"I want to make sure of it," said Miss Ophelia. "You may die, or fail, and then Topsy be hustled off to auction, spite of all I can do."

"Really, you are quite provident. *Well, seeing I'm in the hands of a Yankee, there is nothing for it but to concede;"* and St. Clare rapidly wrote off a deed of gift, which, as he was well versed in forms of law, he could easily do, and signed his name to it in sprawling capitals, concluding by a tremendous flourish.

"There, isn't that black and white, now, *Miss Vermont?"* he said, as he handed it to her.

"Good boy," said Miss Ophelia smiling. "But must it not be witnessed?"

"O, bother,—yes. "Here," he said, opening the door into Marie's apartment. *"Marie, Cousin wants your autograph; just put your name down here."*

(268–69, emphasis added)

Stowe clearly illustrates St. Clare's less than serious attitude when he calls Ophelia a "Yankee" and "Miss Vermont"; when he ignores her request by reading the newspaper and by asking "What's your hurry?"; and finally when he argues that her actions will upset the entire Abolitionist Society. Ophelia rejects St. Clare's dismissive attitude and resolutely asserts her voice until she insures Topsy's freedom. Stowe implies that Ophelia even knows some legal procedures by reminding St. Clare to ascertain a second witness. Thus, through Ophelia, Stowe establishes models of resistance who, despite not being taken seriously, learn to combat silence and condescension with words.

Just as Mr. Shelby, Mr. Bird, and Augustine St. Clare dismiss women's abolitionist efforts by reiterating their proper roles as angels in the house, Henrique, Marie, and Augustine St. Clare dismiss Eva's increasingly political activism. Unsurprisingly, these Southern slave owners contrast the abolitionist fictional adults—in abolitionist juvenile works by her literary foremothers such as

Townsend, Jones, and Follen—who took earnestly children's morality, intellect, and political activity and thereby urged children to pity the slaves and to voice their objections to slavery. However, Eva slowly fights the silencing and engages in behavior prescribed for "real" child abolitionists despite familial opposition and condescending remarks that endeavor to keep Eva in her place as an innocent child, an apolitical wife, and an upper-class Southern mistress. Eva may embody Trensky's image of the saintly child and Tompkins's religious ideal manifested in Rachel Halliday, but like Ophelia, Mrs. Shelby, and Mrs. Bird, she combats attempts at silencing with protests.

Stowe casts Eva as a young girl whose abolitionist voice evolves slowly. At first, Eva has difficulty "talking politics" since she has not mastered its vocabulary. Early in the novel, Eva responds by "sobb[ing] convulsively" (204) to her father's story about his slave, Scipio. She recognizes that she cries because "these things *sink into my heart*" (204), but she cannot fully explain her views to her father:

> "I can't tell you papa. I think a great many thoughts. Perhaps some day I shall tell you."
>
> "Well, think away, dear,—only don't cry and worry your papa," said St. Clare. "Look here,—see what a beautiful peach I have got for you!"
>
> Eva took it, and smiled, though there was still a nervous twitching about the corners of her mouth. (204)

Eva responds with sighs and tears because she possesses the empathy but not the language to express her abolitionist sentiments. Nor does St. Clare help her to find the words; rather, he offers Eva a soothing but dismissive response. When he gives Eva a gift (a peach) to console his daughter and to stop *his* pain, St. Clare echoes the scene in which he jokingly gives Ophelia a gift (Topsy). Stowe calls attention to the silencing nature of his actions by describing Eva's mouth. Rather than soothe her twitching mouth by coaxing Eva into expressing her ideas—or at least why she cries—by giving his daughter the peach, St. Clare literally (since the peach requires oral consumption) and figuratively silences any potential expression of her feelings about slavery. After this scene, however, Stowe depicts a child in a slow battle to assert her abolitionist voice through words and deeds that claim slaves' rights to justice, education, equality, and freedom.

Whereas Eva initially has difficulty expressing herself to her father, she develops a stronger verbal arsenal in her battle against her peer and cousin Henrique St. Clare, who has clearly learned the importance of voice, how to assert his, and how to deny it to others. Stowe immediately suggests that Henrique assert his twelve-year-old muscles to silence those below him. When Dodo, Henrique's young mulatto slave, tries to explain the dust on his master's horse, Henrique responds by silencing him: "'You rascal, shut your mouth!' said Henrique, violently raising his riding-whip. 'How dare you speak?'" (231). When Dodo attempts to speak a second time, Henrique silences him again: "Henrique struck him across the face with his riding-whip, and, seizing one of [Dodo's] arms, forced him on to his knees, and beat him till he was out of breath" and then adds, "I'll teach you your place!" (231). Similarly, when Tom tries to defend the child, Henrique states, "You hold your tongue till you're asked to speak!" (231). By speaking, Dodo oversteps his designated "place" (i.e., silence) in the hierarchy and not only receives a verbal reminder of his transgression, but also a physical one: a wound across his face and possibly also across his mouth.

Though he does not whip his cousin, Henrique does silence Eva whenever she employs persuasive tactics to awaken his conscience to antislavery senti-ments. When Eva witnesses Henrique physically abusing Dodo, she begins on a "political" level by aligning herself with the slave and criticizing Henrique's unjust action. She states, "But you beat him,—and he didn't deserve it" (232). However, rather than recognize his own unjust behavior, Henrique says, "O, well, it may go for some time when he does [deserve it] . . . but I won't beat him again before you, if it troubles you" (232). Henrique not only justifies his behavior, but also suggests that he will continue it outside Eva's presence regardless of her debate over the (in)appropriate punishment. Since the appeal to justice fails, Eva tries to make her cousin recognize his wickedness by asking Henrique to identify with the slave: "Would you think you were well off, if there were not one crea-ture in the world near you to love you?" (236). She asks Henrique to imagina-tively transform himself into a slave so that he may identify with and feel the slave boy's pain. When even this approach fails, Eva urges Henrique to love his servants as she loves hers. In response, Henrique exclaims "How odd!" and dis-misses Eva's reference to Biblical injunctions—the first time religion enters the conversation—claiming that the Bible "says a great many such things; but then nobody ever thinks of doing them,—you know, Eva, nobody does" (237). Iden-tification with the slave and religion do not remedy the situation because Hen-rique reveals how they are easily dismissed as excessive and frivolous, much like women. Finally when Eva asks him to love Dodo for her sake. He responds, "'I could love anything, for your sake, dear Cousin; for I really think you are the loveliest creature that I ever saw!' And Henrique spoke with an earnestness that flushed his handsome face" (237). By focusing on Eva's beauty and ignoring her demands for justice or her Christian politics, Henrique presses her into the proper role for women of her background: apolitical, young Southern belles. He ultimately tries to control Eva's unconventionality by calling attention to her physical beauty, just as Senator Bird tries to deflate his wife's politics by calling her "my fair politician" (69). Stowe suggests, however, that Eva refuses this role: "Eva received it with perfect simplicity, without even a change of feature; merely saying, 'I'm glad you feel so, dear Henrique! I hope you will remember'" (237). Her refusal to call attention to Henrique's remark—and therefore his attempt to silence her—shifts the emphasis away from sexual implications[41] and back to Christian and abolitionist principles that try to insure security for others, rather than for herself. Thus, although Henrique proves a difficult test case for Eva's early political rhetoric, she does not surrender to his excuses. Rather, like Dodo, she steps outside her "place" and speaks like an abolitionist.

Eva also encounters much resistance and silencing for her Northern-style abolitionist views from her mother. Just as Eva tries to insure security for the slaves, as a nineteenth-century mother Marie St. Clare should insure Eva's security rather than her own. However, Stowe creates a jealous and failed mother figure. Stowe writes that when Augustine St. Clare names Eva after his mother, "[t]he thing had been remarked with petulant jealousy by his wife, and she regarded her husband's devotion to the child with suspicion and dislike" (134). Marie openly complains about not being taken seriously and that St. Clare "never realizes, never can, never will, what I suffer, and have, for years" (148; see also 150). Furthermore, she complains to Ophelia that Augustine "indulges every creature [Eva and the slaves] under his roof but his own wife" (149). Marie's feelings of displacement cause her to view Eva as "a nuisance and a rival for her husband's love" (Trensky 393), and consequently one to supplant and to silence.

Eva's supposed violation of her "place" in the family hierarchy and Marie's sense of displacement fuel their mother-daughter contest over the slave's "place" in the master-slave hierarchy. Marie calls Eva "such a strange child" (Stowe, *Uncle* 148) when Eva offers to remain at her mother's beside because Mammy, the slave woman, does not feel well and needs sleep (148). Eva disagrees with her mother, who states, "it's always right and proper to be kind to servants, but it isn't proper to treat them *just as* we would our relations, or people in our own class of life" (158). In response, Eva argues that if Mammy were truly sick, she would let her sleep in her own bed "because it would be handier to take care of her, and because, you know, my bed is better than hers" (158). Through such a statement, Eva challenges the concept of "place"—spatial, racial, and economic—for herself and the slaves and begins to resemble Rachel Halliday, the abolitionist Quaker woman[42] who nurses Eliza in her own bed (121) and who provides George, Eliza, and Harry with the first opportunity to sit "down on equal terms at [a] white man's table" (122). But Marie expresses disgust for Eva's views when she says, "That's just a specimen of the way the child would be doing all the time, if she was left to herself" (149). However, Marie St. Clare, who lives to keep slaves in their "place," fails to place nonconforming Eva into her "place" as the innocent, silent child, and demure Southern slave mistress. Rather, Eva's exchanges with her mother reveal an increasingly nonreligious, abolitionist speech and actions.

Eva not only raises the issue of all men's and women's rights to the same experiences despite race and class, but also broaches the controversial subject of educating and freeing the slaves,[43] for which she forms a capitalistic plan. Just as Gillian Brown argues that "[t]he contagion of the market had already entered" Dinah's kitchen (15); Stowe argues that the marketplace mentality and vocabulary prematurely enters Eva's mindset. Upon hearing that she will inherit the jewels that her mother wore at her "coming out" ball, Eva's abolitionist spirit leads her to conceive a philanthropic plan, like the real children who raised pennies to free the slaves. Again, her assertions make no reference to religion; instead, Stowe writes:

> "Are these worth a great deal of money, mamma?"
> "To be sure, they are. Father sent to France for them. They are worth a small fortune."
> "I wish I had them," said Eva, "to do what I please with!"
> "What would you do with them?"
> "I'd sell them, and buy a place in the free states, and take all our people there, and hire teachers, to teach [the slaves] to read and write." (*Uncle* 229–30)

Eva wishes to use the money to liberate and educate,[44] and consequently to empower. Stowe creates an abolitionist girl who desires to transform the diamonds—a commodity intended to beautify and perhaps objectify—into a financial and political transfer that would decommodify a people. Unlike Ophelia who at least attempts "to get in the kitchen with Dinah to eliminate hurryscurryation" (Brown 16), Marie, could exert influence to empower the slaves. Instead, she heartily objects to educating them, calls Eva an "odd child" for even considering it (Stowe, *Uncle* 229), and laughs at Eva stating, "Set up a boarding school! Would you teach them to play on the piano, and paint on velvet?" (230). When Eva disagrees with her mother's views, Marie dismisses her daughter: "Come, come, Eva; you are only a child! You don't know anything about these things . . . besides, your talking makes my head ache" (230). By dismissing and trying to silence her daughter, Marie represents the antithesis of the mothers in the recovered juvenile works who encourage children's discussion and abolitionist efforts.[45]

Critics like Bardes and Gossett, who only perceive Eva's business plan as a "vision of useful action" (55), dismiss and silence Eva's abolitionism because they fail to note how the issue of educating the slaves represents an important abolitionist act of resistance that at least two additional juvenile versions of *Uncle Tom's Cabin* replicate. Even though Eva dies before she inherits the jewels to carry out her proposal, Eva chooses to reject her mother's wish, to disobey the slave code laws that prohibited educating slaves,[46] and to assert the power of language and voice[47] when she decides to teach Mammy to read. In one of *Uncle Tom's Cabin's* most subversive moments, Stowe writes, "after that, [Eva] assiduously gave Mammy reading lessons" (230). Without her mother's consent, Eva cannot bring about full-scale change, but she does effect some change. Thus, Eva behaves like Stowe's abolitionist Ophelia who gives voice to a plan and subversively executes it.

Similarly, the two recovered juvenile adaptations of *Uncle Tom's Cabin* reinforce subversive activity. First, "Little Eva, the Flower of the South" (1853) initially appears to embody Southern, idealized views of slavery with its images of dedicated servants who refuse their freedom; yet, it contains several subversive qualities and reveals itself as an embattled text. After a brief introduction, the author immediately establishes the image of little Eva violating Southern law by educating the slaves. Her behavior inverts the scene in Frederick Douglass's *Narrative*, where he tricks and manipulates the children into teaching him the alphabet. The author writes, "Here you see, is little Eva teaching the colored boys and girls the alphabet" (2). The illustration shows Eva pointing to the letter "A" on a blackboard (Figure 4). Later, the author reveals that while some slaves prefer to listen to her read from the Bible, "she has learned [sic] some of them to read" (4). Consequently, when Eva's parents give Sam a Bible for saving Eva's life, he can presumably read it. As a young Southern abolitionist, she subverts Southern laws that dictated slave silence; nevertheless she receives the title, the "Flower of the South." Second, *Little Eva's First Book for Good Children* (1853) also presents young readers with a revolutionary and subversive girl educator. While British and American publishers may have used Eva as a marketing strategy, they linked the ideal female child with slavery and education. The book suggests that the good child helps abolish slavery—at least psychological slavery—by breaking the laws to educate and empower others. The author, therefore, implicates a "bad" child who does not educate or empower, but rather upholds discriminatory laws and maintains the slaves' oppressive silence. By associating Eva with this alphabet, speller, and reader (which includes poems and fiction with religious and political lessons), the author links her to the acquisition of language and voice. This suggests a new, nonconformist generation that rejects slavery by educating the slave.

Yet, in the original *Uncle Tom's Cabin*, Stowe does not end with the image of Eva as educator. While the conversations with Henrique center on justice and love, and those with her mother on "place" and education, Eva's repeated interaction with her father focuses on strategies for emancipating the slaves, which likewise expose her abolitionist—not religious—vocabulary. Like the real and fictional young abolitionists who equated participating in the market economy through fund raising with liberating slaves, Stowe offers another image of Eva maneuvering a capitalistic system. Even before Tom saves Eva from drowning, she promises to save him from plantation life in the deep South by telling Tom that she will ask her father to purchase him "this very day" (Stowe, *Uncle* 128), which reveals her understanding of the value and power of money and the concept of ownership. After Tom rescues Eva from drowning, Stowe presents St. Clare haggling with the slave trader over Tom. However, Eva hastens the transaction when she asserts that her father has enough money to purchase Tom: "'Papa, do buy him! It's no matter what you pay,' whispered Eva softly, getting up on a package, and putting her arm around her father's neck. 'You have money enough, I know. I want him. . . . I want to make him happy'" (130). Eva uses her childlike wiles to work within the masculine capitalistic system to do the right thing, a strategy some abolitionists would see as a positive step toward Tom's liberation.[48] Furthermore, by modifying Eva's statement of desire from "I want him" to "I want to make him happy," Stowe

EVA, TEACHING THE ALPHABET.

Here you see, is little Eva teaching the little colored boys and girls the alphabet. See how pleased they are, for they all love Eva, and would do anything to please her; and Eva takes a great deal of pleasure in teaching them and making them happy. She is teaching them the letters one by one, which she marks on the black-board.

FIGURE 4. Eva teaching the slaves from "Little Eva, the Flower of the South" (1853) (courtesy of the American Antiquarian Society).

prevents her from becoming a full-fledged slave mistress who visits a slave market in order to commodify a people. Rather, Stowe aligns her with abolitionists who desire to improve the slaves' life experience. Thus, Eva comes closest to removing Tom from the marketplace and thereby enacts Brown's paradigm of sentimental possession: "translat[ing] possessive individualism into a secure proprietorship by detaching it from the market" (52).

Stowe repeats Eva's knowledge that money produces redemption by having her facilitate Tom's communication with Mrs. Shelby and Chloe so as to effect his liberation and thereby guarantee his complete detachment from the marketplace. In this scene, Tom's illiteracy prevents him from writing a letter home. Eva tries to help him, but must admit that "[l]ast year I could make all the letters, but I'm afraid I've forgotten" (Stowe, *Uncle* 205). Although Eva can teach Mammy to read, her inability to write risks silencing both Eva and Tom. Good intentions aside, she cannot independently effect Tom's liberation. Luckily, St. Clare enters and while he does not want to "discourage" them, neither does he empower them by teaching them how to form the letters. Rather, he writes the letter after Eva explains its importance: Mrs. Shelby "is going to send down money to redeem [Tom]" (206). By instilling the word "redeem" with economic rather than Biblical connotations,[49] Eva's oral request seemingly initiates the process of Tom's redemption because when Mrs. Shelby and Chloe receive the letter, they both further what Eva initiates. Chloe secures permission to leave her family to hire herself out to a baker so that "every cent of [her wages can] be laid aside for [Tom's] redemption" (222). Furthermore, even though Mr. Shelby tells his wife that she is "the finest woman in Kentucky; but still [she] doesn't have sense to know that [she doesn't] understand business,—women never do, and never can" (220), she agrees to hire *herself* out to give music lessons (220), and in a sense becomes like the slave, Chloe. Stowe suggests that women know more about how to do business than the men think.

The discussions Eva engages in with her family members about morality, education, and economics each reveal a difficult but growing abolitionist voice that is fully realized in the final father-daughter contest concerning the slaves' emancipation. Stowe creates a scene very different from the first exchange when Eva cannot speak about slavery. She contrasts Eva's physical deterioration and her ensuing death with Eva's emotional growth and increasing consciousness of slavery's politics. During the final interchange, Stowe suggests that Eva's voice and abolitionist agenda have matured, while her father's attitudes toward her and slavery have remained unchanged:

> "Papa," said Eva, with sudden firmness, "I've had things I wanted to say to you a great while, I want to say them now, before I get weaker."
> St. Clare trembled as Eva seated herself in his lap. She laid her head on his bosom, and said,
> "It's all no use, papa, to keep it to myself any longer. The time is coming that I am going to leave you. I am going, and never to come back!" and Eva sobbed.

"O, now, my dear little Eva!" said St. Clare, trembling as he spoke, but speaking cheerfully, "you've got nervous and low-spirited; you mustn't indulge such gloomy thoughts. See here, I've bought a statuette for you!"

"No, papa," said Eva, putting it gently away, "don't deceive yourself!—I am *not* any better, I know it perfectly well." (240)

Like the first scene when he dismisses his daughter with a gift, St. Clare wishes to ameliorate her by giving Eva another gift, this time a statuette (240). St Clare recognizes the "womanly thoughtfulness about [Eva] now" (229); nonetheless he minimizes her concerns and attempts to preserve his "little girl" by giving Eva a new toy. On the contrary, Stowe suggests the extent of Eva's maturation when she does not accept the statuette as she previously accepted the peach, signaling that this time St. Clare cannot silence Eva. Her discussions with Henrique, her mother, and her father help Eva to achieve a higher level of consciousness and to find the words to express her feelings toward slavery. Previously, in response to hearing Prue's story, "[Eva] did not exclaim, or wonder, or weep, as other children do. Her cheeks grew pale, and a deep, earnest shadow passed over her eyes. She laid both hands on her bosom, and sighed heavily" (189). Conversely, during this final father-daughter interchange, Eva demands that vocalization and action replace the existing silence and supposed beneficial ignorance. For example, when her father regrets letting her hear the stories about slaves, Eva says:

O, that's what troubles me, papa. You want me to live so happy, and never to have any pain,—never suffer anything,—not even hear a sad story, when other poor creatures have nothing but pain and sorrow, all their lives;—it seems selfish. I ought to know such things, I ought to feel about them! Such things always sunk into my heart; they went down deep; I've thought and thought about them. Papa, isn't there any way to have all slaves made free? (241)

Now, however, Eva admits to feeling sad about her friends' condition and finally states "I wish, papa, they were all *free*" (241) because she understands that even her own family members can act cruelly to slaves. Though earlier she could only cry about the slave's fate, now Eva's words confirm her rejection of a woman's apolitical, silent position and affirm the need to effect change.

Clearly, Eva recognizes the importance that language plays in trying to end slavery because she urges her father to speak publicly against slavery:

Papa, you are such a good man, and so noble, and kind, and you always have a way of saying such things that is so pleasant, couldn't you go all around and try to persuade people to do right about this? When I am dead, papa, then you will think of me, and do it for my sake. I would do it, if I could. (241)[50]

When Eva talks about engaging in abolitionist activities, she does not use religious rhetoric as she does with Uncle Tom, with Topsy, or with the slaves when she gives away her locks of hair. Rather, just as Ophelia and Alfred St. Clare debate political activism with Augustine, Eva expresses her desire to move her father to activism because she realizes that, as a dying child, she can make no change other than her willingness to die for them. Even after Augustine tells her not to talk of dying, Eva continues to speak and to express her desire that her father free Tom (242). This young abolitionist consciously talks of freedom in concrete, realistic, and nonreligious terms. By asking her father to grant her quasi-deathbed promise, Eva continues her abolitionist efforts by arousing her father's conscience about the appropriateness of freeing Tom and the other St. Clare slaves.

Eva's difficulties with converting her family members to adopt antislavery sentiments, however, never hinder her from acting independently and from within her own belief system. Stowe, who knew Follen,[51] consciously or unconsciously patterns Eva after Follen's idea that children can engage in private, benevolent activism. Eva, this "true democrat" (154), insists that she desires "to do something for them" (i.e., the slave) (239). She perceives and treats the slaves not as "others" but according to Follen's mandate that children "[l]earn to look upon every human being as equally with yourself the child of God, however degraded he may be, however the world may cast him off" ("How Shall Children Do Good" 113). For example, Eva's tears for Prue and Scipio and her kind words to Topsy and Dodo effect more consolation than the spare change that Henrique gives Dodo after whipping him. In addition, Eva's final attempt to create a democracy and abolish racial and class lines occurs when she gives the slaves locks of her hair. Just as the Birds give Eliza "poor little Henry's" clothes (Stowe, *Uncle* 75) and challenge the dichotomies of white/black and slave/free, Eva shifts her "place" because she gives these supposed "outsiders" what is usually reserved for family members; consequently, she makes them "insiders."

Exclusive of the fact that Stowe martyrs Eva like many of the adult abolitionists who willingly died for the cause, Stowe's young female abolitionist replicates the behavior encouraged of young abolitionists. Proponents of juvenile abolitionism did not expect children to make Eva's sacrificial pronouncements: "I've felt that I would be glad to die, if my dying could stop all this misery. I *would die* for them, Tom, if I could" (240). However, editors of the *Slave's Friend* encourage children to collect money to free the slaves, just as Eva desires to sell the jewels. The *Slave's Friend* and Hannah Townsend invite children to speak to others about slavery's evils, which Eva does. Eliza Follen advocates that children engage in acts of private benevolence, which Eva does. Thus, although Eva's death casts her as a angel, her life manifests qualities of a model juvenile abolitionist. Unfortunately, while Stowe encourages women to combat silence, she replicates the typical gender sphere split by preventing Eva from maturing into an abolitionist woman and allowing George Shelby, although unable to free Tom, to free his father's slaves.

FICTIONAL JUVENILE ABOLITIONISTS: AFTER STOWE

Harriet Beecher Stowe's success with *Uncle Tom's Cabin* may have opened doors for women interested in writing abolitionist juvenile works to create primarily female protagonists. Before Stowe's Little Eva, domestic abolitionists appear to strike a balance between boy and girl protagonists; however, after *Uncle Tom's Cabin*, the recovered authors cast *girls* as the primary forces for restoring American ideals through their deeds and their *voices*.[52] Aunt Mary, M.A.F., Maria Goodell Frost, and Anna Richardson adopt the then popular and accepted image of Little Eva, but heighten her subversiveness. Examining these girls only from a religious perspective would replicate the skewed views critics have held of Eva. However, scrutinizing these "little women's" abolitionist voices reveals heroic, nonconformists who use their voices for political activism that liberates the slaves and themselves.

One of Eva's first literary descendants in both saintliness and activism appears in Aunt Mary's poem, *The Edinburgh Doll* (1854), which depicts two young female abolitionists, Mary and her toy doll, willingly sacrificing themselves for the slave. The poem begins with an ambiguous and disturbing quality in that the unnamed narrator—who eventually identifies herself as Mary's doll— states that she has traveled on the ocean from 'Scotia and "was uncased and brought to light" (10) in Boston's Horticultural Hall. Placed on display, she experiences the "gaze" (40) of over fifty potential buyers (48). The speaker's language has innuendoes of a middle passage and a slave-market experience that make the reader question whether the poem espouses proslavery or abolitionist sentiments. However, the poem's antislavery stance becomes clear when the doll explains that the bazaar represents an international abolitionist effort (51; 53; 56; 69–70) in which children participate. Aunt Mary writes:

> And this is why they've worked and toiled,
>   And sent their precious gifts so far;
> This is why Mary begged that I
>   Might come for sale to the bazaar. (69–72)

Mary's doll not only appears proud to participate in the antislavery bazaar, but also approves of Mary's actions.

The doll's owner, Mary, represents the second heroic female who clearly echoes Harriet Beecher Stowe's portrait of the self-sacrificing, abolitionist Eva. The reference to Eva and Uncle Tom (32) and the passages expressing religious sentiments suggests that Aunt Mary had Stowe's Eva in mind when she created Mary. Like Eva, Mary[53] recognizes how slavery violates Christianity. She states:

> "And it is so, indeed!" she cried;
>   "Have those oppressors ever read

Of the good Jesus—he who died
    For all the souls his hands have made?

"And have they heard that he hath said
    Of every man, 'he is thy brother?'
And do they know that sweet command,
    'My children, love ye one another?'"

She scarcely could believe that those
    Who knew their Master's will so well,
Should slight it thus, and, sighing, said,
    "Then Satan in their hearts must dwell." (85–96)

While Eva utters similar sentiments about Christian love, Mary highlights the Christian oppressor's hypocrisy. The child's anxiety over the violated Christian ethics spurs her to donate her doll to the Boston Anti-Slavery Bazaar. She also designs additional clothing to increase the doll's value, an act that attracts over fifty perspective buyers. These gestures affirm the shift from religious sentiment to public, abolitionist politics. In her realization that religious sentiments alone cannot guarantee the slaves' liberation, Mary participates in the market economy and employs capitalistic efforts.

Like Eva, this young female abolitionist dies before she can witness the slaves' redemption; but unlike Eva, Mary successfully involves others in abolitionism. Whereas Augustine St. Clare dies before he can fulfill his daughter's abolitionist intentions, Mary's mother executes her intentions. Disturbingly, the author says that the mother includes a letter with the doll addressed "to the doll's new mistress" (Extract). The word "mistress" seems to replicate a master-slave relationship and suggests that Mary's mother learned more than St. Clare, but not as much as her daughter. Nevertheless, the mother acts as a conduit for the child's activism. Furthermore, the narrator-doll stresses the importance of children's activism when she states:

And to the children I would say,
    Whate'er your hands may find to do,
O, do it quickly now, I pray,
    For short may be the time for you. (205–208)

Though the doll reminds each child of his/her mortality, she offers powerful incentive, especially to girls, to act and to be remembered as positively as Mary, "[a] little saint" (184), who gains this title because of her abolitionist work.[54]

In 1856, four years after Stowe's creation of the widely popular Little Eva, the American Reform Tract and Book Society sponsored a contest offering a one hundred dollar premium "for the best manuscript for a religious Anti-Slavery Sunday School book, showing [children and youth] that American chattel slave-holding is a sin against God, and a crime against man, and that it ought to be immediately repented of and abolished" (Frost, *Gospel* v). From the forty-eight manuscripts H. Bushnell, John Jolliffe, and George Weed received, the committee awarded the premium to Maria Goodell Frost's *Gospel Fruits; or, Bible Christianity Illustrated*, but it also recommended about fifteen for publication (vi), many of which have not yet been (and possibly cannot be) recovered. Apparently, with Stowe as her literary precedent and with this contest as license, Maria Goodell Frost adopted and adapted Stowe's schema of a young abolitionist girl protagonist who possesses both religious and political awareness. More importantly, as opposed to Stowe and Aunt Mary who "kill" their young female abolitionist, Frost creates a more realistic young female[55] who develops a political voice and brings her activism to fruition.

Maria Goodell Frost's *Gospel Fruits* (1856) won the American Reform Tract and Book Society award perhaps because it illustrates the society's belief in the intersection of Christian and abolitionist ethics. Frost establishes her political views, stating:

> It is the design of this little work, to show what *true religion* is, and that it can not exist without a sympathy for the oppressed; or, in other words, that the Gospel spirit is perfectly antagonistic to Slavery.
> It is maintained that the salvation of the soul *includes* a salvation from the sins of *selfishness and prejudice*, which are the *parents of Slavery*.
> At the same time, it strenuously insists that a change of heart, by the Holy Spirit, is essential to a full and acceptable development of Anti-Slavery principles. (Preface ix)

Her statement attacks the proslavery advocates' corrupt economic and racial views and their use of the Bible to support their institution. She challenges readers to redefine Christianity and to examine their consciences and hearts for a stronger foundation to abolitionist reform. Through a cast of malleable girls, all of whom attend Miss Chester's Grove Street Sabbath School, Frost exposes the need for reform. Kate is Frost's young abolitionist who engages in abolitionist acts because she thinks she is "being good." Conversely, Adeline—proud, prejudiced, and proslavery—attends Sunday school in body but not in spirit. Frost focuses much attention on Adeline's need for and eventual conversion; however, she also suggests that Kate must undergo a more difficult conversion that will allow her to believe that true abolitionism stems from religious beliefs rather than from applause for outward actions. Thus, Frost politicizes religion by suggesting that the ideal abolitionist child (i.e., individual) cultivates expressions of compassion and acts of benevolence that stem from deep religious convictions and a sincere love of the "other."

Through Kate, Frost creates a young girl who initiates her peer community's recognition of the necessary link between religion and politics. Addressing a gender-specific audience, Kate resembles the abolitionist women who discussed slavery's moral hypocrisy during female antislavery society meetings or women's sewing circles. Kate introduces her peers to a politicized religion when she brings an antislavery workbag to Sunday school. The narrator states:

> It was a very pretty pink workbag, with a bright, shining clasp; upon one side was engraved the figure of a kneeling slave, with fettered hands and limbs, and underneath, the words, "Am I not a man and a brother?" Upon the other side were the beautiful lines of Cowper. (13)

Kate faces much opposition to the abolitionist principles her purse emblematizes. Adeline drops it saying, "As I live, there is a *nigger* on it!" (13); Julia Arnot states, "Well, I am sure I would not have a nigger on my workbag" (13), and several other Sunday school classmates taunt her, mishandle the bag, and call the slave Kate's "beau" (14). However, Kate's insistence that "[i]t is not a nigger. . . . It is a poor slave, a colored man, in chains" (13) effects some change. For example, Hellen May, who had never realized that "antislavery [sentiments] had anything to do with religion" (15), learns from Kate that "it represents a principle. The principle of the golden rule is violated by slavery; anyone can see that by looking at this picture. Who would like to be fettered and chained down as this man is, so like a brute?" (15). Kate's workbag and words help Hellen May and several peers to remove the taboo from "abolitionist" by linking it to religion, an established and acceptable part of their lives.

Frost strengthens Kate's abolitionist voice by suggesting that she does not spout empty sentiments, but puts her belief in principles of equality and acceptance into practice when faced with Jane Brown, her new classmate. Though free because Mrs. Brown has paid for her own and her daughter's freedom, Jane Brown's presence evokes racist sentiments from those she encounters. Enrolled in the white Sunday school after her family moves to the town, Jane expects peer rejection: "[her] whole aspect was subdued and sorrowful, as if she knew and felt, with her child's heart, that she was an outcast, unloved, and everywhere unwelcome" (22–23). Kate's classmates resent Jane and voice unkind sentiments. Adeline Roberts, Lizzie Benton, and Anna Porter refuse to allow Jane to sit near them, and Julia claims that Jane should attend the black church school: "that is the place for her" (22). Kate, however, combats separatism and enacts the same rejection of slavery and racism that she expresses when the girls taunt her about her purse. She invites Jane to sit with her, vows her friendship, and speaks words of kindness, "the first civil words [Jane] had ever received from a white child" (27). Furthermore, she helps Jane to find, appropriately, the Bible passage about love. Later, Kate willingly surrenders her birthday gifts so that her mother can use the money to purchase new clothing for Jane, and she promises to help Jane overcome her language difficulties stemming from her inadequate education (58). Rather than martyring herself for Jane, Kate reflects the behavior encouraged of "real" juvenile abolitionists: making financial sacrifices as well as extending compassion and respect to individuals whom others dehumanize.

To Frost, however, well-intentioned abolitionist behavior means little without heartfelt conversions firmly rooted in religious ethics and Christian love. Appropriately enough, Frost begins the conversion process with the Sunday school pupils. Mrs. Chester realizes that her pupils must, to differing degrees, reform their hearts. At one extreme, Kate confidently insists that she loves all (27). Jane voices a more moderate stance, admitting that she finds it difficult to love the racists who pinch her, pull her hair, or make faces at her (25). At the other extreme, Adeline adamantly argues for the impossibility of loving all, insists on disliking people for their appearance, and pronounces that she cares nothing about the unhappiness she inflicts upon those whom she dislikes (25). Adeline's sentiments receive the sharpest critique from Mrs. Chester: "So disagreeable, Adeline! Did you ever know a person about whom you could find nothing to love—in whose whole character there was no redeeming quality? I do not think that God ever made such a person" (24). Yet Mrs. Chester identifies each girl's need to undergo a conversion: "Your hearts need to be changed by the influence of the Holy Spirit; you must be renewed, born again, before you can enjoy the true spirit of Christian love" (26). Frost suggests that only this true spirit will serve abolitionist principles.

Having established the premise by which the children must live, Frost demonstrates how Kate upholds this Christian-abolitionist love ethos. Mrs. Chester invites her Sunday school class to an overnight stay at the country house, "Clover Side," and she bids the girls to control their behavior: "I hope . . . that each little girl will try . . . to see how much happiness she can make for others. . . . Try to govern your dislikes, and they will not appear so great" (56). While Mrs. Chester voices the principles, Kate enacts them, which inspires her peers to change. First, realizing that Adeline and her classmates resent Jane's participation in the class trip, Kate asks Jane to travel with her. Kate explains that she and Jane can ride in her father's carriage since "Mr. Chester's rockaway could not accommodate all the party, and while there, she would make it her business to shield Jane from insults and ridicule, in short should be her guardian" (50). Adeline, however, sustains her racial and religious prejudices. Openly irritated that Mrs. Chester invites Jane, Adeline becomes jealous when Mrs. Chester smiles approvingly when Hellen volunteers to ride with Jane and Kate. However, while Hellen begins to implement principles of love toward the racial "other," Adeline remains hostile and cruelly states, "We're waiting for the abolition stage, I suppose," to which the girls respond with laughter (55). Nor does Adeline "govern her dislikes" during lunch. When Mrs. Chadler and the children wonder whether Jane will eat with the class, Mrs. Chester says, "Certainly, she is one of my class, and is to be treated in all respects, like the rest, while she stays" (60). Kate and Hellen sit on either side of Jane and "ingeniously managed to keep Jane from hearing the unkind remarks that were being made at her expense" (61). However, Adeline refuses to sit at the table, announcing: "I don't eat with niggers!" (61). Rather than remove Jane, Mrs.

Chester, who models Christian love and abolitionism, punishes Adeline's behavior by making her eat in the back parlor (62). From these incidents, the other girls begin to view Kate, not Adeline, as the model to imitate and they begin to welcome Jane, defend her, and invite her on excursions to the dairy and into the woods. Thus, Kate's behavior helps to "free" Jane from prejudice and her peers from religious hypocrisy.

Frost uses Kate and Adeline's responses to Jane as a microcosm for a community that must experience the recognition of the intersection between religion and social relations and the same, slow transformation necessary for the heart to motivate behavior. Like the schoolroom, Frost describes a community's struggle between external behavior and religious principles, encapsulated in the images of the religious revival and abolitionist fair. Mrs. Brooks, an African American woman from the community, gives voice to the conflict. Unlike Susan Brown (Jane's mother), Brooks refuses to send her children to the white Sunday school because she condemns how the power structure uses the Bible to defend slavery and to perpetuate segregation. She, therefore, doubts the religious revival's ability to sustain feelings of acceptance and equality: "It isn't all gold that shines; now mark my word, as soon as the meetin's over, that nigger pew will be sot right up" (75). She is right. Frost illustrates that the revival's impact fades as does white benevolence toward the African American community. The community does not undergo the true conversion that the girls begin to experience. Rather, it reinstitutes segregated church pews that suggest the hypocritical divorcing of religion from racial equality. Frost argues that to end slavery and prejudice, American communities must experience permanent revivals of the heart, which would then lead to truly benevolent actions.

In a text perhaps aimed more at adult rather than juvenile audiences because of its frequent digressions to the community's racial-religious conflicts, Frost nevertheless offers its young readers another glimpse of the young abolitionist female. Like Mary from *The Edinburgh Doll*, Kate and her peers participate in an antislavery fair. Mrs. Chester worries that the excitement over the fair will cloud the children's newly gained religious insights and the reason for holding the fair, to raise funds for an all-black church.[56] Mrs. Chester states:

> This business of the fair troubles me. I had rather the money would be raised in a more quiet manner. It seems too much like the world's way of doing things. We should give from the heart, and not because we can, by giving, purchase a pleasure for ourselves. The children came to me to ask if they might have a table, and very tremblingly I gave my consent. (96–97)

Adeline assists as fortune teller, a commentary on the child's distance from true "faith." Kate, however, offers her young fairgoers tangible testimonials, much like her abolitionist workbag, of slavery. She announces, "Every thing in this corner is *antislavery*. . . . The candy is all made of free labor sugar, and here are antislavery needle-books, and antislavery holders, the dolls too, are all abolitionists; who buys an abolition doll?" (106). Just as Kate's workbag causes some of her peers to recognize slavery's violation of religious principles, so too these tangibles affect her young female customers whose purchases of candy, needle books, and dolls benefit the African American community.

Despite the strength and voice with which she endows Kate, Frost casts her as a flawed abolitionist until she undergoes a true change of heart. Kate and Adeline, models for the need to politicize religion, experience conversions that are chiasmic: Adeline learns to love the "others" she previously looked down upon and Kate realizes her hidden, selfish motives for her benevolence: "I wanted to please you [mother], and be thought a very good child, therefore, I did many things that God would approve, but *not because* he approved them" (152). Having recognized their faults, Adeline and Kate become "active and earnest laborers in the Grove Street School" after Mrs. Chester devotes herself to missionary work (188). Frost suggests that understanding how to use religion to promote good racial politics permits both girls to become truly compassionate and effective community leaders.

Gertrude Lee; or, The Northern Cousin (1856), by M.A.F.—"a lady" from Troy, New York who did *not* win the premium perhaps because of her more subversive, feminist message—represents a complex example of a post–Seneca Falls, post–*Uncle Tom's Cabin* juvenile abolitionist novel with a young female political activist. Recall that Stowe's Eva dies a symbolic death for slavery after she fails to persuade (1) her cousin, Henrique, not to abuse his slave, (2) her mother to free and to educate the slaves, and (3) her father to defend abolitionism. Unlike Stowe, M.A.F. gives readers a different little girl—not a divinely inspired or politically silenced "Eva," but one whose knowledge about slavery comes as part and parcel of her parents' progressive attention to Gertrude's "physical, intellectual, and moral" instruction (10). Consequently, Gertrude successfully abolishes slavery in her extended family both literally (they cease owning slaves) and figuratively (she frees them and herself from the silences imposed on slave owners, children, and women).

Stowe's Eva develops her antislavery sentiment in reaction against her proslavery mother and her deistic father; conversely, Gertrude's parents "spared neither time nor pains, in securing the proper development of her physical, intellectual, and moral nature" (10). M.A.F. stresses that Gertrude's education has created a "thinker" (16) and a talker, characteristics usually given to the boys.[57] Nor do her parents, unlike the St. Clares, silence the reality of slavery. Rather, even before her grandparents invite Gertrude to spend a year with them in Charleston, South Carolina, her mother and father, who moved to Connecticut to sever their ties to the slave-holding South, tell Gertrude about slavery. Her mother, like the abolitionist mother-educators (see chapter 3), takes Gertrude to abolitionist lectures (73) and instills in her the Bible's rejection of slavery. Gertrude states:

> My mother has been my instructor in the Bible, and my father has assisted her, as his time and engagements in business would admit. . . . But for my dear mother, I should have known as little of [the Bible] as you do. She taught me, that slavery was an abomination and a curse, and, fearful lest I should some time or other fall into the same error with her dear friends at the South, she taught me all those passages of Scripture, which show conclusively that slavery is wrong—that it is a sin against God and man. (93–94)

Her mother gives Gertrude a little Bible in which she records her wish that Gertrude become "a diligent student of its holy pages, and an obedient servant to the *Most High*" (29). As a result of her mother's political-religious efforts,

> [t]he downtrodden *slave* was not forgotten in her nightly orisons, and when the morning Sun rode forth . . . she remembered that God caused Him to shine alike upon the "just, and the unjust," the black, and the white; and her heart breathed a prayer, that *HE* would hasten the deliverance of the oppressed. (11)

However, when Gertrude explains to Grace, her ten-year-old cousin, why she rejects slavery, she suggests that her mother's Biblical teachings represent only the first step toward abolitionist thinking. Gertrude's complete awakening requires a mother's teaching, an acknowledgment of her sinful condition, and an independent, firsthand experience with slavery:

> All these [biblical passages] were treasured in my memory, but they never reached my heart and caused me to feel deeply upon the subject until last winter, when it pleased God to open my eyes to my own sinful condition, and to make me, as I trust, his child. Since then I have felt like making the cause of the oppressed, my own. More than ever, since I came to the South, have I realized their awful condition, and felt as if I could mourn and weep over their wrongs. (94)

Thus, like Eliza Follen's "Picnic at Dedham" in which Hal discovers his own abolitionist views when away from his antiabolitionist parents but in the company of his aunt and uncle, Gertrude does so while visiting her proslavery relatives. Consequently, by situating her protagonist in this new environment, M.A.F. suggests that the slaves' liberation will come neither from her prayers nor from divine intervention. Instead, M.A.F. transfers the responsibility for liberating the slaves from God to Gertrude, a young abolitionist who uses her experiences with the religious and political dimensions of abolitionism to free the slaves in her extended family.

Upon her arrival at her grandparent's Charleston plantation, Gertrude shifts from praying for the slaves to behaving in ways that initiate their liberation. For example, Gertrude repeatedly refuses to become another child for whom her grandmother's slave girl must dress and care in preference for "personal independence"

(30). She says "I should be sinning against God were I to give myself up to indo-lence and slothfulness, and allow the powers which He has given me, to become weakened and evenly destroyed, by disuse; whereas they should be strengthened, daily, by reasonable use" (30–31). She enacts the principles she learned from her mother, which M.A.F. documents by narrating a conversation during which Mrs. Lee and Mrs. Howard discuss the economic-religious element of slavery. Unlike Mrs. Howard, whose scorn for labor lends to her defending it, Mrs. Lee quotes Proverbs (xiii: 11; x: 16; and xxi: 25), which encourages work (35). She argues that if the Howards have more work than they can handle, they should hire servants rather than keep slaves. She then states:

> The fact that you own slaves, can never release you from your obligation to God; especially since slavery is in direct opposition to the will of God, and conse-quently a sin against him. It is evident from the nature of your question, that by the commission of this one great sin, you are led insensibly into the commission of a thousand others which grow directly out of it. Labor is honourable; it is enjoined upon us as a duty in the Sacred Scriptures, yet the fact that you own slaves is made an excuse for its omission. (36)

Although Mrs. Lee fails to persuade Mrs. Howard to internalize her politicized religious lesson, she succeeds with Gertrude, whose refusal to have a slave dress her symbolically liberates the slave girl.

However, Gertrude, a child socialized into abolitionist thinking, not only challenges slavery on a personal level, but also socializes and liberates others as she breaks the silence about slavery.[58] Unlike Eva, who encounters difficulty per-suading others of slavery's wrongs, Gertrude successfully influences those around her, beginning with her Southern cousins, raised "to be seen, but not heard" when it comes to slavery. By persuading her cousins (sickly from having been waited upon by slaves) to wake early, to learn to dress themselves, and to run in the fields with her before the adults awaken, Gertrude destroys one lit-eral silence. The Howard children make "an attempt to be active and industri-ous" (55): Grace runs and dresses herself and Arthur learns to paint nature scenes. When Arthur states, "I would give anything, Gertrude, if I had been brought up as you have" (66), he probably refers to his newly acquired indepen-dence and freedom because as Gertrude breaks their dependence on slaves, she liberates the slaves from some of their imposed labor and her cousins from their enslavement to slavery.

Moreover, M.A.F.'s feminist inclinations surface as she creates Gertrude in the image of her abolitionist foremothers who transcended their designated pri-vate sphere by publicly lecturing to mixed audiences to inspire antislavery beliefs. While outdoors and away from the adults during their early morning excursions, Gertrude initiates religious and secular discussions that awaken Arthur and Grace's consciousness about slavery. For example, while the children wait for breakfast after their first morning run, Gertrude notices an advertisement in their grandfather's newspaper for the sale of slaves between ages of "twelve to twenty-five" (68). Gertrude's shock at the separation of parents from children sparks Arthur to remember the loss of "Bridget, our nursery maid' (69) sold away from her husband and two children to pay his grandfather's debts. Arthur recalls how the adults

> turned their heads the other way to hide the tears, and [tried] to act as though they did not care any thing about it. I remember that I wondered then, why they did so, but I have just solved the problem. . . . It was because they were afraid I would ask them if it wasn't wrong to sell her away from her children. (70–71)

As a result of this discussion, Arthur realizes that the adults have kept him and his little sister intentionally ignorant of slavery and have silenced the children's questions to prevent queries about their own actions. When Arthur learns that the Bible denounces slavery, he acknowledges his ignorance and the conflict between his instinct and the adult's silence:

> I don't know much about the Bible . . . but something right here in my heart has *whispered* a thousand times that slavery is wrong, though I never *dared* say a word about it. I never heard *anyone speak* against it, before you. But if the Bible says it is wrong, Gertrude, why don't the ministers preach that it is wrong? They say it is right, and they own slaves, too. Our minister has four. (71–72, emphasis added)

Although Gertrude cannot explain this contradiction between the minister's behavior and Christ's teachings, Arthur exposes the code of silence. Gertrude's presence breaks it and allows the Howard children to progress from whispering, to speaking, to wondering "what I could do to hasten their emancipation" (95), and to challenging the adults' self-imposed silence about their proslavery beliefs.

Having helped her cousins recognize their imposed ignorance, Gertrude advocates ending the slaves' imposed ignorance. Gertrude's desire initially stems from her belief that it is her duty to enable the slave to read the Bible. However, M.A.F. suggests a shift from religious to political motivation[59] and from silence to voice when Gertrude's discussions with her cousins help her to realize the adult's political motives for keeping the slaves ignorant. Gertrude recalls:

> My mother took me to hear a fugitive slave lecture, last winter, and he told what trials he had in escaping from slavery, because he was so ignorant. . . . My mother explained to me, after we went home, the reason why slaves were not allowed to read, and told me that I had good proof in the story of this man, that ignorance of a way of escape was all that could keep men in bondage, and that even this sometimes fails. (73–74)

The children soon realize that masters do not educate the slaves because they recognize the power of knowledge and that literate slaves would flee (74). The children cannot rest knowing this and spend an hour each day educating the slaves (75). However, unlike Eva who educates Mammy against her mother's will, Gertrude, fearful "that even so slight an interference with their arrangements, without permission, might be displeasing to her friends" (56–57), asks her grandfather's permission to teach the "house" slave children to read. Although the grandfather thinks their behavior admirable, the other Howards criticize him for this "*strange whim* . . . which had induced him to consent to such a gross impropriety" (77) and "eagerly watched, as though to ascertain whether much evil could be the result of one year's instruction" (77).

Gertrude—and eventually her cousins—have some success with awakening the adults' consciences; but what eventually jolts the family into acknowledging slavery's evils are not Little Eva-like tears, locks of hair, or death, but Gertrude's *shout*. She witnesses Kate, her African American friend who was kidnapped in Connecticut, being sold at a Charleston slave auction. M.A.F. describes the pivotal scene as follows:

> Gertrude looked at her [the fourteen-year-old slave girl] steadily as they neared the court-house; their eyes met, and a mutual recognition took place. The pleading, beseeching, yet utterly hopeless look of the doomed girl, was enough to break a heart of stone. Gertrude screamed aloud, and would have sprung from the carriage, had not her uncle held her back. With a look of unutterable anguish, she explained, "*and can I not save her!* She is free. I have known her from my infancy." "Who is she?" "She is the daughter of a widow woman who lives in our neighborhood in Connecticut." "Are you sure?" "Yes, certainly I am." (81)

Gertrude's public shout at the Charleston slave market is perhaps the loudest noise in the novel and helps to break the ultimate silence about slavery. Gertrude does not have the political influence or the money to make the necessary maneuvers to free Kate, but her shout and subsequent persuasive skills (she "begged her uncle to buy [Kate], and rescue her from such a fate" [82]) serve as the instruments to free Kate and many more.

Gertrude's shout presses the adults to examine their stance on slavery and to move from silence to speech. The scene at the slave market causes them to shift from watching for the dangers of educating the slaves to gaining increased compassion for the slave. Furthermore, Arthur and Gertrude notice a change in the adults and Arthur now speaks openly about slavery. He realizes:

> They gave him their ears, and offered no opposition to his views, which was more than he had even hoped for. He could not account for it, for he was well aware that his punishment for such an offense, six months before, would have been a severe chastisement, and perhaps a stern prohibition of the use of his tongue on such a dangerous subject. (106)

Ironically, the adults no longer silence Arthur because they can no longer silence themselves. Mr. and Mrs. Howard initially do not "disclose to the other this state of feeling, lest it should be disapproved, and made the subject of ridicule and reproach" (88). Burdened with guilty consciences and the image of the enslaved child, they shift from individual silence to a family confessional. At a family gathering, the grandfather and young Mr. Howard divulge their changed hearts and discuss slavery's violation of American religious and political principles (115–20). Mr. Howard also takes personal responsibility: "WE are the authors of the dreadful *ignorance* which prevails on this plantation, and which has incapacitated the slaves for independent life, and *we* must remove it" (121). The adults come to the same realization as the children did much earlier—that the slaves can take even better care of themselves when free (92). Unlike Stowe's Eva who dies before her father writes the papers to free his slaves, or George who arrives too late to free Uncle Tom, Gertrude's voice brings change: the Howards educate and liberate their slaves, move North, and adopt abolitionist principles.

Ultimately, Gertrude's action also frees herself. M.A.F. specifically states that Gertrude was a thinker and talker because she asked her parents questions and received a response. Her year-long stay in the South could have undermined her earlier training, as it does to Miss Palmiter, the children's Northern teacher who adopts proslavery sentiments until Gertrude's presence and influence help her to return to her abolitionist beliefs. The fact that another Northerner, Miss Palmiter, loses her voice while living in Charleston, makes Gertrude's ability to retain her voice all the more important for securing her independence. Thus, M.A.F. calls to mind Angelina Grimké's *An Appeal to the Women of the Nominally Free States*, which establishes a connection between women's voice and freedom and states that if the patriarchy denies women the right to act, it would make women "the white slaves of the North" (qtd. in Yellin 35). Therefore, Grimké advocated that women speak out publicly against slavery because "to be free is to act, to open one's lips in voice and in hope" (35).

The image of forceful, young, American girl abolitionists like Eva, Mary, Kate, and Gertrude garnered such popularity that it influenced English authors, who had, twenty years earlier, offered domestic abolitionists the first examples of abolitionist juvenile literature. On the eve of the American Civil War, British children received a lesson in American racial politics through the image of a young, abolitionist American girl. In her small book entitled *Little Laura, The Kentucky Abolitionist: An Address to the Young Friends of the Slave* (1859), written for children from the British Islands who want to help the American slave (1), Anna H. Richardson records the true story of young Laura B.'s abolitionist efforts. Laura's family works to abolish slavery by printing an antislavery newspaper. However, when the proslavery mob attempts to silence this expression by burning the press (2), supportive neighbors help the family rebuild it and the newspaper offices at which time Laura "learned to handle type, and was as busy as any one in helping her dear father" (3). By handling the type, Laura participates in the construction and perpetuation of antislavery voices. Furthermore, this activity enables Laura, to an extent, to enter into a public, political discourse that challenges patriarchal ideas of separate spheres.

Richardson, however, reports that Laura also engages fully in a public, political discourse. When Laura becomes physically ill from working at the press, the family sends her to school, where some children decide not to associate with the "abolitionist." Laura does what domestic abolitionists like Hannah Townsend in *The Anti-Slavery Alphabet* tells children to do—to help end slavery by speaking to their peers. Through Laura's frequent discussions with her schoolmates, they begin to express pity for the slave (6) and to adopt abolitionist ideas such that "the odium attached to the word 'Abolitionist' has been assuaged in some circles" (7). By negating the negative implications associated with "abolitionism," Laura again changes the public's perception of a political language. Richardson presents her readers with a child who speaks first through the "silent" medium of the newspaper and then through the public medium—much like her foremothers who challenged the ideology of separate spheres by writing for abolitionist newspapers and speaking publicly despite criticism.

Richardson's narrative transforms the private family affair and the behavior of one model child into a concern for young British readers, aware that the British formerly held slaves (9). She asks the readers to hear Laura's story and "ask if YOU cannot assist her worthy family in their efforts to set the Negro free, in at least one of the Slave States" (5). Richardson adds:

> We should like you, dear young friends, to talk over this matter with your parents and teachers, and if they *quite* approve of your collecting small sums on the slave's behalf, it would give us very great pleasure to forward these to Mr. B. as "collected by the children of England, Scotland, and Ireland, in remembrance of his departed daughter." A great many little sums put together would form a large one, and we are much inclined to believe that in making this kind effort, you will be led to think more and more of the suffering slave. (9)

Richardson urges the children to break the silence—"to talk over this matter with your parents and teachers"—and to act. Through contributions to the family and their cause, "very many of you might learn to walk in [Laura's] footsteps" (9). Thus, Richardson presses children to act like Laura, an American heroine who uses her voice to foster abolitionist principles.

By addressing the popular question, What could children do to end slavery? domestic abolitionists politicized childhood as they intermingled child subjects with abolitionist messages and abolitionist agendas. Children could pray, raise money, talk, and even shout to effect the changes necessary to restore American principles of democracy and equality. Perhaps the greater anxiety that these women reveal was the potential to do nothing, an alternative they clearly rejected. These domestic abolitionists suggest that when "fathers," politicians, and petitions fail to bring the desired change, women will not hesitate to spur tears that inspire activism, to redefine histories that challenge patriotism, and to inspire children to change the status quo. Furthermore, by giving voice to specifically female protagonists, these women validate their own participation in abolitionist politics. If young American girls could effect change, imagine what women could do.

Notes

INTRODUCTION

1. The primary archives include: Duke University, the American Antiquarian Society, the Massachusetts Historical Society, the Boston Public Library, the Library Company of Philadelphia, Harvard's Houghton, Schlessinger, and Weidner Libraries, the Schumburg Collection, and the University of Madison Wisconsin's Cairns Collection.

2. Donnarae MacCann also claims that juvenile works for children between 1830 and 1865 were "scarce" and that "[i]t was a minuscule number [of abolitionists] who entered the children's book field, and those who did rarely wrote an abolitionist narrative or textbook that was not to some degree ambivalent in its attitude towards Blacks" ("White Supremacy" 26; 126).

3. MacCann briefly discusses Child's "Jumbo and Zairee" (51–53), "The Little White Lamb and the Little Black Lamb" (54), and "Lariboo" (54–55); Julia Coleman and Matilda Thompson's works in *The Child's Anti-Slavery Book* (56–60); and Follen's *May Morning and New Year's Eve* (61–62).

4. See also Ann T. Ackerman's dissertation "Victorian Ideology and British Children's Literature, 1850–1914" (1984), which discusses examples of slavery with regards to abolition and imperialism (289–305).

5. See also Anne Scott MacLeod, "Children's Literature and American Culture: 1820–1860" (1978); "Nineteenth-Century Families in Juvenile Fiction" (1988); and *American Childhood: Essays on Children's Literature of the Nineteenth and Twentieth Centuries* (1994).

6. The twelve women in Kelly's study are: Maria Cummins, Gilman, Caroline Lee Hentz, Maria Jane Holmes, Maria McIntosh, Sarah Parton, Catherine Maria Sedgwick, E. D. E. N. Southworth, Harriet Beecher Stowe, Mary Virginia Terhune, Susan Warner, and Augusta Evans Wilson (viii).

7. For information on Elizabeth Margaret Chandler, see: Bowerman, "Elizabeth Margaret Chandler," in *Dictionary of American Biography*; *Allibone's Critical Dictionary of*

English Literature. British and American Authors Living and Deceased from the Earliest Accounts of the Latter Half of the Nineteenth Century; Dillon's two articles, "Elizabeth Margaret Chandler and the Spread of Antislavery Sentiment to Michigan" and "Elizabeth Margaret Chandler," in *Notable American Women, 1607–1950: A Biographical Dictionary;* Hersh's *The Slavery of Sex: Feminist Abolitionist in America* (74); Kunitz and Haycraft, *American Authors, 1600–1900: A Biographical Dictionary of American Literature;* and Lutz, *Crusade for Freedom: Women of the Antislavery Movement* (8–10).

　　8. For information on Eliza Lee Cabot Follen, see MacLeod, *A Moral Tale* (111–13); Schlesinger, "Two Early Harvard Wives: Eliza Farrar and Eliza Follen" (June 1965); Moe, "Eliza Cabot Lee Follen" (1980), and MacCann, "The White Supremacy Myth in Juvenile Books about Blacks, 1830–1900" (141–45).

　　9. Women's conservative or liberal stance regarding women's sphere helped determine the activities in which they participated. The most radical and liberal women defied tradition and became public speakers/lecturers to both single-sex and mixed audiences. Other liberal forms of public involvement included activities such as fund raising, publishing texts, lobbying, and petition-signing drives (Bogin and Yellin 2;12). Since petitioning was a constitutional right (Bogin and Yellin 13) when women did not have the right to vote, Boston and Philadelphia women "[u]sing the only tool available to them for reaching the representatives of the people, . . . helped force abolition onto the nation's political agenda" (Bogin and Yellin 13; see also Soderlund 77). Van Broekhoven suggests that women began petitioning in 1835 but that "mass petitioning campaigns by American women were still new in 1837" (180; 181). These petitions emphasized that women were making familial, moral, and apolitical requests. Yet, "[d]espite the religious and deferential language, women's organizing and petitioning against slavery quickly became controversial" because women were moving outside their appropriate sphere (Van Broekhoven 184; 185–88). However, the increasing political pressure in the 1840s for legal legislation to end slavery reduced female petitioning because then it was seen as women overtly acting according to political rather than moral tactics (Van Broekhoven 190–91; 196–98).

　　10. Women encountered mob violence at the 1838 convention and were burned out of Pennsylvania Hall (Yellin, *Abolitionist* 16).

　　11. Bogin and Yellin (8); See also Lapsansky (222–30).

　　12. Catherine Beecher "condemned the sisters for overstepping the boundaries of the female sphere and for attempting to usurp the authority of the clergy" (Williams, "Female" 173).

　　13. The Massachusetts Association of Congregational Ministers issued a pastoral letter denouncing the Grimkés' behavior as "a scandalous offense against propriety and decency" (Hansen, "Boston" 53).

　　14. See Bogin and Yellin (9–10) and Swerdlow (41).

　　15. Although Bogin and Yellin argue that abolitionist women wrote and published texts like speeches, pamphlets, constitutions, and resolutions (2), they ignore the existence of juvenile works by women.

　　16. Coultrap-McQuin states that women's literary works "were supposed to be used for the entertainment of others; in this sense at least, her literary career did not challenge the expectations of her sphere" (14).

17. See Mary Kelley, *Private Woman, Public Stage: Literary Domesticity in Nineteenth-Century America* (1984).

18. See Shaw's "The Pliable Rhetoric of Domesticity" for a discussion of the increased presence of issues related to motherhood in antebellum periodicals (76–77).

19. See George Boas, *The Cult of Childhood* (1966).

20. Anne MacLeod argues that the intense concern that "public virtue depends on the character of private citizens" not only appears repeatedly in the juvenile literature, but also affirms this period's intense belief in the ability of literature to shape character (*American Childhood* 89, 90).

21. Lynn Rosenthal argues that, for the British, "the development of children's literature as a genre was an essentially middle-class phenomenon that paralleled the emergence of a sufficiently large middle-class reading public, whose increased sense of its own leisure extended to the child. Although lower-class children were sometimes described in the literature (frequently as objects of charity), it was with the formation of the character of the middle class that writers for children were primarily concerned" (xiii–xiv).

22. Barbara Welter writes: "Anti-intellectualism was implicit in the cult which exalted women as creatures who did not use logic or reason, having a surer, purer road to the truth—the road of the heart" (71). A virtuous woman, therefore, remained at home and affected moral development through heartfelt, rather than intellectual, persuasion.

CHAPTER 1.
DOMESTIC ABOLITIONISTS AND THEIR PUBLISHERS

1. Smedman argues that Godey held a separatist mentality "[b]ecause, according to its editorial policy, *Godey's Ladies Book* abstained from politics and economics as subjects inappropriate for women, it did not enter into the controversy between the States; thus, an acknowledged power bypassed its opportunity to influence action" (210).

2. Charlotte Tucker, the daughter of an authority on Indian finances and a mother with connections to James Boswell, eventually became a missionary and traveled to India, where she continued to write extensively (Crawford et al. 399).

3. Clara Balfour suggests that Amelia Opie participated extensively in humanitarian efforts and worked for the antislavery cause (qtd. in Ackerman 295). According to the *NUC*, American publishers frequently published her prolific writings. See also Margaret C. Gillespie, *History and Trends* (90–91).

4. Elisabeth Inglis-Jones and Elizabeth Harden concur that Edgeworth published *Popular Tales* for the middle and lower classes (Inglis-Jones 84; Harden 40).

5. According to Cutt, "Mrs. Sherwood substitutes the Evangelical assumption that all learning is of necessity rooted and directed towards religion. Education thus becomes preparation for eternity; rational and moral elements are subordinated to lessons of faith, resignation, and implicit obedience to the will of God; and the material concerns of everyday life are thinned out" (37–38).

6. W. & J. Gimlan, from Massachusetts, also published this title as *Dazee; or, the Recaptured African* (1822).

7. The catalogue printed in Phelps's 1834 edition states, "A. Phelps, keeps constantly on hand, for sale, at his bookstore [in] Greenfield, Mass., a general assortment of interesting books for children and youth" (lower cover).

8. Anna H. Richardson published *Little Laura, the Kentucky Abolitionist: An Address to the Young Friends of the Slave* in 1859.

9. We can no longer recognize Drysdale as the first American woman to publish abolitionist juvenile literature because Fredrika Teute has documented that Margaret Bayard Smith published "Old Betty" in 1823.

10. According to Bingham, the ASSU

> published hundreds of volumes as well as thousands of tracts, magazines, and journals, which generally were cheerful in tone and provided instruction about religious matters, the importance of charity to the poor, kindness to animals, the dangers of idleness, and the virtues of work. Far from being subtle, the material reflected the spirit of reform which was abroad in the land and the hope the future held for good, hardworking people. (*Fifteen Centuries* 156)

11. In April 1829, Garrison became co-editor with Benjamin Lundy of the Baltimore-based *Genius of Universal Emancipation.* However, when he broke with Lundy's support for gradualism, he left the *Genius* to start the *Liberator,* which he published weekly until December 31, 1865, despite repeated financial difficulties (Cain 4–5; Grimké *William* 141–42; Goodheart & Hawkins 41).

12. Although an unfair comparison, John Scott argues that Garrison's "books and pamphlets and newspapers reached, relatively speaking, only a handful of people" as opposed to Stowe's *Uncle Tom's Cabin,* which reached the hundreds of thousands (119).

13. Mitford's *Our Village: Sketches of Rural Character and Scenery* appeared in American presses as late as 1871 in Philadelphia.

14. Garrison may have been instrumental in allowing even more women to express their sentiments when he published the *Slave's Friend* from 1836–1838. This monthly, pocket-sized publication was available at the Anti-Slavery Office on 144 Nassau Street in New York and was also widely distributed by mail. As Yolanda Federici states:

> The general informational articles on a variety of subjects, such as the invention of the printing press, travel, railroads, ended with a tract-like statement against slavery. Some of the traveler's accounts were in dialogue. These were heart-rending reports of the mistreatment of black children, called "colored"; what happened to recaptured fugitive slaves whose children were born in prison; stories of slave traders who stole as many as one hundred adults and children from their native land to be sold in the United States where many arrived disease-ridden after the dreadful voyage. (1)

However, the absence of signatures in these articles makes it difficult, if not impossible, to determine which expressed women authors' political sentiments.

15. *The Casket* later became know as *Graham's American Magazine,* which published some of America's literary giants.

16. The publication history of Lundy's *Genius of Universal Emancipation* proves interesting and complex. Started in Mount Pleasant, Ohio, in January 1821, the lack of money and a press prompted Lundy to move to Greeneville, Tennessee, where he published and distributed the *Genius* amid proslavery hostility from September 1821 until August 1824. Hoping for more subscriptions and/or wider circulation, he moved the paper to Baltimore. Although suspended from January to September 1829, the newspaper resumed with Garrison as co-editor until March 1830. Once Lundy became its sole editor, the *Genius* changed locations several times: from Baltimore to Washington D.C. to Philadelphia to Lowell, Illinois, and was interspersed with suspensions until Lundy's death in August 1839 (Del Porto 49–69; Dillon 45–260; Dillon, *Benjamin* 245–60).

17. Garrison's feminist beliefs and his opposition to using persuasion and nonresistance instead of political action caused a rift in the American Anti-Slavery Society in 1840 (Cain 127). As a result, Lewis Tappan and others formed the American and Foreign Anti-Slavery Society. See also Garrison's speech, "Women's Rights" (Cain 132–33).

18. This reciprocation between Lundy and Garrison seemed a common trend. Phillip Lapsansky argues that Lundy's *Genius* was the first American newspaper to publish the image of the kneeling female slave in Chandler's May 1830 edition of the "Ladies Repository." Two years later, Garrison used this image in the *Liberator's* "Ladies Department" (205–206).

19. In "The Sugarplums," "Oh Press Me Not to Taste Again," and "Christmas," Chandler depicts children fighting slavery by refusing to consume slave-made goods, a plan that Jones reveals Chandler also advocated to women (2).

20. Chandler's works reached an even larger audience when many were set to music (Jones 15). See reprints in George Clark's *The Liberty Minstrel* (1845).

21. Though Townsend's parental origins remain unclear, historians agree that she married Daniel Longstreth on December 25, 1832, and had seven children (Jordan 1536; Jones 84).

22. Merrihew & Thompson also published Elizabeth Lloyd and the 1839 *Proceedings of the Anti-Slavery Convention of American Women.*

23. See Hansen's *Strained Sisterhood* (76–77).

24. See Horton, *Black Bostonians* (40–42, 46, 50).

25. See Hansen's essays in Yellin's *Abolitionist Sisterhood* (47–48) and in *Strained Sisterhood* (17).

26. Papashvily states: "Mrs. Follen wrote juveniles, teachers' manuals and poetry, translated Fénelon [a French religious philosopher], served actively in the antislavery movement, edited a children's magazine, collected the works of her deceased husband in twenty-five volumes and tutored her son and other young men for entrance to Harvard University" (46–47). See also Debra Gold Hansen, *Strained Sisterhood* (77, 78).

27. Schlesinger reveals that *The Child's Friend* "cost one dollar and fifty cents, which at this time no doubt limited its subscribers to the well-to-do" (164). However, by 1857, the four hundred subscribers paid two dollars per issue [1.5 (1844): title page; 29 (1857): 240].

28. Tebble argues that Crosby and Nicholas published many children's books and purchased Jewett's business in 1857 (437).

29. Jewett may have started the trend of juvenile adaptations of Stowe's *Uncle Tom's Cabin*. The Cairns Collection at the University of Madison, Wisconsin, has an extensive collection of the work's nineteenth- and twentieth-century international juvenile adaptations.

30. Jacob Blanck made this identification from information included in "Topics of the Week" in London's *Literary Gazette, A Weekly Journal* ("Harriet" *BAL*).

31. Before *Uncle Tom's Cabin*, Stowe seems to have published only one other children's book, *Primary Geography for Children on an Improved Plan* (1833). In 1855, Stowe authorized its British and American republication as *A New Geography for Children*. After *Uncle Tom's Cabin*, however, Stowe published children's literature regularly (Lenz 338–50).

32. Jewett published *The Lamplighter Picture Book* at his Boston and Cleveland branches and Sheldon, Lamport, and Blackeman published it in New York. This book's blend of small-print prose designed for older readers and large-print poetry for younger readers closely follows the format in *Pictures and Stories from Uncle Tom's Cabin*.

33. Biographical information on Thompson remains elusive. If cataloguers are correct, the Julia Colman who contributed to this book may be the same one who was later very active in the temperance movement. According to Carol Mattingly, Colman led the Department of Temperance Literature for the Women's Christian Temperance Union from 1875–90, gave public lectures across the country, and wrote over five hundred books and pamphlets (68). See also Bordin 197 n105.

34. Like Jewett, Lee and Shephard's business failed in the 1857 panic and due to the deaths of two partners. Lee eventually joined forces with Crosby & Nicholas. But according to Tebble, "[Lee] was not particularly interested in the Unitarian religious books which were their stock in trade. Lee was far more interested in their children's books, particularly those written by 'Oliver Optic.' Under his stimulation, this part of the list was increased sharply, so that he had more than a hundred titles on it and fifty-two others on the press by the end of 1860" (421). However in February 1, 1862, Lee & Shepard resumed business.

35. See "American Tract Society" in *American Anti-Slavery Society Annual Report* (1859), which documents the American Tract Society's 1857 resolution to exclude all political references to slavery from its publications (171).

36. Historians disagree about the origins of the Eliza story. John Scott argues that Stowe heard the story directly from Rankin, who "was famous in antislavery circles because he was the first person in Ohio to befriend and give aid to a fugitive black woman called Eliza Harris" (57). However, Russell Nye argues, "The true origin of Eliza crossing the ice probably lies in Mrs. Stowe's narrative blend of her own experiences, the numerous stories of similar escapes she gathered from Van Zandt, [Levi] Coffin, and the abolition journals, the Cincinnati incident from Mrs. Bailey's magazine [*A Friend of Youth*, an antislavery magazine], and perhaps Rankin's story of 1834" (101).

37. Other vice presidents included: A. A. Guthrie, Reverend G. W. Perkins, Reverend E. Goodman, Reverend J. Blanchard, and Reverend C. B. Boynton, who wrote *A Journey through Kansas* (1855).

38. The 1852 directors list included: William Lee, A. E. D. Tweed, A. S. Merill, S. C. Foster, and Dr. James Walker. Walker met Theodore Weld and was an agent for the American Bible Society. He edited the abolitionist newspaper, *The Watchman of the Valley,* from 1840–42 (Coyle 664). The following men, excluded from the first list, were later directors who represented diverse religious orientations: Reverend H. M. Storrs and Reverend H. Bushnell (Congregationalist); Reverend R. H. Pollack and Reverend J. J. Blaisdell (Presbyterians); and Professor M. Stone (Baptist).

39. Stowe based Rachel and Simeon Halliday in *Uncle Tom's Cabin* on the Coffins (Scott, *Woman* 60).

40. See John Rankin's *A Remedy for Universalism* (1848) and Ron W. Wilson's *The True Missionary Spirit* (1847).

41. See Reuben Diamond Mussey's *Essay on the Influence of Tobacco on Life and Health* (1839).

42. See Miss E. T. Knowlton's *Poems for Children* (1849).

43. Weed, ["Advertisement"] on the back page of *Aunt Sally;* and Weed, ["Advertisement"] on the back page of *God against Slavery.*

44. The American Antiquarian Society's copy has the following inscription: "Presented to Ola, by his teacher Clara Brett. 1st prize, in 2nd class."

45. The American Antiquarian Society's copy has the following inscription: "Norman Rob, a present from his grandmother, S. Comstock."

46. Frost's success with *Gospel Fruits* may have prompted her to publish *The Children of the Covenant; or, The Christian Family* (1867) with the Western Tract Society.

47. The back pages of Reverend William Patton's *What It Is to Preach the Gospel* (185?) and *The Constitution of the American Reform Tract and Book Society, with Reasons for Its Organization* (1853) indicate that the ARTBS's depository was located at 180 Walnut Street. Therefore, it must have moved to 28 West Fourth Street some time after 1853.

48. See the American Antiquarian Society's catalogue record for *Not a Minute To Spare.*

CHAPTER 2.
SENTIMENTALIZED VICTIMS AND ABOLITIONIST TEARS

1. Qtd. in Dudley, *Slavery: Opposing Viewpoints* (207).

2. According to his discussion about the relationship between reading and material objects in antebellum New England, Zboray states: "Printed handkerchiefs commonly featured a wide range of texts like almanacs, broadsides, elegies, hymns, maps, primers and even words and music for the "Little Eva Song; Uncle Tom's Guardian Angel" (594).

3. Ammidon sent similar versions of this letter to the Portland FASS (July 14, 1835); the New York FASS (July 21, 1835); the Concord, NH FASS (July 22, 1835); and the Putnam, Ohio, FASS (July 22, 1835) (Female Anti-Slavery Society Papers, MHS).

4. Ann Douglas claims: "The tragedy of nineteenth-century northeastern society is not the demise of Calvinist patriarchal structures, but rather the failure of a viable, sexually diversified culture to replace them. 'Feminization' inevitably guaranteed, not simply the loss of the finest values contained in Calvinism, but the continuation of male hegemony in different guises. . . . Sentimentalism, with its tendency to obfuscate the visible dynamics of development, heralded the cultural sprawl that has increasingly characterized post-Victorian life" (13).

5. Tompkins argues that many literary critics have claimed that these women authors "dish[ed] out weak-minded pap to nourish the prejudices of an ill educated and underemployed female readership" (124).

6. See *Good Little Girls Book* (1848) and *The Happy Changes; or, Pride and Its Consequences* (1854). Sarah Josepha Hale's fictional sketches of children who exemplified "models of virtuous living" were to reform erring readers who encountered the amorality inherent in the turbulent society (MacLeod, *Moral Tale* 15–16, 17, 21; see also MacLeod, "Children's Literature . . .").

7. Angela Davis cites the example of Jenny Proctor, who remembered working in the cotton patch when she turned ten (*Women, Race, and Class* 6).

8. Signed W.M. in the *Liberator's* "Juvenile Department," September 3, 1831, and republished in Garrison's *Juvenile Poems, for the Use of Free American Children of Every Complexion* (1835). I have been unable to verify whether W.M. was a woman; however, since women wrote most of the poems submitted to Garrison's "Juvenile Department" and since the poem employs similar strategies and images as subsequent works, I conjecture a female authorship.

9. Eliza Follen reissued her books several times after her husband's death to support herself; however, because copies remain unavailable, I cannot confirm that these 1846 poems also appeared in the 1831 and 1848 editions.

10. This poem appears as "Lines in Hearing of the Terror of the Children of the Slaves at the Thought of Being Sold" in Follen's *The Liberty Cap* (1846). Furthermore, in 1855, Follen republished it as "On Hearing of the Sadness of the Slave-Children from the Fear of Being Sold" when printed for the Anti-Slavery Tract for gratuitous distribution for the American Anti-Slavery Society (8).

11. This also appears as "The Slave Boy's Wish" in Julia Colman's "Little Lewis" (1859), which makes an explicit reference to Follen (29).

12. Follen's poem "Lord Deliver" casts a slave calling on God to grant him/her the right to remain in America as a free person. Follen suggests a hopeful, not denunciatory, tone.

13. Catherine O'Connell argues, "The white reader can feel the suffering of an Other only when the Other has become them" (34).

14. Catherine O'Connell suggests that *Uncle Tom's Cabin* "does not rest with modeling a sympathetic response for readers, but attempts to involve them emotionally in the scene; they must cry too for the sentimental message to be effectively transmitted" (16).

15. Originally published in the *Liberator* in 1831 and credited to E.T.C. It has a companion poem, "The White Infant's Reply to the Little Slave" by C.T.E. and published in

the *Liberator* in 1831. The inversion of the first and last initials of the author's name may have been a printing error. Both were republished in Garrison's *Juvenile Poems, for the Use of Free American Children of Every Complexion* (1835).

16. The adult version has forty-nine chapters, but this juvenile version only abridges chapters 1–15.

17. Jewett may have anticipated widespread circulation based on the success of the adult *Lamplighter*, which sold "40,000 copies in its first month alone and 60,000 more before it had been out for a year" (Baym, "Introduction," *Lamplighter* ix).

18. This work's format resembles *Pictures and Stories for Uncle Tom's Cabin*, which Jewett also published. Jewett used larger-font poems to increase their accessibility to the young reader as he suggests in the preface to *Pictures and Stories for Uncle Tom's Cabin* ([2]).

19. Jean Fagan Yellin notes that "The Abolitionist Emblem" also appeared in the juvenile magazine *The Slave's Friend*, but she interprets the image as a violated mother (*Women and Sisters* 15). Thus far, no similar emblem using a slave child has surfaced.

20. See also Cousin Ann's "Henry Box Brown," which the *National Anti-Slavery Standard* recognized as an antislavery work based on the *Narrative of Henry Box Brown* (1849). Rather than giving excerpts from Brown's autobiography, Cousin Ann uses the third person and recounts the story of a Richmond slave, Henry Brown, who worries about his wife and children sold to the Carolinas (22). Brown ultimately decides to run away, hiding in a small box during a trip to Philadelphia, the city of brotherly love. Although Brown's difficult journey ends in freedom, Cousin Ann emphasizes Brown's unhappiness because he could not forget the violation to the family bonds.

21. "The Slave" was originally published in the *Liberator's Juvenile Department* on March 3, 1832, and signed D.C.C. from Portland (34).

22. This work is most likely by a woman because it appears in the same volume as *Jemmy and His Mother* (1858), authored by an anonymous, "Madame" (33). Furthermore, its female narrator is consistent with a strategy that other domestic abolitionists employ.

23. Jones claims, "fewer than two out of three black children survived to the age of ten in the years between 1850 and 1860" (35). See also Fox-Genovese's discussion of slave children's deaths (323–34).

24. In Fox-Genovese's discussion of infanticide, she claims, "Perhaps that knowledge [the view of the child as the master's property] led some of the more desperate to feel that, by killing an infant they loved, they would be in some way reclaiming it as their own" (324).

25. See Deborah White's discussion of the "mammy" in *Ain't I a Woman?* (56–61).

26. See Fox-Genovese's discussion of African motherhood (322). See also Deborah White's discussion in *Ain't I a Woman?* (106–108).

27. Lynn Lyerly argues: "Through [Evangelical] religion, slave women defined motherhood as a sacred relation and not as an economic activity" (203). Lyerly also suggests that Methodist preachers defended the slave mother-child relationship because "[m]otherhood in general was viewed by Methodists as a sacred office, and the love of a mother for her child was the closest earthly analog to the unconditional love of God for humanity" (218).

28. This poem was first published on January 21, 1832, in the *Liberator* and then republished in Garrison's *Juvenile Poems, for the Use of Free American Children of Every Complexion* (1835). This is not the same poem as Frances Ellen Watkins Harper's "The Slave Mother: A Tale of the Ohio," based on Stowe's Eliza from *Uncle Tom's Cabin*.

29. Phyllis Moe states "the ensuing idyll of family life, which includes stories told during a party, suffers from a contrived plot and the heavy-handed contrast of good and evil so typical of early nineteenth-century children's literature" (*American Women Writers* 59)

30. See Deborah White's discussion in *Ain't I a Woman?* about the special dangers that fugitive mothers and children experienced (71–74).

31. Amy Lang claims, "The success of *Uncle Tom's Cabin* depends on the placement of the chattel slave in a developmental scheme which makes immanent his middle-class character and thus brings him, provisionally at least, into the world of the reader" (142).

32. See Ann Shapiro's discussion of mothers in *Uncle Tom's Cabin* and her claim that Eliza assumes "the conventional values of white society after she and Harry are safe and reunited with George" (25).

33. The prose sections delete portions from the adult version, but the remaining parts contain the same wording as the original.

34. The preface to *Pictures and Stories from Uncle Tom's Cabin* states:

> The purpose of the Editor of this little Work, has been to adapt it for the juvenile family circle. The verses have accordingly been written by the Authoress for the capacity of the youngest readers, and have been printed in a large bold type. The prose parts of the book, which are well suited for being read aloud in the family circle, are printed in a smaller type, and it is presumed that in these our younger friends will claim the assistance of their older brothers or sisters, or appeal to the ready aid of their mamma. ([2])

35. See Stowe, "Letter to the Abolitionist Eliza Cabot Follen" [December 16, 1852].

36. These narratives resemble *Incidents in the Life of a Slave Girl*, in which many people help Brent attain her freedom, rather than Douglass, who ascertains his freedom on his own.

37. See MacCann's discussion of white supremacy in this work ("White Supremacy" 59–60).

38. See also Anne P. Adam's short story "Christine," which exemplifies later works in which violated maternity leads to psychological suffering with deadly consequences.

39. MacCann argues that although Colman depicts a "strong" mother figure, she does not grant the same positive treatment to her other slave characters ("White Supremacy" 58–59).

CHAPTER 3.
THE ABOLITIONIST MOTHER-HISTORIAN

1. Mary Cable writes: "Traditional child-rearing methods were not abandoned easily, but by 1830 changes were clearly on the way. The Republic was young and rambunc-

tious. It had achieved its independence not through submission and a broken will but through self-assertion—a lesson not lost on bright children, who were urged to be patriotic and to learn their country's history" (90).

2. This fictional mother figure's presence challenges the argument (in *No Mothers in Novels* [1864]) that mother figures are absent from both novels and children's literature ("Publishing Department" 21–22).

3. See also Mrs. J. Bakewell's *The Mother's Practical Guide in the Physical, Intellectual, and Moral Training of Her Children* (111–12).

4. See also Tompkins (143–45) and Ann Douglas (74–75).

5. Swerdlow explains that the passage of two "motherhood resolutions" by the Anti-Slavery Convention of American Women may have been an attempt to reconcile an ongoing debate over how to increase women's participation in the abolitionist debate. However, Swerdlow does not address how the resolutions helped to transform republican motherhood into abolitionist motherhood.

6. See Cott (63–100) and Baym in *American Women Writers* (30).

7. Swerdlow asserts that Boston, New York, and Philadelphia women "saw themselves as republican mothers responsible for the virtue and character of future generations" (39).

8. Their drive to educate children in this way was not as radical as it may seem. Barbara Greenleaf argues that the nineteenth-century Romantics abandoned the emphasis on discipline and self-control that permeated eighteenth-century views (62), which had *already* replaced the Calvinistic belief in a child's innate depravity (MacLeod, *American* 94). The Romantics perceived children as innocents who, according to David Grylls, possessed "a more profound awareness of enduring moral truths" (35). However, historians Bingham and Scholt suggest that rather than follow Rousseau's advice to allow natural child development, "in practice youngsters were often burdened with pressure of information" (142).

9. We must add political, domestic storytelling to Ruth Bogin and Jean Fagan Yellin's argument that "petitioning by women became a way to expand the public's conception of women's legitimate activities" (17).

10. This supports Baym's idea that maternal historians claim: "if home was their provenance, then whatever in the world affected the home was their provenance also. And every important historical event had an impact on the home" (31).

11. See the anonymous "Extract from a Journal" (1828 and 1829) in Lydia Maria Child's *Juvenile Miscellany.*

12. This issue of the *Child's Friend,* seemingly dedicated to American independence, makes no overt reference to slavery or how slavery violates American democratic principles. Yet the same issue includes "The Liberty Wherewith Christ Hath Made Us Free," which never mentions American slavery but uses the rhetoric of slavery (chains, bondage, servants, etc.) to discuss sin.

13. See Mrs. J. Bakewell's strict recommendations on suitable books for children in *The Mother's Practical Guide in the Physical, Intellectual, and Moral Training of Her Children* (1850). She does not recommend novels; instead, she believes children should only read texts "true to nature, and the moral of which is evidently good" (101).

14. Hale's patriotism is evident as she persuaded Abraham Lincoln to establish Thanksgiving as a national holiday, organized women in the Bunker Hill Monument Association to raise thirty thousand dollars to complete the Boston Monument, and attempted to define American literature by demanding original, rather than pirated, essays and fiction (see Schilpp 37–48; Okker 70–71, 84–109).

15. Bradburn's and the other domestic abolitionists' constructions of the mother figure challenge the negative image that Cornelia Meigs argues exists in juvenile literature. She states:

> Rousseau went further [than Locke] and declared that they [children] must not be led, but accompanied in that search for knowledge, with the wise preceptor and friend always at hand to supply information when they asked it, to make things clear at the critical moment when self-instruction tends to turn into confusion. . . . There began, perforce, to emerge a stock literary character, the parent or relative or friend or teacher who knew everything, who could answer all the questions—provided the right ones were asked— who was always at hand to make a profitable lesson out of everything, to render every experience educational and almost always dull. (88)

16. Bradburn implies that children can convert adults, and she uses the example of African children arguing that the converted will train their own children to hold similar beliefs. This transmission will persist through the generations such that the children become the vehicles for change and reform (11).

17. See MacCann's brief reference to "Aunt Judy's Story: A Story from Real Life" ("White Supremacy" 60).

18. See Mary Patricia Jones's brief discussion of poetic meter in this poem (66).

19. See chapter 2 for an extended discussion of "Mark and Hasty."

20. Jones extends the father's reluctance to speak of slavery in the following comments: "Charlie talked a great deal with his father, and I think some of my young friends would like to know what their conversations were about; but in this little book I shall tell them only what his mother said about slavery" (*The Young Abolitionist* 58).

21. See "A Massachusetts Slave," in which Anne Wales Abbott corrects historical misconceptions as she documents her great-grandfather's ownership of slaves, especially the rebellious Dinah (1847).

22. Elijah P. Lovejoy was a martyr for abolitionism. Forced out of St. Louis, Missouri, he moved to Alton, Illinois. In 1837, he was killed while protecting his printing press and defending the freedom of speech it represented (Filler 102–105).

23. S.C.C. is most likely a woman, since this text reflects the characteristic domestic abolitionists text, especially with the inclusion of a feminist mother figure.

CHAPTER 4.
THE JUVENILE ABOLITIONISTS

1. This question appears repeatedly in abolitionist literature. See Angelina Grimké, *Appeal to the Christian Women of the South* (1836) and *Appeal to Women of the Nominally*

Free States (1837); Elizabeth Lloyd, *An Appeal to the Bondwomen, to Her Own Sex* (1846); Harriet Beecher Stowe, *Uncle Tom's Cabin* (1852) and "Appeal to the Women of the Free States" (1854); Elizabeth Margaret Chandler, "An Appeal to the Ladies of the United States" in *Essays, Philanthropic and Moral* (1836); and Maria Weston Chapman, "How Can I Help to Abolish Slavery?" (1855), which encourages adults to hasten the coming of "millennial glory" (1) by joining an antislavery society that supports "unconditional emancipation" through public condemnation instead of supporting those who advocated colonization, secret underground railroads, or segregated schools and businesses (2–4).

2. Bertram Wyatt-Brown notes that Lewis Tappan persuaded the antislavery society to budget $30,000 for a "national pamphlet campaign, one of the most ambitious in evangelical history" (143). One of the four of these abolitionist newspapers was the *Slave's Friend,* published by the American Anti-Slavery Society from 1836–1838. Its editor claims that "About two hundred and fifty thousand copies of the *Slave's Friend* have been published, and we suppose they have been read by at least fifty thousand children. Many of them have been deeply interested, stirred up to duty, and have formed antislavery societies" (2.5 [1837]: [65–66]). All subsequent references to the *Slave's Friend* will be cited parenthetically, indicated by *SF.*

3. According to Wyatt-Brown, "Early in 1832, [Lewis] Tappan began to negotiate with a reluctant circus owner for the lease of a theater near Five Points on Chatham Street [in New York City]" (70–71). Located "in the midst of the slums, discouraging 'decent' people from attendance" (71), Tappan transformed the theater into the Chatham Street Chapel, where the Female Anti-Slavery Society also had a division (Swerdlow 30n2).

4. Tappan helped form the first antislavery society in 1833, but he separated from Garrison in 1840 (*Dictionary of American Religious Biography* 540). However, Lewis Tappan was not the only abolitionist in the family; the women were involved as well. Tappan's wife, Susan Aspinwall Tappan, Jr. and his oldest daughter, Juliana A. Tappan, were participants at the 1837–1839 Anti-Slavery Conventions of American Women (*Proceedings* . . . 1837, 1838, 1839). While they "also distributed petitions to free District of Columbia slaves, made items for the popular Anti-Slavery Bazaars, and corresponded with Maria Weston Chapman's circle in Boston," they rejected women like "Angelina and Sarah Grimké, who spoke before 'promiscuous assemblies' of men and women" (Wyatt-Brown 173).

5. *The Child's Friend* contains four articles about children's charity for poor children: "The Child's Mission" (Dec. 1854 or 1855?), "The Anniversary of the Children's Mission" (1855), "Friendless and Homeless Children" (1857), and "The Children's Mission to the Children of the Destitute" (1857). The Children's Mission in Boston was started by "the children of the Unitarian Sunday schools" to make donations to help sponsor missionary work among the neglected city children (268). Each article informs juvenile readers of the good they can do even through penny donations. Such actions benefit the poor children and teach young donors about benevolence. The authors state: "The germ of kind action, the real interest, and *real* we are sure it is, will never die. In a wider sphere, these hearts, and these heads, and these hands, will busy themselves still with the welfare of their less fortunate brethren" ("The Child's Mission" 269). "The Anniversary of the Children's Mission" cites that the children organized fairs, donated pennies, and made clothes and other things for sale to raise funds (32–33). In "The Children's Mission to the Children of the Destitute," Anne Wales Abbot, the editor, states:

> This is a society supported by the contributions of children, and its object is not merely to rescue exposed children from vice, ignorance, and degradation, but to foster the spirit of Christian benevolence in the minds of the young who are growing up in more fortunate circumstances . . . [and] answers an excellent end in enabling children to perceive how they can, by self-denial and personal exertion, do more for the wretched than give them a mere sentimental pity. (238)

See also Anne Wales Abbot's "Friendless and Homeless Children" (99).

6. See *SF* 2.10 (1837): [back cover] and 2.11 (1837): [back cover].

7. Tappan started this journal in 1828 and sold it to David Hale and Gerard Hallock in 1831 ("Lewis Tappan," *American* 628).

8. The Massachusetts Historical Society has bracketed Boston as the location for this group. The first recorded meeting was held on July 28, 1837. However, the incomplete nature of the records, which begin and end *in medias res,* suggests that it may have started before this date (Juvenile Anti-Slavery Society Papers, MHS).

9. See *SF* 2.12 (1837): [23–27].

10. Bartlett's name does not appear in the *Biography and Genealogy,* a master index of *Allibone, Who's Who,* and *Dictionary of American Biography.* The references to himself suggests that he may be a youth; however, his identity remains uncertain.

11. Robert Bartlett letters to the Juvenile Anti-Slavery Society, January 19, 1838 (Juvenile Anti-Slavery Society Papers, MHS).

12. The *Slave's Friend* used the Chatham Street Chapel group as a model upon which other groups could base themselves. I suspect, therefore, that their published constitution became the basis of other groups' constitutions.

13. The cost of the *Slave's Friend* was one cent for one copy, ten cents for 12 copies, 80 cents for 100 copies and $6.50 for 1,000 copies. According to Robert Shaw, between 1835 and 1840, one dollar was the equivalent of $13.00 in 1990. Therefore, one cent in 1835 equaled thirteen cents in 1990 (291).

14. Evidence of children's efforts appears in reports like "The Little Tract Distributor," which tells of a young boy who distributed antislavery tracts to steamship passengers. The author comments, "How much good, little children can do, if they have a mind to do it. If they all feel and act right on the subject of slavery, all the people in the United States will be immediate abolitionists one of these days" (*SF* 1.6 [1836]: [82]).

15. Shirley Samuels claims that the *Slave's Friend* implied that children could make a difference also by selling copies of this publication, thereby "an equivalence is established between the circulation of texts and the circulation of money, as if reading and capitalism indicated each other" ("Identity" 164–64).

16. *National Anti-Slavery Standard,* November 12, 1840, p. 90.

17. The Executive Committee of the American-Anti-Slavery Society appointed Wright to work with the children (*SF* 2. 7 (1837): [back page]). Ruchames states that Wright "was a hatmaker turned minister who was ordained in 1823. . . . He joined the New England Anti-Slavery Society in May 1835, and met Garrison for the first time in

November of the same year" (109). Wright, an extreme radical, had a firm "belief in the absolute equality of the sexes and in the dignity and rights of children" (Lerner *Grimké Sisters* 177).

18. The petition states: "let the names of every youth of the city and country (which is old enough to understand its object) be appended to it, or at least furnish them with the opportunity of signing" (December 23, 1836).

19. Their visits were on July [22, 1837], October 20, 1837, and January 5, 1838, respectively (Juvenile Anti-Slavery Society Papers, MHS).

20. Nathaniel Southard, editor of The *Anti-Slavery Almanac,* also edited *The Youth's Cabinet,* a weekly newspaper (*SF* 3.3 (1838): [49]).

21. Lydia Maria Child edited *The Oasis* (1834), a collection of antislavery articles and poetry through which she "wish[es] to familiarize the public mind with the idea that the colored people are *human* beings—elevated or degraded by the same circumstances that elevate or degrade other men. . . . If it were otherwise, we could not look upon their wrongs so coldly as we do" (Preface vii). She also defends abolitionist efforts, stating: "The abolitionist merely wish that colored people should have the same opportunities for instruction, the same civil treatment at public places, the same chance to enlarge their sphere of usefulness, that is enjoyed by the lowest and most ignorant white man in America" (ix). She concludes that antislavery "will soon become the universal public sentiment of New England—a sentiment that cannot be repressed, and will not be silent" (xvi). The anthology contains works by Lydia Maria Child, D. L. Child, Eliza Follen, John Greenlief Whittier, Miss E. H. Whittier, "Florence," Reverend S. J. May, Miss H. F. Gould, and by an ex-slave named James Bradley. See especially "The Infant Abolitionist" by Florence and "Miss [Prudence] Crandall's School," by Reverend S. J. May, who records the true story of Prudence Crandall's establishment of the Canterbury School in Connecticut, to which she wanted to enroll black girls because she abhorred slavery. The town was in a great uproar, and both jailed and ostracized Crandall. Her trial passed through lower courts and eventually reached the Supreme Court. Her story made all the newspapers at the time. Elizabeth Margaret Chandler wrote a poem "To Prudence Crandall" (1834), which may suggest how well known the story was.

22. Juvenile Anti-Slavery Society Papers, MHS.

23. "From Greenland's Icy Mountains" was a missionary hymn that urged singers to spread Christianity to redeem those in heathen lands.

24. This title does not appear in her collected works; however, George W. Clark's *The Liberty Minstrel* (1845) "contains her anti-slavery poems that were set to music" (Dillon 320). Mary Jones's dissertation suggests that there was a poem called "Praise and Prayer" that was set to music (15). Perhaps that was the title to which the girls referred.

25. Published in the *Genius of Universal Emancipation* in June 1831 and in the *Liberator* on May 7, 1831. Also reprinted in Garrison's *Juvenile Poems for the Use of Free American Children of Every Complexion* (1835). The poem may have been accessible to an even larger audience after it was set to music (Jones 15).

26. "Oh Press Me Not to Taste Again" was reprinted in Garrison's *Juvenile Poems for the Use of Free American Children of Every Complexion* (68–69). This volume also contains several anonymous works that deal with this issue of slave sugar production. See "The

Petition: Of the Sugar Making Slave—Humbly Addressed to the Consumers of Sugar" (66–67); "An Answer to the Question, 'Do You Take Sugar in Your Tea?'" (67–68); and "The Sugar Cane" (69–70).

27. Also reprinted in Garrison's *Juvenile Poems for the Use of Free American Children of Every Complexion*.

28. Abel C. Thomas wrote the only other recovered antislavery alphabet, *The Gospel of Slavery: A Primer of Freedom* (1864?). This alphabet is aimed at an older audience that could clearly include adults. A relief print and poem accompanies each letter of the alphabet. A highly political prose commentary that attacks the proslavery argument appears below each poem. For a general discussion of nineteenth-century alphabet books, see Lou McCulloch, "Alphabet Basics" in *Children's Books of the Nineteenth Century* (73–85).

29. See chapter 3 for complete discussion of this text.

30. In "How Shall Children Do Good?" [1844], Eliza Follen advocates that children participate in slavery only indirectly. However, two years later, in *The Liberty Cap* (1846), she posits more direct activism.

31. Abolitionist fairs were actually held in Dedham, a Boston, Massachusetts suburb. A broadside and Elizabeth Follen's letter to Joseph Congdon, Esq. reveal that the female abolitionist, like Follen and Chapman, played a leading role in organizing the antislavery fair on July 4, 1846.

32. Lucinda MacKethan argues that the slave's letter to a master was "[o]ne of the most artful devices employed by any of the slave narratives, it involves a reversal of one of the stock elements of the narratives as a genre" in that it served as one of the metaphors through which slaves gained mastery over former slave owners (67).

33. See Henry Louis Gates, *The Signifying Monkey* (1988); Lucinda MacKethan, "Metaphors of Mastery in the Slave Narratives" (59–60); and Keith Byerman, "We Wear the Mask: Deceit as Theme and Style in the Slave Narrative" (70–82).

34. See Lucinda MacKethan's discussion of word tricks that ex-slaves used to gain some control over the white master (62–63).

35. In *Women and Sisters*, Yellin's brief discussion of Lydia Maria Child's *The Kansas Emigrants* (1856), Frances Ellen Watkins Harper's "The Two Offers" (1859), and Anne Dickinson's *What Answer?* (1869) reveals that by the 1850s "antislavery feminists and their supporters were presenting women like themselves in fiction" (69).

36. See Bardes and Gossett, "Finding a Voice to Answer a Moral Call" (*Declarations* 38).

37. See Stowe, "An Appeal to the Women of the Free States" (1854). Faced with the impending passage of the Kansas-Nebraska Act (n1 428), Stowe calls women to prevent the passage of this law by engaging in religious and political activism. She urges women to "make this subject a matter of earnest prayer" (429), but also to

> make exertions to get up petitions, in their particular districts, to our
> national legislature. They can take measures to communicate information in
> their vicinity. They can employ lectures to spread the subject before the peo-

ple of their town or village. They can circulate the speeches of our members in Congress, and in many other ways secure a full understanding of the present position of our country. (429)

38. This silencing is ironic considering that Evangelicals were active participants in abolitionism.

39. See also Isabelle White's analysis of Eva's death in "Sentimentality and the Uses of Death" (103–108).

40. Yellin says that Angelina Grimké "us[ed] the language of evangelical abolitionism" (*Women* 53).

41. See Isabelle White's brief commentary on Eva's sexuality in "Sentimentality and the Uses of Death" (107).

42. Stowe carefully situates the Rachel Halliday chapter immediately before the first chapter on Eva. By doing so, she highlights the fact that Quakers blended their religious beliefs with that of the abolitionists. This juxtaposition suggests that we should see Eva as both religious *and* abolitionist, especially since Evangelicals incorporated abolitionism into their reform agenda. Therefore, we cannot ignore Eva's political side as many critics who focus on her religious nature have done.

43. Augustine debates the issue of educating the slaves with his brother and with Ophelia. If we see their conversations as political, then we must view Eva's conversation in this political vein as well. Ironically, while the men remain passive, Eva and Ophelia do the most toward literally educating the slaves.

44. Eva's educational and capitalist politics parallel those of George Shelby, who teaches Tom to read (parental permission uncertain) and ties a coin around Tom's neck as a token of his commitment to locate the money to "redeem" him. Furthermore, one of the novel's last images depicts George trying to purchase Tom from Simon Legree. Having arrived too late, George vows to God that "I will do *what one man can* to drive out this curse of slavery from my land!" (Stowe, *Uncle* 365), and then he frees his slaves.

45. See also Isabelle White's brief discussion of this scene in "Sentimentality and the Uses of Death" (107).

46. Elizabeth Fox-Genevese states, "slave codes rigorously prohibited teaching slaves to read and write and well over 90 percent of the slaves remained illiterate" (156). Furthermore, although Stanley Elkins ignores that fact that Douglass's autobiography suggests that slave literacy was discouraged in Maryland, he states:

> Every Southern state except Maryland and Kentucky had stringent laws forbidding anyone to teach slaves reading and writing, and in some states the penalties applied to the educating of free Negroes and mulattoes as well. It was thought that "teaching slaves to read and write tends to dissatisfaction in their minds, and to produce insurrection and rebellion"; in North Carolina it was a crime to distribute among them any pamphlet or book, not excluding the Bible. The same apprehensions applied to instruction in religion (60).

Finally, James Breeden cites a Georgia planter's 1851 prize essay that argues against educating the slaves because "the spirit of bigotry and fanaticism which are abroad in the country, seeking to disseminate a spirit of insubordination in the bosom of the slave, by the circulation of incendiary publications, inducing him to throw off the authority of those to whom his services are due, at once precludes the idea of such policy [i.e., Educating the slaves]" (12). Breeden also cites a Mississippi editor who writes, "To instruct our Negroes in the truth of the Bible, it is not necessary to teach them to read" (226).

47. Yellin points out that in *Appeal to the Christian Women of the South,* Angelina Grimké urged Southern women to educate their slaves even though doing so was a crime (*Women* 33). Elkins acknowledges that there were risks and rewards for "the planter (pro- or antislavery) who might resolve to educate his slaves, law or no law" (200). William Goodell's *American Slave Code in Theory and Practice* cites that slaves were usually whipped if found teaching other slaves to read or learning on their own. If a white person was discovered educating a slave, s/he would pay a fine and/or be imprisoned. For example, Goodell cites an 1818 Savannah city ordinance which fined a white offender $30 per offense. In North Carolina, offenders paid a $200 fine (321), while in Georgia they paid $500 and were "imprisoned at the discretion of the Court" (321–22).

48. For an opposing view, see Jacobs' *Incidents in the Life of a Slave Girl,* in which she suggests that purchasing her freedom is merely a compromise within a corrupt system.

49. "Redeem" has religious connotations—as Christ came to redeem mankind. However, by saying that Mrs. Shelby will send money to redeem Tom, Eva associates redemption with capitalism and women. The *Oxford English Dictionary* focuses on these economic terms, defining the word as: (1) "to buy back (a thing formerly possessed); to make payment for (a thing held or claimed by another); (2) to free (mortgaged property), to recover (a person or thing put in pledge), by payment of the amount due, or by fulfilling some obligation; (3) to ransom, liberate, free (a person) from bondage, captivity, or punishment; to save (one's life) by paying a ransom; (4) to rescue, save, deliver."

50. Eva's desire to participate in activism through her father may echo Stowe's desire to participate in abolishing slavery through her book. Like the pleasant-speaking father, Stowe's book presents the horrors of slavery in a fictional form with plenty of seemingly nonthreatening women and children. Like St. Clare, the book would "go all around and try to persuade people to do right about this" (241). Finally, just as Eva begs her father to speak for her when she is dead (i.e., when her voice is silenced), Stowe may have used the book to speak for her in order to avoid direct public criticism.

51. In a reply to Eliza Lee Cabot Follen's letter, on December 16, 1852, Stowe writes:

I hasten to reply to your letter, the more interesting that I have long been acquainted with you, and during all the nursery part of my life made daily use of your poems for my children" (Norton 413).

Stowe may, therefore, have been familiar with poems like "Billy Rabbit to Mary" and "Soliloquy: Of Ellen's Squirrel and His Liberty;—Overheard by a Lover of Nature and a Friend of Ellen. (1846)

52. Gay Schwartz Herzberg states that exemplary youths "enhance[d] the stories of women, since most of these dynamic and influential children were girls" (99). However, she neither documents nor provides examples to support her claim.

53. The name "Mary" calls to mind the Virgin Mary, who sacrifices her Son to save others as this child sacrifices her child.

54. While Aunt Mary states, "may [the poem] be the means of wakening among *the children*, a zeal for the cause of suffering humanity" (*Extract* 2), she specifically stresses girls' activism when she wishes that "of each who reads this simple story may it be said, as with truth it might be said of little Mary, '*She* hath done what *she* could.'" (*Extract* 2, emphasis added).

55. Cornelia Meigs writes, "Many realistic stories for girls were written in America during the 1860s and 1870s" [204].

56. Frost muddies the reader's interpretation of this apparent act of benevolence and activism by suggesting that the white community raises the church funds "to help keep the colored people in their place by themselves" (91).

57. M.A.F. states, "Thus, an active mind is ever originating ideas within itself. Who shall say what such a mind may accomplish?" (33)

58. The narrator has faith in children's ability to effect change. She writes, "The child's influence lives. . . . Let not any child of twelve years suppose that he has not a work to do—a mission to perform, the accomplishment of which may result in [much?] good" (49).

59. See also David Van Leer's brief analysis of reading in Douglass's *Narrative of the Life of Frederick Douglass* (123).

Works Cited

Primary Sources

Abbot, Anne Wales [ed]. "A Massachusetts Slave." *The Child's Friend* 8.5 (Aug. 1847): 233–38.

———. "Friendless and Homeless Children." *The Child's Friend* 29 (1857): 97–101.

———. "The Children's Mission to the Children of the Destitute." *The Child's Friend* 29 (1857): 238–40.

Abbott, John S[tevens] C[abot]. *The Mother at Home; or, The Principles of Maternal Duty Familiarly Illustrated.* New York: American Tract Society, 1833.

The Abolitionists: Means, Ends, and Motivations. Ed. Lawrence B. Goodheart and Hugh Hawkins. 3rd ed. Lexington, Mass.: Heath, 1995. 44–49.

Adams, Anne P. "Christine." *Autographs for Freedom.* Ed Julia Griffiths. Auburn: Alden, Beardsley, 1854. 139–46.

The African Orphan Boy, and Other Books for Children. New York: American Tract Society, 1800.

The African Woman. Philadelphia: American Sunday School Union, 1830.

A Lady. *A Home in the South; or, Two Years at Uncle Warren's. Written for the American Reform Tract and Book Society.* Cincinnati: American Reform Tract and Book Society, [c1857].

A.L.L. "A Sermon for Children." *The Child's Friend* 24 (1855): 214–16.

American Anti-Slavery Society. "Declaration of Sentiments (1833)."

"American Tract Society." *American Anti-Slavery Society Annual Report.* New York: [np], 1859. 170–71.

Ammidon, Melissa. "Letter to the Lowell Female Anti-Slavery Society, July 14, 1835." Boston Female Anti-Slavery Society Papers. Massachusetts Historical Society.

Aunt Mary. *The Edinburgh Doll and Other Tales for Children.* Boston: John P. Jewett, 1854.

Aunt Sally; or, The Cross, the Way of Freedom. Cincinnati: American Reform Tract and Book Society, 1858.

Bakewell, J. [Mrs.]. *The Mother's Practical Guide in the Physical, Intellectual, and Moral Training of Her Children.* New York: Lane & Scott, 1850.

Barclay, Kate. *Minnie May: With Other Rhymes and Stories.* Boston: John P. Jewett, 1856.

———. "The Ride." *Minnie May: With Other Rhymes and Stories.* Boston: John P. Jewett, 1856. 12–14.

———. "The Sale." *Minnie May: With Other Rhymes and Stories.* Boston: John P. Jewett, 1856. 19–20.

———. "The Slave." *Minnie May: With Other Rhymes and Stories.* Boston: John P. Jewett, 1856. 31–32.

Bartlett, Robert. "Letters from Robert Bartlett to the Juvenile Anti-Slavery Society, Oct. 20, 1837, Jan. 5, 1838, Jan. 19, 1838; Juvenile Anti-Slavery Society Papers. Massachusetts Historical Society.

Boynton, C[harles] B[randon]. *A Journey through Kansas with Sketches of Nebraska.* Cincinnati: Moore, Wilstach, Keys, 1855.

Bradburn, Eliza Weaver. *Pity Poor Africa: A Dialogue for Children in Three Parts.* 2nd ed. London: John Mason, 1831.

———. *The Story of Paradise Lost for Children.* New York: Carlton & Porter, 1800(?).

Brown, Henry Box. *Narrative of Henry Box Brown Who Escaped from Slavery Enclosed in a Box Three Feet Long and Two Wide and Two and a Half High.* Boston: Brown & Stearns, 1849.

Bullard, Asa, comp. *Aunt Lizzie's Stories. Sunnybank Stories.* 10. Boston: Lee & Shephard, 149 Washington Street, 1863.

Butts, Harriet Newell Greene. *Ralph; or, I Wish He Wasn't Black.* Hopedale, Mass.: E. Gay, 1855.

C.T.E. "The White Infant's Reply to the Little Slave." *Liberator* 26 Mar. 1831: 51.

Chandler, Elizabeth Margaret. "An Appeal to the Ladies of the United States." Lundy 17–21.

———. "Christmas." Lundy 124–25.

———. "Looking at the Soldiers." Lundy 109–10.

———. "Oh Press Me Not to Taste Again." Lundy 108–109.

———. "The Child's Evening Hymn." Lundy 72.

———. "The Sugarplums." Lundy 108.

———. "To Prudence Crandall." Lundy 176–77.

———. "What Is a Slave Mother?" *Genius of Universal Emancipation* May 1831: 13.

———. "What Is a Slave Mother?" *Liberator* 4 June 1831: 90.

Channing, William Ellery. "Letter from William Ellery Channing to Catharine Maria Sedgwick," Aug. 23, 1827. W. E. Channing Papers. Massachusetts Historical Society.

Chapman, Maria Weston. "How Can I Help to Abolish Slavery?" Tract no. 14. New York: American Anti-Slavery Society, 1855. In Anti-Slavery Tracts Series 1: Nos. 1–20, 1855–1856. Westport, Conn.: Negro UP, 1970.

Charter; Being a Plain Statement of Facts in Relation to the Legislature of Pennsylvania to Grant a Charter to the American Sunday School Union, The. Philadelphia: American Sunday School Union, 1828.

Child, Lydia Maria, ed. Preface. *The Oasis*. Boston: Allen & Ticknor, 1834.

———. *Juvenile Miscellany*. Boston: John Putnam, 1826–1834.

Child, Lydia Maria. *An Appeal in Favor of That Class of Americans Called Africans*. New York: Allen & Ticknor, 1833.

———. *Anti-Slavery Catechism*. Newburyport, Mass.: C. Whipple, 1839.

———. *Biographical Sketches of Great and Good Men for Children*. Boston: Putnam & Hunt, 41, Washington Street, 1828.

———. Evening in New England. Intended for Juvenile Amusement and Instruction, as an American Lady. Boston: Cummings, Hilliard, 1824.

———. *The Evils of Slavery, and the Cure of Slavery. The First Proved by the Opinions of Southerners Themselves, the Last Shown by Historical Evidence*. Newburyport, Mass.: C. Whipple, 1839.

———. "Jumbo and Zairee." *A Lydia Maria Child Reader*. Ed. Carolyn L. Karcher. Durham, N.C.: Duke UP, 1997. 153–59.

———. *Juvenile Miscellany*. Boston: John Putnam, 1826–34.

———. "Letter to the Editor of the Liberator." *Lydia Maria Child, Selected Letters, 1817–1880*. Ed. Milton Meltzer and Patricia G. Holland. Amherst: U of Massachusetts P, 1982. 68–69.

———. *The Mother's Book*. Boston: Carter, Hendee & Babcock, 1831.

The Child's Book on Slavery; or, Slavery Made Plain. Cincinnati: American Reform Tract and Book Society, 1857.

The Child's Friend. Boston: L. C. Bowles, 1843–1858.

Clark, George, comp. *The Liberty Minstrel*. New York: Leavitt & Alden, 1845.

Colman, Julia, and Matilda Thompson. *The Child's Anti-Slavery Book: Containing a Few Words about American Slave Children and Stories of Slave Life*. New York: Carlton & Porter, 1859. Florida: Mnemosyne, 1969.

Colman, Julia. "Little Lewis: The Story of a Slave Boy." Colman and Thompson 2–61.

Constitution and Preamble (1836?). Junior Anti-Slavery Society of Philadelphia Papers, HSP.

Constitution of the American Reform Tract and Book Society, with Reasons for Its Organization. Cincinnati: Board of Directors, 1853.

Cousin Ann. "Henry Box Brown." *Cousin Ann's Stories for Children*. Philadelphia: J. M. McKim, 1849. 22–26.

———. "Howard and His Squirrel." *Cousin Ann's Stories for Children*. Philadelphia: J. M. McKim, 1849. 13–14.

———. "Tom and Lucy: A Tale for Little Lizzie." *Cousin Ann's Stories for Children*. Philadelphia: J. M. McKim, 1849. 14–17.

Croft, S. C. [Mrs. S. Croft]. *Not a Minute to Spare*. Cincinnati: Western Tract & Book Society, 1867.

Douglass, Frederick. *Narrative of the Life of Frederick Douglass, An American Slave: Written by Himself.* New York: Signet, 1968.

Drysdale, Isabel. *Evening Recreations: A Series of Dialogues on the History and Geography of the Bible. Written for the American Sunday School Union. Revised by the Committee of Publication*. Philadelphia: American Sunday School Union [1830?].

———. "The Negro Nurse." *Scenes in Georgia*. Philadelphia: American Sunday School Union, 1827. 27–42.

E.T.C. "From an Infant Slave to the Child of Its Mistress, Both Born on the Same Day." *Liberator* 12 Mar. 1831: 43.

Earnest Laborer; or, Myrtle Hill Plantation. Being Sketches and Incidents Drawn from the Experience of a School Teacher, A Book for Senior Scholars. New York: Carlton & Porter, 1864.

Edgeworth, Maria. "The Grateful Negro." *Popular Tales*. 4th ed. Boston: Samuel H. Parker, 1823.

Editor [?]. "The Anniversary of the Children's Mission." *The Child's Friend* 25 (1855): 33–37.

Editor [?]. "The Child's Mission." *The Child's Friend* 25 (Dec. 1855): 33–37.

Editor [?]. "Independence Day." *The Child's Friend and Youth's Magazine* 23 (1854): 25–26.

Fifty-Second Annual Report of the American Sunday School Union, The. Philadelphia: American Sunday School Union, 1876.

Florence. "The Infant Abolitionist." *The Oasis*. Ed. Lydia Maria Child. Boston: Allen & Ticknor, 1834. 201–202.

Follen, Eliza Lee Cabot. "And the Days of Thy Mourning Shall Be Ended." New York: American Anti-Slavery Society, 1855. 5–6. Anti-Slavery Tracts Series 1: Nos. 1–20, 1855–1856. Tract No. 8. Westport, Conn.: Negro UP, 1970.

———. *Anti-Slavery Hymns and Songs*. New York: American Anti-Slavery Society, 1855. Anti-Slavery Tracts: Series 1: Nos. 1–20, 1855–1856. Westport, Conn.: Negro UP, 1970.

———. "Auld Lang Syne." New York: American Anti-Slavery Society, 1855. 4. Anti-Slavery Tracts Series 1: Nos. 1–20, 1855–1856. Tract No. 8. Westport, Conn.: Negro UP, 1970.

———. "Billy Rabbit to Mary." *Hymns, Songs, and Fables for Young People*. Rev. and enl. from the last ed. Boston: William Crosby & H. P. Nichols, 1848. 91–92.

———. "Children in Slavery." *Hymns, Songs, and Fables for Young People*. Rev. and enl. from the last ed. Boston: William Crosby & H. P. Nichols, 1848. 54–55.

———. "Dialogue." *The Liberty Cap*. Boston: Leonard C. Bowles, 1846. 23–30.

———. "How Shall Children Do Good?" *The Child's Friend* 2.4 (July 1844): 109–13.

———. *Hymns, Songs, and Fables for Children*. Boston: Carter, Hendee & Babcock, 1831.

———. "Lines on Hearing of the Terror of the Children of the Slaves at the Thought of Being Sold." *The Liberty Cap*. Boston: Leonard C. Bowles, 1846. 22.

———. "Lord Deliver." *Anti-Slavery Hymns and Songs*. New York: American Anti-Slavery Society, 1855. 7. Anti-Slavery Tracts Series 1: Nos. 1–20, 1855–1856. Westport, Conn.: Negro UP, 1970.

———. *May Morning and New Year's Eve*. Boston: Whittmore, Nichols, & Hall, 1858, c1857.

———. "On Hearing of the Sadness of the Slave Children from the Fear of Being Sold." *Anti-Slavery Hymns and Songs*. New York: American Anti-Slavery Society, 1855. 8. Anti-Slavery Tracts Series 1: Nos. 1–20, 1855–1856. Westport, Conn.: Negro UP, 1970.

———. "Picnic at Dedham." *The Liberty Cap*. Boston: Leonard C. Bowles, 1846. 10–21.

———. "Remember the Slave." *Hymns, Songs, and Fables for Young People*. Rev. and enl. from the last ed. Boston: William Crosby & H. P. Nichols, 1848. 50–52.

———. *Sequel to "The Well-Spent Hour"; or, The Birthday*. Boston: Carter & Hendee, 1832.

———. *Sequel to "The Well-Spent Hour"; or, The Birthday*. Boston: J. Munroe, 1848.

———. "Soliloquy: Of Ellen's Squirrel, on Receiving His Liberty;—Overheard By a Lover of Nature and a Friend of Ellen." *Hymns, Songs, and Fables for Young People*. Rev. and enl. from the last ed. Boston: William Crosby & H. P. Nichols, 1848. 76–77.

———. "The Land of the Free and the Home of the Brave." New York: American Anti-Slavery Society, 1855. 1–2. Anti-Slavery Tracts Series 1: Nos. 1–20, 1855–1856. Tract No. 8. Westport, Conn.: Negro UP, 1970.

———. *The Liberty Cap*. Boston: Leonard C. Bowles, 1846.

———. "The Little Slave's Wish." *Hymns, Songs, and Fables for Young People*. Rev. and enl. from the last ed. Boston: William Crosby & H. P. Nichols, 1848. 69–71.

———. "The Melancholy Boy." *The Child's Friend* 2. 2 (1844): 37–41.

———. *The Well-Spent Hour*. New ed. Boston: J. Munroe, 1838.

———. "Three Little Kittens." *Little Songs, for Little Boys and Girls*. Boston: Leonard C. Bowles, 1833.

———. "To Mothers in the Free States." New York: American Anti-Slavery Society, 1855. 1–4. Anti-Slavery Tracts Series 1: Nos. 1–20, 1855–1856. Tract No. 8. Westport, Conn.: Negro UP, 1970.

———. *True Stories about Dogs and Cats*. Boston: Whittmore, Niles, & Hall, 1856.

———. *Twilight Stories*. Boston: Wittemore, Niles, & Hall, n.d.

———. "Where Is Thy Brother." New York: American Anti-Slavery Society, 1855. 1. Anti-Slavery Tracts Series 1: Nos. 1–20, 1855–1856. Tract No. 8. Westport, Conn.: Negro UP, 1970.

Frost, Maria Goodell. *Gospel Fruits; or, Bible Christianity Illustrated; A Premium Essay.* Cincinnati: American Reform Tract and Book Society, 1856.

———. *The Children of the Covenant; or, The Christian Family.* Cincinnati: Western Tract and Book Society, 1867.

Garrison, William Lloyd. *Juvenile Poems, for the Use of Free American Children of Every Complexion.* Boston: Garrison & Knapp, 1835.

———. "To the Public [1831]." *The Abolitionists: Means, Ends, and Motivations.* Ed. Lawrence B. Goodheart and Hugh Hawkins. 3rd ed. Lexington, Mass.: Heath, 1995.

Genius of Universal Emancipation. Baltimore, Md.: Benjamin Lundy, 1826–1839?

Gilman, Caroline Howard. "The Plantation.'" *The Rose-Bud Wreath.* Charleston: S. Babcock, 1841. 133–47.

———. "The Planter's Son." *The Rose-Bud Wreath.* Charleston: S. Babcock, 1841. 63–69.

———. "Wishes." *The Rose-Bud Wreath.* Charleston: S. Babcock, 1841. 26–27.

Godey's Lady's Book. Philadelphia: L. A. Godey, 1840–1859.

Grandmother's Stories for Little Children. Boston: John P. Jewett, 1854.

Grimké, Angelina. *An Appeal to the Women of the Nominally Free States.* New York: W. S. Door, 1837.

———. *Appeal to the Christian Women of the South.* New York: American Anti-Slavery Society, 1836.

Hale, Sarah Josepha (Buell). *The Gift for Good Little Girls, Containing Good Little Girls Book.* New York: Edward Dunigan, 1848.

———. *The Happy Changes; or, Pride and Its Consequences.* New York: John McLoughlin, 1854.

———. "Independence." *The School Song Book. Adapted to the Scenes of the School Room. Written for American Children and Youth.* Boston: Allen & Ticknor, 1834.

———. *Liberia; or, Mr. Peyton's Experiments.* New York: Harper, 1853.

———. "My Country." *Poems for Our Children: Designed for Families, Sabbath Schools, and Infant Schools. Written to Inculcate Moral Truths and Virtuous Sentiments.* Boston: Marsh, Capen, & Lyon, 1830. 14–15.

———. *Northwood; or, Life North and South: Showing the True Character of Both.* New York: H. Long, 1827.

———. *Poems for Our Children: Designed for Families, Sabbath Schools, and Infant Schools: Written to Inculcate Moral Truths and Virtuous Sentiments.* Boston: Marsh, Capen & Lyon, 1830.

Harper, Frances E. W. *The Complete Poems of Frances E. W. Harper.* Ed. Maryemma Graham. New York: Oxford UP, 1988.

The History of Adjai, the African Slave Boy Who Became a Missionary. New York: Carlton & Porter, 18??.

History of Little Richard. New York: Carlton & Porter, Sunday-School Union, 1856.

Jacobs, Harriet A. *Incidents in the Life of a Slave Girl, Written by Herself.* Ed. Jean Fagan Yellin. Cambridge, Mass.: Harvard UP, 1987.

Jemmy and His Mother: A Tale for Children and Lucy; or, the Slave Girl of Kentucky. Cincinnati: American Reform Tract and Book Society, 1858.

Jewett, John P. A Pocket Guide. [The American Antiquarian Society.]

Jones, Jane Elizabeth. *Address to the Women's Rights Committee of the Ohio Legislature*. Columbus: Harris & Hurd, 1861.

———. *The Wrongs of Women: An Address Delivered Before the Ohio Women's Convention, at Salem, April 19th, 1850. Ohio Women's Convention Proceedings*. Cleveland, Ohio: Smead & Cowles, 1850. 30–48.

———. *The Young Abolitionist; or, Conversations on Slavery*. Boston: Published at the Anti-Slavery Office, 1848.

Knowlton, E. T. [Miss]. *Poems for Children*. Cincinnati: George L. Weed, 1849.

"Lady" [Sarah Buell Hale?]. *The Lamplighter Picture Book; or, The Story of Uncle True and Little Gerty: Written for Little Folks*. Boston: John P Jewett; Cleveland, Ohio: Jewitt, Proctor, & Worthington; New York: Sheldon, Lamport, & Blakeman, 1856.

Liberator. Boston, Mass.: Garrison & Knapp, 1831–1865.

"Liberty Wherewith Christ Hath Made Us Free." *The Child's Friend* 23 (1854): 25–26.

Little Eva: The Flower of the South. New York: Vincent L. Dill [between 1853 and 1855?].

Little Eva's First Book for Good Children. Exeter [England]: Drayton and Sons, High Street, c1855.

Little Eva's First Book for Good Children. New York: Stereotyped by Vincent L. Dill, 24 Beekman Street, 1853 & 1855.

"The Little Tract Distributor." *The Slave's Friend* 1.6 (183?): [82–83)].

Lloyd, Elizabeth. *An Appeal for the Bondwomen, To Her Own Sex*. Philadelphia: Merrihew & Thompson, 1846.

Lois [the Authoress]. *Harriet and Ellen; or, The Orphan Girls*. Cincinnati: American Reform Tract and Book Society, 1865.

Low, Mary; Stowe, Harriet Beecher, *A Peep into Uncle Tom's Cabin*. Boston, MA: Sampson Low; Jewett, 1853.

Lowell, Maria. "The Slave Mother." *The Liberty Bell: By the Friends of Freedom*. Boston: Mass. Anti-Slavery Fair, 1846.

The Lucky Stone. Philadelphia: American Sunday School Union, No. 316, Chestnut Street, 18—?

Lundy, Benjamin, ed. *Poetical Works of Elizabeth Margaret Chandler; with a Memoir of Her Life and Character by Benjamin Lundy, and Essays, Philanthropic and Moral, by Elizabeth Margaret Chandler, Principally Relating to the Abolition of Slavery in America*. Philadelphia: Lemuel Howell, 1836.

M.A.F. *Gertrude Lee; or, The Northern Cousin. "By a Lady."* Cincinnati: American Reform Tract and Book Society, 1856.

Margery. "Aunt Margery's Letter to Young Folks." *Liberator* 19 May 1832: 79.

Martyrs of the South. New York: Carlton & Porter, 1853.

"Maternal Instruction." *Godey's Lady's Book* 30.9 (March 1845): [n.p.].

May, Reverend S. J. "Miss [Prudence] Crandall's School." *The Oasis.* Ed. Lydia Maria Child. Boston: Allen & Ticknor, 1834. 180–91.

McIntosh, Maria Jane. *Woman in America: Her Work and Her Behavior.* New York: D. Appleton, 200 Broadway, 1850.

———. *Blind Alice; or, Do Right, if You Wish to Be Happy.* 2nd ed. New York: Dayton and Saxton, 1841.

Medora. "On Hearing a Child Say Father." *Liberator* 17 Mar. 1832: 42.

Minute Book (1836–1846). Junior Anti-Slavery Society of Philadelphia Papers, HSP.

Mitford, Mary Russell. *Our Village: Sketches of Rural Character and Scenery.* London: Whittaker, 1824.

———. "The Two Dolls." *Liberator* 9 April 1831: 58.

Mussey, Reuben Diamond. *Essay on the Influence of Tobacco on Life and Health.* 3rd ed. Cincinatti: George L. Weed, 1839.

"Old Caesar." *Grandmother's Stories for Little Children.* Boston: John P. Jewett, 1854. 23–32.

Opie, Amelia (Alderson). *The Negro Boy's Tale: A Poem, Addressed to Children.* London: Harvey & Darton, 1824.

———. *The Negro Boy's Tale: A Poem, Addressed to Children.* New York: Samuel Wood, [1825?].

Paul, Susan. *Memoir of James Jackson, the Attentive and Dutiful Scholar, Who Died In Boston, October 31, 1833, Aged Six Years and Eleven Months.* Boston: James Loring, 1835.

Philo Paidos. "Answer to the Letter of the Little Slaves, by the Sabbath School Children." *Liberator* 17 March 1832.

———. "Letter: The Little Slaves to the Sabbath School Children of New England." *Liberator* 17 March 1832.

Proceedings of the Anti-Slavery Convention of American Women, Held in Philadelphia, May 1st, 2d and 3d, 1839. Philadelphia: Merrihew & Thompson, 1839.

Proceedings of the Anti-Slavery Convention of American Women, Held in the City of New York, May 9th, 10th, 11th, and 12th, 1837. New York: William S. Dorr, 1837.

"Publishing Department." American Tract Society Thirty-Ninth Annual Report. n.p.: n.p., 1864. 21–22.

Rankin, John. *A Remedy for Universalism.* Cincinnati: Weed, 1843.

Richardson, Anna H. *Little Laura, the Kentucky Abolitionist: An Address to the Young Friends of the Slave.* Newcastle: Printed by Thomas Piff and Company, 1859.

S.C.C. *A Visit to the Country: A Tale, by the Author of Letters to A Mother, Ellen, Happy Valley etc.* Boston: William Crosby, 1839.

———. *Louisa in Her New Home.* Author of the "Wonderful Mirror." Philadelphia: Pennsylvania Anti-Slavery Society, 31 N. Fifth Street, 1854.

———. "The Wishing-Cap." *The Child's Friend* 9 (1847): 66–69.

———. *The Wonderful Mirror. By the Author of A Visit to the Country.* Boston: n.p., 1855.

The Seventh Annual Report of the American Sunday School Union. 2nd ed. Philadelphia: American Sunday School Union, 1831.

Sherwood, Mary Martha (Butt). *The Babes in the Wood of the New World.* New York: Mahlon Day at the New Juvenile Bookstore, no. 376. Pearle Street, 1831.

———. *Dazee; or, the Recaptured African.* Newburyport, Mass.: Printed by W. & J. Gilman, 1822.

———. *The History of Little Henry.* Andover, Mass: Mark Newman, 1818.

———. "The Poor Little Negroes." *Choice Gems for Children Selected from Mrs. Sherwood's Writings. Never before Published in This Country.* Boston: James Loring, No. 132 Washington Street, 1827. 41–46.

———. The Re-Captured Negro. Greenfield, Mass.: Ansel Phelps, 1834.

Sigourney, Lydia Howard. *Letters to Mothers.* Hartford, Conn.: Hudson & Skiner, 1838.

"The Slave Mother." *Liberator* 21 Jan. 1832.

Smith, Margaret Bayard. *My Uncle's Family, or, Ten Months at the South.* Cincinnati: American Reform Tract and Book Society, 1860.

Stowe, Harriet Beecher. "Appeal to the Women of the Free State [Feb. 23, 1854]." Ammons 424–29.

———. "Letter to the Abolitionist Eliza Cabot Follen. [Dec. 16, 1852.]." Ammons 413–14.

———. *Pictures and Stories from Uncle Tom's Cabin.* Boston: John P. Jewett, 1853.

———. *Uncle Tom's Cabin: Authoritative Text, Backgrounds and Contexts, Criticism.* Ed. Elizabeth Ammons. New York: Norton, 1994.

Thomas, Abel Charles. *The Gospel of Slavery: A Primer of Freedom.* New York: T. W. Strong, 1864?

Thompson, Matilda G. "Aunt Judy's Story: A Story from Real Life." Colman and Thompson 106–53.

———. "Mark and Hasty; or Slave-life in Missouri." Colman and Thompson 69–104.

Torrey, Charles. *Home; or, The Pilgrim's Faith Revived.* Cincinnati: John P. Jewett & George L. Weed, 1845.

Townsend, Hannah. *The Anti-Slavery Alphabet.* Philadelphia: Printed for the Anti-Slavery Fair, Merrihew & Thompson, 1846 & 1847.

A Tract for Sabbath Schools. Cincinnati: American Reform Tract and Book Society, 1857.

Tuthill, Louisa Caroline. *When Are We Happiest? or, The Little Camerons.* Boston: William Crosby & H. P. Nicholas, 1848.

U.I.E. "Helen, George, and Lucy: The Eclipse." *Liberator* 29 Jan. 1831: 18–19.

———. "The Family Circle; or, the Story of Helen, George, and Lucy." *Liberator* 22 Jan. 1831: 13.

W.M. "Address of a Little Slave Boy to His Master's Son." *Liberator* 3 Sept. 1831: 143.

Wakefield, Priscilla (Bell). *A Brief Memoir of the Life of William Penn: Compiled for the Use of Young Persons.* New York: Mahlon Day, 1821.

Warner, Susan [pseud. Elizabeth Wetherell]. *The Wide, Wide World.* 13th ed. New York: G. P. Putnam, 1852.

What Will Become of the Baby? With Three Other Stories about Children in Heathen Lands. New York: Carlton & Porter, Sunday School Union, 1855.

Wilson, Harriet. *Our Nig; or, Sketches from the Life of a Free Black: A Novel.* London: Allison & Busby, 1984.

Wilson, Ron. W. *The True Missionary Spirit, As Exemplified in the Life and Triumphant Death of John Milton Campbell, Late Missionary to Africa.* Cincinnati: George L. Weed, 1847.

Zillah. "A Dialogue between a Mother and Her Child." *Liberator* 1 Sept. 1832: 138.

———. "A True Tale for Children." *Liberator* 7 July 1832: 106.

———. "For the Children." *Liberator* 18 Aug. 1832: 131.

SECONDARY SOURCES

Ackerman, Ann Trugman. "Victorian Ideology and British Children's Literature, 1850–1914." Diss. North Texas State U, 1984.

Adams, John R. *Harriet Beecher Stowe.* Boston: Twayne, 1989.

American Antiquarian Society. [Catalogue Record.] *Not a Minute to Spare.* By S.C. [Mrs. S. Croft]. Cincinnati: American Reform Tract and Book Society [between 1856 and 1858].

Ammons, Elizabeth, ed. *Uncle Tom's Cabin: Authoritative Text, Backgrounds and Contexts, Criticism.* Harriet Beecher Stowe. New York: Norton, 1994.

Andrews, William. *To Tell a Free Story: The First Century of Afro-American Autobiography, 1760–1865.* Urbana: U of Illinois P, 1986.

Baker, Augusta. *Books about Negro Life for Children.* New York: New York Public Library, 1963.

———. *The Black Experience in Children's Books.* New York: New York Public Library, 1984.

Balfour, Clara L. *Women Worth Emulating.* New York: American Tract Society [1877?]. 74–89.

Bardes, Barbara, and Suzanne Gossett. *Declarations of Independence: Women and Political Power in Nineteenth-Century American Fiction.* New Brunswick: Rutgers UP, 1990.

Baym, Nina, ed. "Introduction." *The Lamplighter.* By Maria Susanna Cummins. New Brunswick: Rutgers UP, 1988. ix–xxxi.

Baym, Nina. *American Women Writers and the Work of History: 1790–1860.* New Brunswick: Rutgers UP, 1995.

———. *Novels, Readers and Reviewers: Responses to Fiction in Antebellum America.* Ithaca: Cornell UP 1984.

———. *Woman's Fiction: a Guide to Novels by and about Women in America, 1820–1870.* Ithaca: Cornell UP, 1978.

Bingham, Jane M. *Writers for Children: Critical Studies of Major Authors Since the Seventeenth Century.* New York: Scribner's, 1988.

Bingham, Jane M., and Grayce Scholt. *Fifteen Centuries of Children's Literature: An Annotated Chronology of British and American Works in Historical Context.* Westport, Conn.: Greenwood, 1980. 131–257.

Biography and Genealogy Master Index. 1996 Cumulation. Disc A: Name Search. Dos Version 1.4. Detroit: Gale, 1996.

Boas, George. *The Cult of Childhood.* London: Warburg Inst., 1966.

Bogin, Ruth, and Jean Fagan Yellin. "Introduction." Yellin and Van Horne 1–19.

Bordin, Ruth. *Women and Temperance: The Quest for Power and Liberty, 1873–1900.* Philadelphia: Temple UP, 1981.

Born, Donna. "Sara Jane Clarke Lippincott (Grace Greenwood)." *American Newspaper Journalists, 1690–1874.* Ed. Perry J. Ashley. Vol. 43. Detroit: Gale, 1985.

Bowerman, Sarah G. "Elizabeth Margaret Chandler." *Dictionary of American Biography.* Ed. Allen Johnson and Dumas Malone. Vol. 2. New York: Scribner's, 1930. 613.

Breeden, James O., ed. *Advice among Masters: The Ideal Slave Management in the Old South.* Westport, Conn.: Greenwood, 1980.

Broderick, Dorothy M. *The Image of the Black in Children's Fiction.* New York: Bowker, 1973.

Brown, Gillian. *Domestic Individualism: Imagining Self in Nineteenth-Century America.* Berkeley: U of California P, 1990.

Byerman, Keith. "We Wear the Mask: Deceit as Theme and Style in the Slave Narrative." *The Art of Slave Narrative: Original Essays in Criticism and Theory.* Ed. John Sekora and Darwin T. Turner. Chicago: Western Illinois U, 1982. 70–82.

Cable, Mary. *The Little Darlings: A History of Childrearing in America.* New York: Scribner's, 1975.

Cain, William E, ed. *William Lloyd Garrison and the Fight against Slavery: Selections from the Liberator.* Boston: Bedford, 1995.

Cohen, William. "James Miller McKim: Pennsylvania Abolitionist." Diss. New York U, 1968.

Commire, Anne, ed. *Yesterday's Authors of Books for Children: Facts and Pictures about Authors and Illustrators of Books for Young People from Early Times to 1960.* 2 vols. Detroit: Gale, 1977.

Cott, Nancy F. *The Bonds of Womanhood: "Woman's Sphere" in New England, 1780–1835.* New Haven: Yale UP, 1977.

Coultrap-McQuin, Susan. *Doing Literary Business: American Women Writers in the Nineteenth Century.* Chapel Hill: U of North Carolina P, 1990.

Coyle, William. *Ohio Authors and Their Books; Biographical Data and Selective Bibliographies for Ohio Authors, Native and Resident, 1796–1950.* Cleveland: World Publishing, 1962.

Crawford, Anne, Tony Hayter, Anne Hughes, Frank Prochaska, Pauline Stafford, and Elizabeth Vallance. *The Europa Biographical Dictionary of British Women: Over 1,000 Notable Women from Britain's Past.* London: Europa, 1983.

Cutt, M. Nancy. *Mrs. Sherwood and Her Books for Children.* London: Oxford UP, 1974.

Davidson, Cathy. *Revolution and the Word: The Rise of the Novel in America.* New York: Oxford UP, 1986.

Davis, Angela. *Women, Race, and Class.* New York: Random, 1981.

Davis, Fred. *Yearning for Yesterday: A Sociology of Nostalgia.* New York: Free (Macmillan), 1979.

Del Porto, Joseph Anthony. "A Study of American Anti-Slavery Journals." Diss. Michigan State College of Agriculture and Applied Science, 1953.

Dillon, Merton L. *Benjamin Lundy and the Struggle for Negro Freedom.* Urbana: U of Illinois P, 1966.

———. "Elizabeth Chandler and the Spread of Antislavery Sentiment to Michigan." *Michigan History* 39 (1955): 481–94.

———. "Elizabeth Margaret Chandler." *Notable American Women, 1607–1950: A Biographical Dictionary.* Ed. Edward T. James. Vol. 1. Cambridge: Belknap of Harvard UP, 1975. 319–20.

Douglas, Ann. *The Feminization of America.* New York: Doubleday, 1977.

Dudley, William. *Slavery: Opposing Viewpoints in American History.* San Diego: Greenhaven, 1992.

Dzwonkoski, Peter, ed. *American Literary Publishing Houses, 1638–1899.* Vol. 49. Detroit: Gale, 1978.

"Elizabeth Margaret Chandler." *Allibone's Critical Dictionary of English Literature. British and American Authors Living and Deceased from the Earliest Accounts of the Latter Half of the Nineteenth Century.* Ed. S. Austin Allibone. 3 vols. Philadelphia: Lippincott, 1858–1871. Reprint. Detroit: Gale, 1965.

———. *American Authors, 1600–1900: A Biographical Dictionary of American Literature.* Ed. Stanley J. Kunitz and Howard Haycraft. New York: Wilson, 1938.

Elkins, Stanley M. *Slavery: A Problem in American Institutional and Intellectual Life.* 3rd ed. Chicago: U of Chicago P, 1976.

Estes, Glenn E. *American Writers for Children before 1900.* Dictionary of Literary Biography 42. Detroit: Gale, 1985.

Federici, Yolanda D. "American Historical Children's Magazines of the Nineteenth and Early Twentieth Centuries." Headnote from the microfilm series from the American Antiquarian Society [nd].

Filler, Louis. *Crusades against Slavery: Friends, Foes, and Reform, 1820–1860.* Algonac, Michigan: Reference Publication, 1986.

Finkelstein, Barbara. "Casting Networks of Good Influence: The Reconstruction of Childhood in the United States, 1790–1870." *American Childhood: A Research Guide and Historical Handbook.* Ed. Joseph M. Hawes and N. Ray Hiner. Westport, Conn.: Greenwood, 1985. 111–52.

Finley, Ruth E. *The Lady of Godey's: Sarah Josepha Hale.* Philadelphia: Lippincott, 1931.

Fisher, Philip. "Making a Thing into a Man: The Sentimental Novel and Slavery." *Hard Facts: Setting and Form in the American Novel.* New York: Oxford UP, 1987. 87–127.

Foster, Frances Smith. *Witnessing Slavery: The Development of Antebellum Slave Narratives.* 2nd ed. Madison: U of Wisconsin P, 1994.

Fox-Genevese, Elizabeth. *Within the Plantation Household: Black and White Women of the Old South.* Chapel Hill: U of North Carolina P, 1988.

Gates, Henry Louis, Jr. *The Signifying Monkey: A Theory of African American Literary Criticism.* New York: Oxford UP, 1988.

Genovese, Eugene, D. "The Children." *Roll, Jordon, Roll: The World the Slaves Made.* New York: Pantheon, 1972. 502–19.

Gillespie, Margaret C. *History and Trends.* Dubuque, Iowa: Brown, 1970.

Ginzberg, Lori. *Women and the Work of Benevolence: Morality, Politics, and Class in the Nineteenth-Century United States.* New Haven: Yale UP, 1990.

Goodell, William. *American Slave Code in Theory and Practice; Its Distinctive Features, Shown by Its Statutes, Judicial Decisions, and Illustrative Facts.* New York: Negro UP, 1968.

Goodheart, Lawrence B., and Hugh Hawkins, eds. *The Abolitionists: Means, Ends, and Motivations.* 3rd ed. Lexington, Mass.: Heath, 1995.

Gray, Janet. "Grace Greenwood." *The Oxford Companion to Women's Writing in the United States.* Ed. Cathy N. Davidson and Linda Wagner-Martin. New York: Oxford UP, 1995.

Greenleaf, Barbara Kaye. *Children through the Ages: A History of Childhood.* New York: McGraw Hill, 1978.

Grossberg, Michael. *Governing the Hearth: Law and the Family in Nineteenth-Century America.* Chapel Hill: U of North Carolina P, 1985.

Grylls, David. *Guardians and Angels: Parents and Children in Nineteenth-Century Literature.* London: Faber, 1978.

Hansen, Debra Gold. *Strained Sisterhood: Gender and Class in the Boston Female Anti-Slavery Society.* Amherst: U of Massachusetts P, 1993.

———. "The Boston Female Anti-Slavery Society and the Limits of Gender Politics." Yellin and Van Horne 45–65.

Harden, Elizabeth. *Maria Edgeworth.* Boston: Twayne, 1984.

Hare, Lloyd C. M. *The Greatest American Woman: Lucretia Mott.* New York: American Historical Society, 1937.

"Harriet Beecher Stowe." *Bibliography of American Literature.* Comp. Jacob Blanck. Ed. and completed Michael Winship. Vol. 8. New Haven: Yale UP, 1990.

Hawthorne, Mark D. *Doubt and Dogma in Maria Edgeworth.* Gainesville: U of Florida P, 1967.

Hedrick, Joan, D. *Harriet Beecher Stowe: A Life*. New York: Oxford UP, 1994.

Hersh, Blanch Glassman. *The Slavery of Sex: Feminist-Abolitionist in America*. U of Illinois P, 1978.

Herzberg, Gay Schwartz. "The Portrayal of Men by Women Writers: A Critical Analysis of the Fiction of Harriet Beecher Stowe." Diss. SUNY Buffalo, 1982.

Hewitt, Nancy A. *Women's Activism and Social Change: Rochester, New York, 1822–1872*. Ithaca: Cornell UP, 1984.

———. "On Their Own Terms: A Historiographical Essay." Yellin and Van Horne 23–30.

Hoffert, Sylvia D. *Private Matters: American Attitudes toward Childbearing and Infant Nurture in the Urban North, 1800–1860*. Urbana: U of Illinois P, 1989.

Horton, James Oliver, and Lois E. Horton. *Black Bostonians: Family Life and Community Struggle in the Antebellum North*. New York: Holmmes, 1979.

Inglis-Jones, Elisabeth. *The Great Maria: A Portrait of Maria Edgeworth*. London: Faber, 1959.

Isenberg, Nancy. *Sex and Citizenship in Antebellum America*. Chapel Hill: U of North Carolina P, 1998.

"James A. Thome." *The Encyclopedia of Cleveland History*. Ed. David D. van Tassel and John J. Grabowski. Published in association with Case Western Reserve U. Bloomington: Indiana UP, 1987.

Jones, Jacqueline. *Labor of Love, Labor of Sorrow: Black Women, Work, and the Family from Slavery to the Present*. New York: Basic Books, 1985.

Jones, Mary Patricia. "Elizabeth Margaret Chandler: Poet, Essayist, Abolitionist." Diss. U of Toledo, 1981.

Jones, Norrence T, Jr. *Born a Child of Freedom, Yet a Slave: Mechanism of Control and Strategies of Resistance in Antebellum South Carolina*. Middletown, Conn: Wesleyan UP, 1990.

Jordan, John W., ed. "Longstreth-Townsend Family." *Colonial Families of Philadelphia*. Vol. 2. New York: Lewis, 1911. 1532–40.

Kasson, Joy. *Marble Queens and Captives: Women in Nineteenth-Century American Sculpture*. New Haven: Yale UP, 1990.

Kelley, Mary. *Private Woman, Public Stage: Literary Domesticity in Nineteenth-Century America*. New York: Oxford UP, 1984.

Kerber, Linda. *Women of the Republic: Intellect and Ideology in Revolutionary America*. Chapel Hill: Published for the Institute of Early American History and Culture by U of North Carolina P, 1980.

Kiefer, Monica. *American Children through Their Books: 1700–1835*. Philadelphia: U of Pennsylvania P, 1948.

Kilgour, Raymond L. *Lee and Shepard: Publishers for the People*. [Hamden, Conn.]: Shoe String, 1965.

King, Wilma. *Stolen Childhood: A Slave Youth in Nineteenth-Century America.* Bloomington: Indiana UP, 1995.

Lang, Amy Schrager. "Class and Strategies of Sympathy." Samuels 128–42.

Lapsansky, Emma Jones. "The World the Agitators Made: The Counterculture of Agita-
tion in Urban Philadelphia." Yellin and Van Horne 91–99.

Lapsansky, Phillip. "Graphic Discord: Abolitionist and Antiabolitionist Images." Yellin
and Van Horne 201–30.

Lehmann-Haupt, Hellmut. *The Book in America: A History of the Making and Selling of
Books in the United States.* 2nd ed. New York: Bowker, 1951.

Lenz, Millicent. "Harriet Beecher Stowe." *American Writers for Children before 1900.* Ed.
Glenn E. Estes. *Dictionary of Literary Biography* 42. Detroit: Gale, 1985.

Lerner, Gerda. *The Grimké Sisters from South Carolina: Pioneers for Woman's Rights and Abolition.* New York: Schocken, 1967.

Lesick, Lawrence Thomas. *The Lane Rebels: Evangelicalism and Antislavery in Antebellum
America.* Metuchen, N.J.: Scarecrow P, 1980.

Lundy, Benjamin, ed. *Poetical Works of Elizabeth Margaret Chandler; with a Memoir of Her
Life and Character by Benjamin Lundy, and Essays, Philanthropic and Moral, by Eliza-
beth Margaret Chandler, Principally Relating to the Abolition of Slavery in America.*
Philadelphia: Lemuel Howell, 1836.

Lutz, Alma. *Crusade for Freedom: Women of the Antislavery Movement.* Boston: Beacon,
1968.

Lyerly, Cynthia Lynn. *Methodism and the Southern Mind, 1770–1810.* New York: Oxford
UP, 1998.

Lystad, Mary. *From Dr. Mather to Dr. Seuss: 200 Years of American Books for Children.*
Boston: Hall, 1980.

MacCann, Donnarae C. "The White Supremacy Myth in Juvenile Books about Blacks,
1830–1900." Diss. U of Iowa, 1988.

MacKethan, Lucinda H. "Metaphors of Mastery in the Slave Narratives." *The Art of Slave
Narrative: Original Essays in Criticism and Theory.* Ed. John Sekora and Darwin T.
Turner. Chicago: Western Illinois U, 1982. 55–69.

MacLeod, Anne Scott. *A Moral Tale: Children's Fiction and American Culture, 1820–1860.*
Conn.: Archon, 1975.

———. *American Childhood: Essays on Children's Literature of the Nineteenth and Twentieth
Centuries.* Athens: U of Georgia P, 1994.

———. "Children's Literature and American Culture: 1820–1860." *Society and Children's
Literature: Papers Presented on Research, Social History, and Children's Literature at a
Symposium Sponsored by the School of Library Science, Simmons College, and the Com-
mittee on National Planning for Special Collections of the Children's Services Division of
the American Library Association, May 14–15, 1976.* Ed. James H. Fraser. Boston:
Godline, 1978. 11–31.

————. "Nineteenth-Century Families in Juvenile Fiction." *The Child and the Family: Selected Papers from the 1988 International Conference of Children's Literature Association. May 19–22, 1988.* New York: Pace U, 1989.

Mahoney, Mary. "Manning and Loring." Dzwonkoski 6.

Mason, Mary Ann. *From Father's Property to Children's Rights: The History of Child Custody in the United States.* New York: Columbia UP, 1994.

Mattingly, Carol. *Well-Tempered Women: Nineteenth-Century Temperance Rhetoric.* Carbondale: Southern Illinois UP, 1998.

McCulloch, Lou W. *Children's Books of the Nineteenth Century.* Des Moines, Iowa: Wallace-Homestead, 1979.

Meigs, Cornelia. *A Critical History of Children's Literature; A Survey of Children's Books in English.* Rev. ed. New York: Macmillan [1969].

Meltzer, Milton, and Patricia G. Holland, eds. *Lydia Maria Child: Selected Letters, 1817–1880.* Amherst: U of Massachusetts P, 1982.

Moe, Phyllis. "Eliza Cabot Lee Follen." *American Women Writers: A Critical Reference Guide from Colonial Times to the Present.* Ed. Lina Mainiero. Vol. 2. New York: Ungar, 1980.

Moser, I. Kathleen. "J. Elizabeth Jones: The Forgotten Activist." Thesis, Kent State University Honors Program. August 1996.

Nelson, Dana. "Sympathy as Strategy in Sedgwick's *Hope Leslie.*" Samuels 191–202.

Nord, David Paul. "The Evangelical Origins of Mass Media in America, 1815–1835." *Journalism Monographs.* Columbia, S.C.: Association for Education in Journalism and Mass Communication, 1984.

Nye, Russell B. "Eliza Crossing the Ice—A Reappraisal of Sources." *Critical Essays on Harriet Beecher Stowe.* Ed. Elizabeth Ammons. Boston: Hall, 1980. 98–101.

O'Connell, Catherine E. "'The Magic of the Real Presence of Distress': Sentimentality and Competing Rhetorics of Authority." *The Stowe Debate: Rhetorical Strategies in Uncle Tom's Cabin.* Ed. Mason I. Lowance, Jr., Ellen E. Westbrook, and R. C. De Prospo. Amherst: U of Massachusetts P, 1994. 13–36.

Okker, Patricia. *Our Sister Editors: Sarah J. Hale and the Tradition of Nineteenth-Century American Women Editors.* Athens: U of Georgia P, 1995.

Papashvily, Helen Waite. *All the Happy Endings: A Study of the Domestic Novel in America, the Women Who Wrote It, the Women Who Read It in the Nineteenth Century.* New York: Harper, 1956.

Racism and Sexism in Children's Books. New York: Council on Interracial Books for Children, 1976.

"Redeem." *Oxford English Dictionary.* Prep. by J. A. Simpson and E. S. C. Weiner. 2nd ed. Oxford: Clarendon P, 1989.

Reynolds, David S. *Beneath the American Renaissance: The Subversive Imagination in the Age of Emerson and Melville.* Cambridge, Mass.: Harvard UP, 1988.

Reynolds, Moira Davison. "Harriet Beecher Stowe: *Uncle Tom's Cabin*." *Nine American Women of the Nineteenth Century: Leaders into the Twentieth.* Jefferson, N.C.: McFarland, 1988. 36–49.

———. *Uncle Tom's Cabin and Mid-Nineteenth-Century United States: Pen and Conscience.* Jefferson, N.C.: McFarland, 1985.

Roberts, Bette B. "Lydia Maria Francis Child." *American Women Writers: A Critical Reference Guide from Colonial Times to the Present.* Ed. Lina Mainiero. Vol. 1. New York: Ungar, 1979.

Rosenthal, Lynne Meryl. *The Child Informed: Attitudes towards the Socialization of the Child in Nineteenth-Century English Children's Literature.* Diss. Columbia U, 1974.

Ruchames, Louis. *The Abolitionist: A Collection of Their Writings.* New York: Putnam, 1963.

Samuels, Shirley, ed. *The Culture of Sentiment: Race, Gender, and Sentimentality in Nineteenth-Century America.* New York: Oxford UP, 1992.

Samuels, Shirley. "The Identity of Slavery." Samuels 157–71.

Schilpp, Madelon Golden, and Sharon M. Murphy. "Sarah Josepha Hale: First Woman's Magazine Editor [1788–1879]." *Great Women of the Press.* Carbondale: Southern Illinois UP, 1983. 37–48.

Schlesinger, Elizabeth Bancroft. "Two Early Harvard Wives: Eliza Farrar and Eliza Follen." *New England Quarterly* 38 (June 1965): 147–67.

Scott, Anne Firor. *The Southern Lady: From Pedestal to Politics, 1830–1930.* Chicago: U of Chicago P, 1970.

Scott, John Anthony. *Woman against Slavery: The Story of Harriet Beecher Stowe.* New York: Crowell, 1978.

Shackelford, Lynne P., and Everett C. Wilkie, Jr. "John P. Jewett and Company." Dzwonkoski 226.

Shapiro, Ann R. *Unlikely Heroines: Nineteenth-Century American Women Writers and the Women Question.* Westport, Conn.: Greenwood, 1987. 1–35.

Shaw, S. Bradley. "The Pliable Rhetoric of Domesticity." *The Stowe Debate: Rhetorical Strategies in* Uncle Tom's Cabin. Ed. Mason I. Lowance, Jr., Ellen E. Westbrook, and R. C. De Prospo. Amherst: U of Massachusetts P, 1994. 73–98.

Sklar, Kathryn Kish. "'Women Who Speak for an Entire Nation': American and British Women at the World Anti-Slavery Convention. London, 1840." Yellin and Van Horne 301–33.

Smedman, M. Sarah. "Sarah Josepha Hale." *American Writers for Children before 1900.* Ed. Glenn E. Estes. Vol. 42. Detroit: Gale, 1985. 207–17.

Smith, Susan. "Caroline Howard Gilman." *American Women Writers: A Critical Reference Guide from Colonial Times to the Present.* Ed. Lina Mainiero. Vol. 2. New York: Ungar, 1980. 128–30.

Soderlund, Jean R. "Priorities of Power: The Philadelphia Female Anti-Slavery Society." Yellin and Van Horne 67–88.

Stone, James Clement. "The Evolution of Civil War Novels for Children." Diss. Ohio SU, 1990.

Stone, Witmore. "John Kirk Townsend." *Dictionary of American Biography.* Ed. Dumas Malone. Vol. 9 (part 2). New York: Scribner's, 1935–36. 617–18.

Sutton, Walter. *The Western Book Trade: Cincinnati as a Nineteenth-Century Publishing and Book-Trade Center, Containing a Directory of Cincinnati Publishers, Booksellers, and Members of Allied Trades, 1796–1880.* Columbus: Ohio State UP for the Ohio Historical Soc., 1961.

Swerdlow, Amy. "Abolition's Conservative Sisters: The Ladies' New York City Anti-Slavery Society, 1834–1840." Yellin and Van Horne 31–44.

"Tappan, Lewis." *American Authors and Books: 1640 to the Present Day.* 3rd rev. ed. W. J. Burke and Will D. Howe. Rev. Irving Weiss and Anne Weiss. New York: Crown, 1972.

———. *Dictionary of American Religious Biography.* Ed. Henry Warner Bowden. 2nd ed. Westport, Conn.: Greenwood, 1993.

Tate, Claudia. *Domestic Allegories of Political Desire: The Black Heroine's Text at the Turn of the Century.* New York: Oxford UP, 1992.

Taylor, Earl R. "American Sunday School Union." Dzwonkoski 13–14.

Tebble, John. *A History of Book Publishing in the United States: The Creation of an Industry, 1630–1865.* Vol. 1. New York: Bowker, 1972.

Teute, Fredrika. "In 'the gloom of evening': Margaret Bayard Smith's View in Black and White of Early Washington Society." *The Proceedings of the American Antiquarian Society* 106.1 (1996): 37–58.

Thesing, Jane Isley. "William Manning and James Loring." *Boston Printers, Publishers, and Booksellers: 1640–1800.* Ed. Franklin V. Benjamin. Boston: Hall, 1980.

Tompkins, Jane. *Sensational Designs: The Cultural Work of American Fiction, 1790–1860.* New York: Oxford UP, 1985.

Trensky, Anne. "The Saintly Child in Nineteenth-Century American Fiction." *Prospects: An Annual Journal of American Cultural Studies* 1 (1975): 389–413.

Van Broekhoven, Deborah Bingham. "'Let Your Names Be Enrolled': Method and Ideology in Women's Antislavery Petitioning." Yellin and Van Horne 179–99.

Van Leer, David. "Reading Slavery: The Anxiety of Ethnicity in Douglass' *Narrative.*" *Frederick Douglass: New Literary and Historical Essays.* Ed. Eric J. Sundquist. Cambridge: Cambridge UP, 1990. 118–40.

Venet, Wendy Hamand. *Neither Ballots nor Bullets: Women Abolitionists and the Civil War.* Charlottesville: UP of Virginia, 1991.

Ward, Martha E., Dorothy A. Marquardt, Nancy Dolan, and Dawn Eaton. *Authors of Books for Young People.* 3rd ed. Metuchen, N.J.: Scarecrow, 1990.

Weed, George L. ["Advertisement."]. *Aunt Sally; or, The Cross, the Way of Freedom.* Cincinnati [American Reform Tract and Book Society], 1858. [back cover].

———. ["Advertisement"] *The Family Relation as Affected by Slavery*. By Charles K. Whipple. Cincinatti [American Reform Tract and Book Society], 1858. 24.

———. *God against Slavery: And the Freedom and Duty of the Pulpit to Rebuke It, as a Sin against God*. By George B. Cheever. Cincinnati [American Reform Tract and Book Society], 1859. [back cover].

Welter, Barbara. *Dimity Convictions: The American Woman in the Nineteenth Century*. Athens: Ohio UP, 1976.

White, Deborah Gray. *Ain't I a Woman? Female Slaves in the Plantation South*. New York: Norton, 1985.

White, Isabelle. "Sentimentality and the Uses of Death." *The Stowe Debate: Rhetorical Strategies in Uncle Tom's Cabin*. Ed. Mason I. Lowance, Jr., Ellen E. Westbrook, and R. C. De Prospo. Amherst: U of Massachusetts P, 1994. 99–115.

"William Goodell." *Dictionary of American Biography*. Ed. Allen Johnson and Dumas Malone. Vol. 4. New York: Scribner's, 1932. 384–85.

———. *Who Was Who in America: Historical Volume, 1607–1896. A Component Volume of Who's Who in American History*. Rev. ed. Chicago: Marquis Who's Who, 1963.

Williams, Carolyn. "The Female Antislavery Movement: Fighting against Racial Prejudice and Promoting Women's Rights in Antebellum America." Yellin and Van Horne 159–77.

Williams, Susan S. "'Promoting an Extensive Sale': The Production and Reception of *The Lamplighter*." *The New England Quarterly* 69.2 (1996): 179–200.

Woodard, Frederick, and Donnarae MacCann. "Huckleberry Finn and the Traditions of Blackface Minstrelsy." *The Black American in Books for Children: Readings in Racism*. Ed. Donnarae MacCann and Gloria Woodard. Metuchen, N.J.: Scarecrow, 1985. 75–103.

Wroth, Lawrence C., and Rollo G. Silver. "Book Production and Distribution from the American Revolution to the War between the States." Lehmann-Haupt 63–138.

Wyatt-Brown, Bertram. *Lewis Tappan and the Evangelical War against Slavery*. Cleveland: P of Case Western Reserve U, 1969.

Yee, Shirley, J. *Black Women Abolitionists: A Study in Activism, 1828–1860*. Knoxville: U of Tennessee P, 1992.

Yellin, Jean Fagan. *Women and Sisters: The Antislavery Feminist in American Culture*. New Haven: Yale UP, 1989.

Yellin, Jean Fagan, and John C. Van Horne, eds. *The Abolitionist Sisterhood: Women's Political Culture in Antebellum America*. Ithaca: Cornell UP, 1994.

Zboray, Ronald, Jr., and Mary Saracino Zboray. "Books, Reading, and the World of Goods in Antebellum New England." *American Quarterly* 48.4 (1996): 587–622.

Index

Memoir Of James Jackson . . . Eleven Months. See Paul, Susan

Merill, A. S., 155n. 38

Methodist Book Concern, 33

Minute Book (1836–1846). See Junior Anti-Slavery Society of Philadelphia

Mitford, Mary Russell, "Two Dolls, The," 18; *Our Village*, 18, 152n. 13

Moe, Phyllis (critic), on Eliza Follen, 26, 150n. 8, 158n. 29

Moser, I. Kathleen (critic), on Jane Elizabeth Jones, 13; on Jones's lost abolitionist lectures, 23; on slavery's corruption of slave holders, 100; on fugitive slaves, 102

Mothers: abolitionist mother-historian, 10, 23, 79–106, 153nn. 18, 19, 20, 159n. 10; as activists, 8, 59–75, 82–85, 102, 105; as intercessor, 57–75; moral influence on children, 8, 61, 81–82; politicized, 10, 37, 79; in periodicals, 151n. 18; republican mothers, 82, 84, 87, 97, 102, 103, 106, 159n. 7; as storytellers, 85, 159n. 9. *See also* slave mothers

Motherhood, republican, 82, 84, 87, 97, 102, 103, 106, 159n. 7

Motherhood resolution, 82–83, 89, 159n. 5

Mother's Book, The. See Child, Lydia Maria

Mott, Lucretia, as leader of PFASS, 6; and Elizabeth Margaret Chandler, 19; and Hannah Townsend, 22; and James McKim, 24

Murray, Mary, 58

Mussey, Reuben Diamond. *Essay on the Influence of Tobacco on Life and Health*, 155n. 41

My Uncle's Family, or, Ten Months at the South. See Smith, Margaret Bayard

National Anti-Slavery Standard, 24, 109, 110

National Enquirer. See Lundy, Benjamin

National Era, 13, 28

National Union Catalogue (NUC), 151n. 3

Nelson, Dana (critic), on views of "the other," 104

Nord, David (critic), on the AASS, 17, 18

Not a Minute to Spare. See Croft, S. C. [Mrs. S. Croft]

Nye, Russell (critic), on the sources for Stowe's *Uncle Tom's Cabin*, 154n. 36

Oasis, The, 113, 163n. 22

O'Connell, Catherine (critic), 42, 47, 48, 58, 64, 70, 156nn. 13, 14

O'Driscoll, C. F. (stereotyper), 36

"Oh Press Me Not to Taste Again." *See* Chandler, Elizabeth Margaret

Okker, Patricia (critic), on women's periodicals, 13, 14; on "Maternal Instruction," 79; on Sarah Hale, 86, 87, 160n. 14

Old Betty, 2–3, 152n. 9

"Old Caesar." *See* Grandmother

"On Hearing a Child Say Father." *See* Medora

"On Hearing of the Sadness of the Slave Children from the Fear of Being Sold." *See* Follen, Eliza Lee Cabot

Opie, Amelia (British), biography, 14; humanitarian and abolitionist work, 151n. 3; *The Negro Boy's Tale*, 14

Opie, John, 14

Optic, Oliver, 3, 154n. 34

Our Nig. See Wilson, Harriet

Page, Thomas Nelson, 3

Panic of 1857, 29

Papashvily, Helen (critic), on stereotyping books, 36–37; on sentimental fiction, 42, 43, 58; on Eliza Follen, 153n. 26

Paul, Susan. 1, 28, 37 *passim;* biography, 25; use of sentimentality, 40; *Memoir of James Jackson*, 25

Paul, Thomas, 25

Peabody, Elizabeth, 86, 89

Peabody, Ephraim, 41, 42

Peep into Uncle Tom's Cabin, 28

Perkins, Rev. G. W., 154n. 37

Philadelphia Anti-Slavery Fair, 22, 23

Philadelphia Sunday and Adult School Union. *See* American Sunday School Union

Philo Paidos, "Letter: The Little Slaves to the Sabbath School Children of New England," 18, 45; "Answer to the Letter of the Little Slaves, by the Sabbath School Children," 45

"Picnic at Dedham." *See* Follen, Eliza Lee Cabot

Pictures and Stories from Uncle Tom's Cabin. See Stowe. Harriet Beecher

Pittsburg Saturday Visitor, 13

"Plantation, The." *See* Gilman, Caroline Howard

"Planter's Son, The." *See* Gilman, Caroline Howard

Poetical Works of Elizabeth Margaret Chandler. See Lundy, Benjamin

"political culture," 1

Pollack, Rev. R. H., 155n. 38